Missouri Compromise

MISSOURI Compromise

BY TRIS COFFIN

Little, Brown and Company · Boston
1947

FIRST EDITION

Published May 1947

Published simultaneously
in Canada by McClelland and Stewart Limited

PRINTED IN THE UNITED STATES OF AMERICA

Missouri Compromise

Chapter I

THE little white cottage on the hill basked, like a drowsy kitten, in the warm morning sunshine. A fresh, growing smell moved out of the woods.

Inside the tiny cottage a tired man awoke with a dull headache. His valet, a solicitous Negro who had hovered over him loyally for a decade, asked if anything was wrong. No, just a headache. He would shake it off. Ah, it was a beautiful day to relax and rest . . . and rest.

At 4:35 in the afternoon, the man passed quietly away. Bill Hassett, the gentle, white-haired New Englander, called Washington. He broke the news simply. "The President has died."

Franklin Roosevelt had no intimation of death. The day before at Warm Springs he talked enthusiastically with Dewey Long, the White House travel expert, on the projected trip to the San Francisco Conference. He inquired, with boyish eagerness, into all the details.

When Bill Hassett called, the White House was empty with silence. Only a few people were around. A picnic had been planned, and many of the employees had already left. Less than a handful of reporters were sprawled out sleepily in the stuffy press room. Mrs. Roosevelt was out. A few shafts of the hot afternoon sun poured through the glass doors of the round Presidential office. All the gadgets were in place on the desk, just as the President had left them.

Up the Hill on Pennsylvania Avenue, Harry Truman sat in the comfortable, old-fashioned Capitol in the friendly comradeship of Senator Alben Barkley, the Democratic majority leader.

This was a long, feverish afternoon in Washington. Harry S. Truman, a pale, frightened man, was called to the White House by Steve Early. Steve was terse in his message. "Come to the White House right away. Something has happened."

Mr. Truman humbly asked a composed Mrs. Roosevelt, "Is there anything I can do for you?"

Mrs. Roosevelt, with her long sense of time, answered, "Is there anything I can do for you?"

More than a hundred reporters swarmed in confusion in the lobby of the West Wing of the White House. Some of the girl secretaries cried softly and unnoticed. The uniformed guards at the gate stood limp with dejection and shock.

A huge silent crowd filled Lafayette Park across the street, and stared into the big hall of the White House. The front doors were open and the big chandelier glistened in the sunlight. The crowds stood in the twilight, and far into the night.

A year later, on the anniversary of Mr. Roosevelt's death, many hundreds walked through a thin rain to the memorial services in Washington churches. They hoped to squeeze some comfort and hope from the reverent words of prayer.

The war had been won, and peace had come. But with peace came new fears – fear of the atomic bomb, fear of inflation, and above all a dim, nameless fear of the future. With fear came, too, its twin, bitterness.

The first few days of shock in Washington after Mr. Roosevelt's death blotted out the measurements of the task ahead. Even Harry Truman knew only a vague apprehension. He had no intimation of the crises to arise within the next two years.

When Franklin Roosevelt passed away, all the thin threads of his diplomacy, strategy, and government snapped. For President Roosevelt was a leader in a highly personal sense.

He was the master producer of a great puppet show. He brought into the White House a revolving circus of men and women with imagination and daring. He drew from them ideas and inspiration. Some of them were young government brain trusters, like the young man out of the West, Bill Douglas . . . bustling, booming Leon Henderson . . . the very shy and serious Ben Cohen. When the President wanted dramatic, ringing lines for his speeches, he brought the tall gawky playwright, Bob Sherwood, into the White House. In those early days when atomic energy seemed just a fantastic dream – particularly to the Army – Mr. Roosevelt talked with Dr. Albert Einstein. Franklin Roosevelt had an acquisitive instinct for brains and daring, drawing them from all parts of the country, all fields, into the White House. For he respected them above all else.

To give the lines of his show the crust of respectability, the President made a point of receiving in the White House such elder statesmen as Bernard Baruch, the park-bench philosopher. When the Administration was making war on American isolationism and preparing to move on the Nazis, Mr. Roosevelt called in a whole procession of respectable citizens to make statements on the steps of the White House against German and Japanese aggression.

The puppets were the government administrators and, less predictably, Congress. These puppets in the departments were a curious lot, a hodgepodge of old friends, political hacks, earnest New Dealers, and colorful characters who struck his fancy.

Secretary of the Treasury Henry Morgenthau, Jr., was a personal friend who tried enthusiastically to outdo his chief in his New Dealism. Mr. Roosevelt gained much pleasure and relaxation in teasing the Secretary and puncturing his ego.

There were the political stand-bys, like former Attorney General Homer Cummings, and that short-time, bewildered Price Administrator, Prentiss Brown. Some men were brought in to give an air of respectability to new projects, like Nelson Rockefeller, who headed the Office of Inter-American Affairs, and Elmer Davis, director of OWI. Others were brilliant young New Dealers, whom Mr. Roosevelt scattered about in such independent agencies as the Securities and Exchange Commission. A few were brought in to keep them where they could be watched, like the politically ambitious Paul V. McNutt. Some represented politically powerful groups – for example Harold Ickes, who was an old Bull Moose independent voter, and Henry Wallace, for the Midwestern farmers. Henry Stimson and Frank Knox were appointed as Secretaries of War and Navy to unite Republicans behind the war and the preparatory period.

All these men of different temperaments, abilities, and convictions were expected to follow directions from the White House. The second and third levels below the agency heads were scattered with individuals passionately loyal to the President. They served, sometimes, not only as liaison, but as bearers of tales, when the top man slipped off the track.

All the groups within the government were kept in balance. None, the New Dealers, the politicians, the old-line bureaucrats, or the businessmen brought in for the war, were ever strong enough to run the show themselves.

When all the new defense and war agencies sprouted out in temporary buildings along the Mall, the New Dealers licked their lips and started to move in. Mr. Roosevelt coldly held them back, giving the right of way to a flood of businessmen and old-line government administrators to keep them from tripping over red tape. Then, he let the New Dealers filter through slowly.

In and around the White House were the directors – men who helped pull the strings. They were the selfless, anonymous, hard-working assistants to the President. Theirs was the almost hopeless job of pulling things together to see that the team went in the same direction . . . of collecting information and bringing it to the President . . . of taking orders out to the agency heads and presenting them tactfully.

The President also used the Bureau of the Budget, little heard of outside Washington, to keep the whole big show of government in balance. The Bureau men operated skillfully behind the scenes in every agency. The Bureau director, colorless Harold Smith, was one of the most powerful men in Washington.

Of all the men in Washington in responsible positions, Franklin Roosevelt trusted very few all the way. He trusted some in specialized lines, but not across the board. Old Admiral Leahy advised him on how to get along with the Army and Navy, but he did not meddle in other affairs, at least under Mr. Roosevelt.

Perhaps the only two men President Roosevelt trusted all the way were Marvin McIntyre and Harry Hopkins. They worked themselves to death for him.

Mr. Roosevelt was ruthless in exploiting the imagination, the talents, the political drawing power of all those in his immense show. The only thing that mattered, and the President was selfless about it, was the success of his programs: first, the economic reforms of the early New Deal, then the swing from isolationism to intervention in foreign affairs, and, greatest of all his dreams, the United Nations.

The puppets were also a kind of guard around the White House – to keep the slings and arrows of public opposition away from the President; to bare their own bosoms. Some, such as Harold Ickes and Leon Henderson, accepted this role with great enthusiasm.

Honest Harold loved nothing better than to roar out with his lance tilted, taking on one or many opponents of the New Deal. When political and business heat blistered the OPA, Leon Henderson cheerfully took it all on himself, and stepped out when it impaired his job as administrator. Others, like Elmer Davis, bore it with a spirit of patient martyrdom.

When the Office of War Information sucked in much of the opposition to the war and was pounded unmercifully by Congress, Davis said philosophically that it was better for the heat to fall on him than on the White House. Henry Wallace took criticism right on the chin that might have reflected on Mr. Roosevelt. He did not turn sour, even when he was cast out in the 1944 Democratic Convention. Some grew bitter. Jim Farley was one. Harry Hopkins never thought about it. He was too busy.

Mr. Roosevelt used a variety of tactics to keep Congress in line. As a great reader of history, the President knew that Congress was normally unfriendly to the White House.

Among the younger men, and a few of their elders, Mr. Roosevelt developed a spirit of crusade. He encouraged and inspired them to do lusty battle for him. Roosevelt and the New Deal were a religion to them. There was that little band of reckless New Dealers in the Senate – long-jawed "Shay" Minton of Indiana, mournful Lew Schwellenbach from Washington, and genial Lister Hill of Alabama.

With the party hacks, Mr. Roosevelt played the tune of party regularity. His way of dealing with the balky Senators and Congressmen was to use political patronage, and to scare the hell out of them by building bonfires. Such bonfires pushed through the Holding Company Act, repeal of the Neutrality Act, and the Lend-Lease Bill.

As a politician – and he was a master – Mr. Roosevelt was one of the first big public figures of the day to recognize the disintegration of the mass backing for either the Democratic or the Republican Party. He himself had a healthy disrespect for politicians, and never trusted them. He used them to get what he wanted in conventions and primaries, but did not rely upon them.

President Roosevelt made a conscious, energetic effort to organize the independent voters behind him, to use their strength not only to elect him and the men he wanted in Congress, but to serve as a pressure for his program.

When war seemed inevitable, Franklin Roosevelt – with his curious, inquiring mind and his scorn for the judgment of most men – moved in on the Army and Navy. The services were the most tightly organized corporations in Washington. They had not been disturbed all through the New Deal. They were a kingdom apart.

Mr. Roosevelt began cultivating the generals and admirals. He looked them over with a sharp, discerning eye. He liked the cool, tempered mind of General George C. Marshall; the ruthless efficiency of General Brehon B. Somervell to run the giant supply show. He spotted Dwight D. Eisenhower as a diplomat and peacemaker.

His next move was to bring into the White House Admiral William Leahy with the shaggy eyebrows and the long, skeptical face. Admiral Leahy became the Chief of Staff to the Commander in Chief, a new position. He sat in for FDR on both the Joint Chiefs of Staff (Army and Navy) and the Combined Chiefs of Staff (United States and Great Britain).

Admiral Leahy was invaluable to Mr. Roosevelt. He would take orders. That was proved when the old Admiral, as our Ambassador to Vichy, followed to the letter instructions direct from the White House. Too, Admiral Leahy was a member of the old services hierarchy. He belonged to the inner circle, and could give orders with authority to such young fellows as Admiral Ernie King and General George Marshall.

It was actually Franklin D. Roosevelt who mapped the broad strokes of strategy for a war spread over four continents and two oceans. He received guidance and expert information from the generals and the admirals. But it was Mr. Roosevelt – in the great loneliness of his position – who made the decisions . . . yes, no, how much, where?

Admiral Leahy served as the go-between for the White House and the military hierarchy. He was also the interpreter. The Joint and Combined Chiefs of Staff were in session most of the time five blocks from the White House.

Mr. Roosevelt picked General Eisenhower to run the European show, not because he was a great general or strategist, but because he was tactful and diplomatic. The problems in winning the European war were as political as they were military – the suspicions and resentments among the Allied nations.

Because the United States was practically the whole show in the Pacific and Asiatic war, the President selected a great showman and military leader, Douglas MacArthur.

MacArthur might have slowed the European war down to a walk by angering the British, Russians, and French, and Eisenhower might have delayed for weeks or months the bold stabs against Japan. Mr. Roosevelt knew what he was doing.

The President devoted almost all his energies during the third and fourth terms to diplomacy and military strategy. He had little interest in anything else, and was impatient when other matters were brought before him.

It was as the statesman that Mr. Roosevelt exercised all his talents to the full – his shrewd cunning, his imagination, all his experience as a politician and a President, and his great personal charm. He drove himself relentlessly. The United Nations became the great passion of his life. Perhaps it was his pride, the idea of succeeding where others had failed. Perhaps it was a challenge to his imagination, the radical idea of bringing all the nations of the world together in a federation. Perhaps it was his sense of philanthropy, ending the pain and suffering that wars have brought to mankind. Perhaps it was a combination of all these.

Franklin Roosevelt stood as the suave, shrewd mediator between those two suspicious power politicians, Winston Churchill and Josef Stalin, who, without him, would have been at each other's throats all the time. He tried to prevent one from getting an advantage over the other. In the worst dark hours of Britain and Russia, he pulled agreements from them that would lay the basis for a future peace, and fed them with supplies, as a mother gives a crying child a stick of candy.

At the Big Three conferences, he was the one who ruled the meetings by charm, by compromise, by full use of the power of the United States. He did not like Winston Churchill personally, and he privately compared Josef Stalin to his Chicago political boss, Mayor Ed Kelly.

Mr. Roosevelt used all his talents to dramatize and sell the United Nations to the world, to build a pressure force to pinch reluctant prime ministers and dictators.

As long as that stubborn Tennessee mountaineer, Cordell Hull, was Secretary of State, Mr. Roosevelt was forced to make compromises on his foreign policy plans. But later, the President put in a more amenable Secretary, handsome Ed Stettinius. The new Secretary of State was an errand boy who operated on detailed instructions from the White House.

This was Franklin Roosevelt, a man whose great gift of personality won the respect – sometimes grudging – and the devotion of politicians, generals, statesmen, and plain ordinary people the world over. He was the master politician. He was a dreamer of almost unlimited imagination, and, at the same time, a realist with a hard understanding of the limitations of other men. Above all, he was a dramatist.

I remember a small incident at Hyde Park on election eve in 1944. I was with Mr. Roosevelt in his tiny, dim study in that sprawling old mansion. He listened with the careful ear of the dramatist to the radio program that would end his campaign for re-election. He nodded his head with appreciation at the high points of the show, and chuckled at the jabs at the Republicans.

I was there as a news reporter for a radio network, and as its representative in case any problems arose in connection with Mr. Roosevelt's part of the program. He was to speak at the tail end of the broadcast.

The President told me very seriously when I came into the study that he was closing his part of the broadcast with a prayer. Mr. Roosevelt then said, "I find that my script is three minutes short. What will you do for the remainder of the time?"

He looked at me inquiringly. I told him that since he was ending with a prayer, I would pause a few seconds, then say in a lowered voice, "I return you to New York."

"What will they do then to finish the time?" he asked eagerly.

I said it was customary to play organ music to fill out the time. The President smiled through his eyes. The drawn, haggard look vanished. He said with great relish, "That's fine. The organ music will make the radio listeners sleepy. They will turn off their sets and go to bed. That way they will miss Governor Dewey's broadcast."

It was plain to me that Franklin Roosevelt had planned it this way.

This was the man Harry S. Truman succeeded!

Chapter II

THE day after President Roosevelt passed away, the Senate soberly listened to the reading of the official document. Franklin Delano Roosevelt was dead. According to the authority of the Constitution, Harry S. Truman was President of the United States.

The new President stood just off the Senate floor, outside his old Vice-Presidential office. He moved to pass through the swinging doors into the Senate. A Secret Service man stopped him. He said politely, "Mr. President, you can't go in there."

Harry Truman was puzzled. "Why not?" he asked. "Those are my boys. That's where I belong."

Leslie Biffle, the curly-haired Secretary of the Senate, quietly motioned the Secret Service man aside. He told the new President, "Mr. Truman, you can't. Don't you understand? You are the President."

Crestfallen, Harry Truman took one last, wistful look at the familiar Senate, and moved away.

Harry S. Truman is the great American dream. He is the country boy who worked reasonably hard, made friends, didn't get into any serious trouble, and grew up to be President. It was as simple as that.

He spent the ten happiest years of his life in the United States Senate. He came into the gloomy old chamber an awed little country politician who had spent almost all his life in one Missouri county as a boy, young farmer, haberdasher, struggling lawyer, and county judge.

The Senate opened up an exciting new world . . . national problems, issues that swept the world, dramatic personalities.

Harry Truman became the tail end on the passionate New Deal kite. He did not fight on the floor by the sides of his New Deal friends. He stood back quietly. But he voted with them, and played poker with them. He was accepted as a friendly, regular guy.

The older Senators paid little attention to Harry Truman.

An integral part of his charm as a Senator was his humility. Senator Truman did not pretend to be a great thinker or leader. One afternoon when the Senate walls echoed to the brave, strong words of a great debate, Mr. Truman walked out of the chamber with his good friend, Senator Schwellenbach. The Missourian said eagerly, "Lew, that was an exciting session, wasn't it?"

The Senator from Washington agreed enthusiastically. The little man beside him said frankly and wistfully, "I wish I understood all of it."

Sometimes, Mr. Truman had a hard time making up his mind on how to vote on specific bills. He looked to Bennett Clark, the senior Senator from Missouri, for advice. At the same time, Senator Truman wanted to go along with his new friends.

In some of the bitter, close New Deal struggles, it often became a question of which side reached Mr. Truman first. One Senate secretary tells of getting up early in the morning to meet Senator Truman at the Washington railway station to cinch his vote.

It was this appealing, friendly little man that the Democrats nominated for Vice-President in 1944. The nomination was as much of a surprise to Mr. Truman as it was to the convention.

After an intolerably hot night in the middle of the convention, Mr. Truman met one of his friends in the Stevens Hotel coffee-shop for breakfast. The friend asked casually, "Who do you suppose they will nominate for Vice-President?"

The Senator smiled mysteriously, like a little boy with a secret. He said, "I know. Me." He seemed as honestly bewildered as his friend.

The next day I sat by Mr. Truman in the steaming convention hall. He watched the proceedings with the cheerful, wide-eyed wonder of the poor orphan boy who, quite by miracle, got an electric train for Christmas. He didn't quite understand it. But it was swell.

Less than a year later, as he left the Capitol on that bright April afternoon, Mr. Truman clutched his good friend, Senator Kilgore of West Virginia, and said simply, "Harley, pray for me."

That winter when the nation was divided by strikes and economic disorders, the President unhappily told Jim Farley, "I didn't want to be President. I wouldn't have accepted the nomination if I had thought Mr. Roosevelt was going to die. I don't want the nomination in 1948. I want to go back to the Senate. That is where I belong."

President Truman is the man who normally could melt into a crowd very easily. When he was a Senator and even Vice-President, he used to ride the streetcar down from Capitol Hill. He did not create even a flicker of interest. He might have been a government clerk, or a sightseer going back to town after climbing the dome of the Capitol.

He is a neat, gray-haired man with smile creases at the edges of his eyes, and a stubborn little chin. He always manages to look as if he had just brushed his hair, scrubbed his face and hands, and put on a newly pressed suit.

The President dresses conservatively, usually favoring double-breasted suits, with an imaginative flair in ties and handkerchiefs to match. He likes a gaudy bow tie, and stirred up a tempest in a teapot among the best-dressed-men club by wearing a dress bow tie with silver stripes.

Harry Truman is probably the most friendly and democratic man in Washington. At the Jefferson Island outings of the Democrats, he has been seen arm in arm with Theodore (The Man) Bilbo, or joking good-naturedly with the club steward. He just likes people.

Unlike Mr. Roosevelt, he sees a constant stream of visitors, and holds the all-time record for honorary memberships. He honestly enjoys trading a few cheerful, casual words with the president of Rotary International.

On his many junkets out of Washington, the President never stays long in the seclusion of his private car. He wanders through the train, joshing with conductors, peering in on the endless poker games among the reporters, and staring at the gadgets in the locomotive with the eager fascination of a boy.

Mr. Truman likes noise and crowds. When he was on Capitol Hill, he went to every baseball game he could. He sat happily in the stands, chewing peanuts, drinking pop, and shouting at the umpire.

When Harry Truman moved downtown, the White House relaxed. It was no longer the headquarters for global strategy and world affairs. It settled down to the pleasant atmosphere of a small-town hotel.

Many of the boys in the press room were won over to this friendly, democratic man. He treated the correspondents like fellow Masons. He took them on his junkets and entered their bull sessions. He answered all their questions frankly. There was a rash of articles about Harry Truman as "the simple, homespun man who wants so earnestly to do the right thing." A good deal was written of his "stanch loyalty" to his friends.

But as the months wore on, sucking him into endless controversies, the reporters learned more about this stranger in the White House. They discovered, for example, blind spots in his loyalty to friends. Four men who perhaps did the most to advance his political career were unceremoniously dumped. They were Hugh Fulton, who built his national reputation as chairman of the Senate Investigating Committee; Bob Hannegan, who talked the Democratic bosses into nominating Mr. Truman for Vice-President; A. F. Whitney, who wheedled reluctant labor chiefs into accepting Truman at Chicago; and Henry Wallace, who stumped the country for him and kept liberal support tied to the new administration for more than a year.

The correspondents found out about a stubbornness that is likely to boil up in a crisis. Harry Truman sets his jaw forward, makes his own decisions, and to hell with the consequences.

He never seemed to understand the awful vastness of the Federal Government, and the terrible necessity to check over the agencies and weigh all the factors before making a decision. It was so easy and so natural for him to listen to a good salesman, take up the idea enthusiastically, and blurt out at a press conference a statement that would make Washington stir uneasily and statesmen turn faintly green.

President Truman crossed up Secretary of State Jimmy Byrnes at least twice.

While a comprehensive seventy-six-page report on reconversion prepared by his own staff was at the printer's, Mr. Truman said very positively that meat shortages would be over "in the near future." A week later, the report was turned over to the reporters. It said solemnly, "We are plagued with shortages of some types of food, and for some items the shortages will become worse this winter. This is especially true of meat."

At one White House news conference following a series of Presidential statements, each contradicted later, in which Mr. Truman had said earnestly that he knew what he was talking about, he gave the reporters a lecture on meat. He said quite unconsciously and with strong feeling that this was something he really knew about THIS TIME.

First a titter, then a roar of laughter, swept the room. The correspondents were laughing at the President of the United States.

The Washington reporters got their first intimate glimpse of Harry Truman on a five-day trip to Missouri six months after FDR's death.

This was home . . . among old friends in a sleepy country town. Not a brass hat in a hundred miles. Not even a governor. These friends were small-town businessmen, the clothing store merchant of the tiny town of Caruthersville, local politicians, including barrel-chested Obey Croaker, the county assessor, and an ex-sheriff.

Appointments to see the President were made largely by Neal Helms, a local politician and county wholesale liquor dealer. Helms would take whoever wanted to meet the President by the elbow and steer him over to Mr. Truman.

The President stood on the porch of the tiny, run-down hotel where he had the one suite with bath. He chewed gum and talked to his old neighbors. The local politicos would come up to Mr. Truman, tug at his sleeve, and say, "Come over here, Harry. I've got something to talk to you about."

A farmer took ten minutes of the President's time trying to find out how he should go about getting a birth certificate. Mr. Truman stood docilely on the porch. This was like old times, when he was just a county judge.

On the Sunday morning of the trip, the President was up at the crack of dawn, six-fifteen. He walked to the Mississippi River and spit in it. Before noon, he had pinned medals on the local Boy Scouts, accepted a membership in the Caruthersville Lions Club, gone to church, received a custom-built hat from Mr. Kohn, the local clothier, shaken hands with at least two hundred persons, and signed his autograph scores of times.

After lunch, the 40 and 8, an organization of middle-aged veterans, drove up in front of the hotel with its imitation locomotive. Mr. Truman playfully grabbed the arm of his Reconversion Director and old Missouri buddy, John Snyder. They raced out to the street and took turns yanking the bell cord of the locomotive.

In the afternoon, he went to the county fair. With obvious, beaming pleasure, he watched the high school drum majorettes. He saw buxom carnival dancers. He presented a drooping floral wreath to the winner of the "Truman Handicap" horse race.

That night, he was served dinner by the Methodist Church ladies. Between courses, he noticed a battered upright piano in the dining room and walked over to it eagerly. He sat straight on the stool, his fingers pounding the black and white keys enthusiastically. He picked out the chords of Paderewski's "Minuet."

With a final flourish, Mr. Truman twirled around on the stool and said with a proud smile, "When I played this, Stalin signed the Potsdam agreement."

The excited Methodist ladies clapped their hands. The local politicians drawled, Yes sir, our Harry has done right well by himself.

To the reporters, it did not seem quite right to disturb this man who was having such a wonderful time. But newspaper editors had questions. Why did the President go off on a five-day junket to Missouri when the world was shaking with big problems?

Charley Ross, the patient, gray-haired White House press secretary, tried to answer the questions. The President's presence was not constantly required in Washington. He was running a cabinet form of government. Matt Connelly, the efficient young executive secretary, tried his hand. Mr. Truman had marked off the areas of responsibility. Strikes? Well, that was Lew Schwellenbach's job. Foreign affairs? Jimmy Byrnes.

George Allen, the master spinner of yarns and constant Truman companion, was more direct. He said genially that Harry just wanted to get away from the pressure of Washington and chum around with his old friends.

On Monday night, the correspondents were invited over to the cottage on Reelfoot Lake in Tennessee, just across the line from Missouri, where the President was resting and taking it easy.

The evening session with the correspondents was billed as an off-the-record bull session.

It was clear and cold in western Tennessee that night. The Secret Service men guarding the driveway to the log cabin warmed their hands over a charcoal fire. The sky looked like a field of white-topped dandelions. The Secret Service men flashed a light on the correspondents as they piled out of their cars, nodded, and let us walk up to the screened porch.

There, against a background of cypress logs, was Harry Truman. His face wore that familiar deep smile. Around him in the comfortable cabin were old friends, men who could slap him on the back and say, "Harry, remember that time back in 1934 . . . or '30." They were, for the most part, local politicians, American Legionnaires, and cotton farmers.

John Snyder, who used to be an assistant cashier in a little Missouri bank, and who was at this time Director of Reconversion, was there. He looked from a distance like a Truman twin – the same gray suit and small stocky figure. He spoke with the same casual Missouri twang.

Les Biffle had been fishing. He wore a plaid wool shirt. George Allen was spread out comfortably in a porch chair.

Over in one corner on the porch a lively group of Tennesseans were arguing with the Missourians over who among them was the best Democrat. At intervals an uneven shout arose, "Tennessee for Tru-man."

The President waved the reporters to the other end of the porch. He explained to us that this was going to be all off the record. We could talk back and forth on any subject in the world. No holds barred.

Mr. Truman grinned, pushed himself up a little straighter, and said, "Go ahead. Any questions?"

They piled up. Frank answers were given. One correspondent asked, "What are you going to do, Mr. President, about giving the atomic bomb secret to the world?"

The President shrugged his shoulders, a characteristic gesture. Sure, there wasn't any big secret about atomic power. Scientists the world over knew the theory. But – and the President made a short, earnest gesture with his right hand – we are the only nation in the world with the practical know-how and the resources to make the bombs.

At this point, an exuberant Tennessean at the other end of the porch bellowed, "Tenn-e-see for Tru-man." There was a loud shushing. The President went on without noticing the interruption.

This practical know-how, the President said, we would keep. As a matter of fact, we couldn't give it away. Practical know-how is grown into a country: the boy who knows how to fix a Ford with a monkey wrench and a screw driver. The world can have this theory. We are now the only people who can *make* atomic bombs. And we'll keep it that way.

The President talked easily, like a man who has made up his mind and is sure of himself. A reporter asked Mr. Truman if he had talked over this atomic decision with our partners, Britain and Canada.

No, he hadn't.

Charley Ross asked quietly, "Do you want this on or off the record, Mr. President?"

There was just the slightest change of expression in Mr. Truman's eyes behind his glasses.

Then – ON THE RECORD. Why not!

More questions flew from the intense crowd of reporters. Was the London foreign ministers' conference a failure?

No, the President didn't think so. We Americans would assume world leadership in about every field. And we would follow the Golden Rule . . . do unto others as you would have them do unto you.

What about our relations with Russia? Mr. Truman shrugged his shoulders again. Two Secret Service men stood stiffly at attention behind him. The language difficulty . . . that was the big barrier. At Berlin, President Truman and Marshal Stalin both had interpreters. It took the four of them to make sure the American and the Russian leader always understood what the other was saying.

An idea occurred to Mr. Truman. He took it on in a burst of enthusiasm. He told us he would like to go see Russia for himself. He had a feeling the Russians knew as little about us as we did about them.

There was a frenzied race among the reporters to reach the long-distance telephone and the telegraph office. The stories were flashed all over the world. Across the world, the news teletypes a few seconds later paused. There was a ringing of bells . . . clang, clang, clang. Then, slowly, the printed words appeared: BULLETIN, TRUMAN SAYS U.S. TO KEEP ATOM BOMB SECRET.

The gathering on the screened front porch in Tennessee melted back again into a get-together of old friends and political bedfellows. George Allen drawled lazily he didn't see much news in the conference. John Snyder nodded solemn agreement.

President Truman was puzzled and disturbed. Why did all the boys have to rush off just as the party was getting under way?

Someone on the front porch, perhaps it was Charley Ross, said, "Mr. President, whenever you say anything, it is news in every country across the world."

Mr. Truman smiled and shook his head. He said reflectively he guessed he just had trouble remembering he was the President.

Chapter III

THE White House press room is a tiny battered alcove in the West Wing littered with old newspapers and crowded with rows of telephones.

A stuffed deer's head hangs over the bulletin board looking over the scene dejectedly. Each morning a White House secretary scurries into the press room, pins a notice on the board, and switches out before any remarks can be made.

It is the daily announcement of the President's visitors. In the Roosevelt days, the list of names was like a weather bulletin. It indicated the state of affairs at the moment and predicted into the future. A visit by the Soviet Ambassador might mean a change in the world temperatures. The list was quickly copied off by the correspondents. Seconds later, teletypes would begin ringing.

Mr. Roosevelt saw fewer and fewer people his last years . . . the strategists who mapped the winning of the war, the architects drawing up plans for the temple of peace, and the special agents coming and going from mysterious missions.

With Harry Truman in the White House, the list of Presidential appointments had become a geography lesson . . . the strawberry queen from Alabama, a cowboy in a big sombrero, a Chamber of Commerce secretary from Indiana, the Minister from Liberia paying a courtesy call.

Many come bearing gifts – strawberries, two dozen brown trout from the streams of Oregon, a handmade chair from Connecticut, a carved bowl from Hawaii.

The routine is the same each time. The photographers are called in. Mr. Truman stands with a warm smile on his face as the cameramen squint into their lenses. There is a final handshake and the next group is called in.

One day during a period of great crisis – coal and railway strike problems, price control wrecked by an angry Congress, the Paris Peace Conference winding up a failure – President Truman saw 400 people, received 32 quarts of strawberries, 2 baseballs, 160 stamps, and a set of recordings.

Sandwiched briefly in between these more social appointments are the business guests. Mr. Truman does not pretend to enjoy them. He sits at his desk in a mood of resigned patience, a look of polite interest on his face.

When Herbert Hoover returned from his round-the-world famine inspection tour he was in the Presidential office for half an hour. The implication was that great decisions were made.

Actually, what happened was that Mr. Hoover talked for twenty-five minutes making a report. The President thanked him courteously in the remaining time.

When Franklin Roosevelt was alive, he used to receive a procession of Congressmen, government officials, men from the arts, labor, business. They all came for encouragement, for inspiration, or to plant an idea. They stopped coming to the White House a few months after his death.

Young Bill Fulbright, the earnest, world-minded Senator and former Rhodes scholar, used to visit Mr. Roosevelt much as a boy comes to a favorite teacher for inspiration and guidance. The President encouraged him to introduce and fight for the famous Fulbright Resolution which laid the groundwork for the United Nations.

A few months after Mr. Truman moved into the White House, Fulbright, disturbed by the division among the Allies, came to see the President. He poured out his fears for a quarter of an hour.

The Senator left the White House more pessimistic than when he entered. He told a friend sadly, "I didn't make a bit of impression on the President. He didn't know what I was talking about."

The Congressional leaders no longer come down to the White

House for regular strategy huddles. Relations between President Truman and individual Senators and Representatives are purely social.

One Senator, a member of an important committee, tells an illustrative incident. His committee was working over a bill which would change the whole economic complexion of the nation. The Senator, as a routine matter, asked the chairman, an old veteran on Capitol Hill, if he had discussed it with the President.

The chairman snorted, "Why should I? I know more about it than he does!"

Under Mr. Truman, the Presidency has become a ceremonial, rather than an operating office, much of the time. He leaves the decisions to individual department heads about three fourths of the time. If the problem has something to do with food, that is up to Secretary of Agriculture Anderson to worry about. That is his business. The other fourth Harry Truman strikes out on his own.

This has led to some curious mix-ups. In the middle of delicate negotiations to prevent coal and railway strikes, John D. Small, the cocky Civilian Production Administrator, handed out a stinging press release. He advocated a law prohibiting strikes for the next six months. Organized labor hit the ceiling. Even Congressional conservatives said that was going too far. Mr. Truman's reaction was that he hadn't seen the statement, didn't know anything about it.

At another time, John Snyder, the thin-lipped little Missouri banker whom the President named to direct reconversion mobilization, was called to appear before a House committee. So was Chester Bowles, who is as warm and engaging as Snyder is cold and drab. Bowles was running the Office of Price Administration at the time.

Bowles argued for a strong, tough rent and housing control program. Snyder finally and unhappily indicated he had his doubts. The committee members scratched their heads. What did the Administration want?

For months admirals and generals quarreled publicly over the

Administration-backed merger of the armed services. General Leslie Groves, the pudgy director of the atomic bomb project, openly – before the Senate Atomic Energy Committee – argued against an atomic control plan approved by the White House.

There is no cracking of the whip over Congress. Mr. Truman dutifully sends his messages to Capitol Hill outlining recommended legislation. Occasionally, supplemental reports are sent up from the White House, or Mr. Truman will make a mild comment at a news conference.

During a press conference in the middle of the OPA fight, he did not even mention price control. A reporter finally asked him if he would comment. Mr. Truman skipped over it lightly. He hoped the House would pass a good bill.

The House wrecked price control in a wild night of voting. Administration leaders who stood on the floor trying futilely to beat down the revolt said privately that if Mr. Truman had stuck his chin out, warned that the blood would be on Congress's head if inflation came, he would not have lost this battle in the House.

The same thing happened when other crucial legislation came up . . . housing, atomic energy control, conscription. The White House did not lend a hand. There was no wide organization of forces within and without the Administration to put on the heat. This was just the opposite of the Roosevelt technique of scheming, making deals and dramatic bids for public support to get bills through a balky Congress.

There were some strange exceptions to President Truman's "hands-off" rule. Inexplicably, Mr. Truman butted right into the middle of some heated arguments. He talked angrily about firing an admiral who opposed the services merger plan, and caustically criticized other naval officers for lobbying against the bill. John Small and General Groves might defy Administration policy on labor and atomic energy, but that was different.

The truth is that Harry Truman is a hero worshiper. His heroes are the generals. He regards them with all the awe and devotion of a small, barefoot boy watching a parade swing by. The World War I Captain of Battery D looks with starry eyes at General George Marshall, the wartime Chief of Staff, and other high-ranking officers.

Harry Truman enjoys playing soldier, reviewing troops, or pinning on medals. His stock comment at the ceremony for Congressional Medal of Honor winners in the White House is the earnest sentence, "I would rather have this medal than be President."

The quiet persuasion of General Marshall and his associates led to Mr. Truman's demanding universal military training, continuation of the draft, and unification of the Army and Navy. He took these bold steps despite public irritation with everything military and a stubborn reluctance by Congress.

He actively lobbied for the Army's bills in his social contacts with Congressmen and brought the subjects up again and again at his press conferences.

Mr. Truman let the House action on price control go by with an irritated shrug of his shoulders. But when the House stymied Army plans by prohibiting the induction of teen-age boys, the President let out a formally written blast that echoed in the Capitol cloakrooms.

The President's international views, which he clings to stubbornly in face of opposition within his own official family, have been influenced by the Army's suspicion of Soviet Russia, and by its pessimistic view that war will always settle arguments between men.

Mr. Truman has been sold on the idea of having the biggest and best Army, the most atomic bombs, and a military-trained youth.

President Truman has a mulish streak in him. He makes up his mind, sets his chin, and all the king's men cannot change him. He clashed several times with Secretary of State Byrnes, and after each one reminded his press conferences, "I decide American foreign policy."

It was this same cussedness that sent him off by airplane through one of the winter's worst storms his first year in the White House. The Secret Service men pleaded with him. No. He had spent every Christmas at home with his mother in Missouri, and rain and snow were not going to stop him this time.

A few weeks after his inauguration, Mr. Truman decided he wanted his old friend, former Senator Lewis B. Schwellenbach, as his Secretary of Labor. Schwellenbach had a lifetime job as a Federal Judge and did not want to come to Washington. He certainly did not want the ticklish job of Secretary of Labor. The President insisted. The Judge finally consented. But he wanted several weeks.

"No," Mr. Truman replied. "I need you now. I've made up my mind."

Schwellenbach packed his bags.

Months later, a delegation of five Senators went to the White House to get Presidential support for a resolution urging international control of the atomic bomb.

The spokesman for the delegation was pink-cheeked Senator Tobey, the New England internationalist. He said afterwards, "I could tell after the first five minutes Harry Truman was against us. So I didn't even take the resolution out of my pocket. It would have been a waste of time."

A big horseshoe covered with gold paint hangs over the door of President Truman's cheerful White House office. It is a symbol of his faith that with a little good luck everything will turn out all right.

Almost from the beginning of his term, Mr. Truman stared into grave problems. But at the gloomy White House conferences he was cheerful, and told his advisers soothingly, "Things will work out."

One of his favorite words is "hope." At a time when reconversion was slowed down by labor disputes, when world peace was uneasy over the angry exchanges between Britain's Bevin and Russia's Vishinsky, the President smiled benignly at his press conference and, by actual count, used his favorite word, "hope," seven times.

Another Presidential news conference just happened to be scheduled at a time of great climax. It was a hot Thursday afternoon in late spring. The coal strike was choking off production. Thousands were being laid off across the nation. John L. Lewis and the operators had just turned down a White House proposal for arbitration. A nationwide railway strike was scheduled for Saturday with no hope of settlement. The Senate was threatening to kick over the traces and pass drastic antilabor legislation. The Administration's program in Congress was blocked, delayed, and mutilated. Secretary of State Jimmy Byrnes was on his way back from Paris with a depressing report on the Peace Conference.

President Truman looked like a man without a care in the world. He stood behind his desk, a sprightly gray-haired man in a double-breasted blue pin-stripe suit, joking with reporters in the front row. He laughed easily. The skin around his eyes and mouth wrinkled into smile creases.

He whisked through two brief announcements, neither of them top news stories. Then he straightened himself up and said he was ready for the questions. They came at him from all directions. He stood on his tiptoes to see who the inquirer was, or calmly fiddled with a paper knife.

Was there any chance of settling the coal strike?

The President replied quietly, "I hope so."

What about the railway strike?

Mr. Truman smiled politely. Yes, he hoped he would settle that one, too.

A cupboard just a step from the President's desk was jammed with knickknacks. One was a motto lettered in English script, "If the trumpet sounds an uncertain note, who will prepare himself for battle?"

On the other side of his desk hanging on the wall is a large oil portrait of Franklin D. Roosevelt. Mr. Truman considers himself a loyal follower. His legislative program was mildly liberal and New Dealish. Mr. Truman backed the British loan and the rest of Roosevelt's international program.

There is no love lost, however, between the New Dealers and President Truman. The Roosevelt protégés are, for the most part, determined men with cold contempt for bumbling little men. Mr. Truman, as a Senator and Vice-President, let them alone. He felt uneasy toward them.

When he became President, he accepted with no profound regret the resignation of scores of New Dealers. He took a particular pleasure in seeing Harold Ickes go. The Old Curmudgeon had a way of making Mr. Truman feel most uncomfortable . . . a purposely obscure phrase, a cold look out of the corner of his eyes.

The President replaced the New Dealers with men he knew, trusted, and understood. Most of them were men of his own temperament – good-natured politicians with a humble beginning, or old friends from Missouri. His loyalty to them has become a byword. His boys can do no wrong.

Mr. Truman's little Missouri friend, John Snyder, unhappily stumbled into one pitfall after another. Demands for his resignation kept piling up. The question was popped to President Truman at a news conference.

He answered crisply that Mr. Snyder had not submitted his resignation. He was a patriotic citizen and would stay there as long as the President needed him.

If this had been Mr. Truman's predecessor in the White House, John Snyder would have been sent on a trip, a mission to investigate woolgathering in Australia.

For a political leader, President Truman is unusually frank and straightforward. His news conferences are jammed because there is always a chance he will make black headlines with a casual remark.

In the fall of his first year, a reporter asked Mr. Truman, "Are we still manufacturing atomic bombs?" He had only a faint hope that the President would answer. The War Department, in reply to similar questions, had only glared.

The President answered matter-of-factly that yes, we were making atomic bombs still.

"What for?" a surprised reporter inquired.

Mr. Truman replied in a conversational tone. For experimental purposes.

The press association men left a collection of bruised reporters behind in their wild rush to get out to the telephones that day.

During the railway labor crisis, Senator Burton K. Wheeler

went to the White House to see if he could get an inkling of which way the wind was blowing. He is a good friend of the railway brotherhoods.

The Senator asked Mr. Truman, "What are you going to do about the strikes?"

The President blurted out, "Oh, let them run their natural course."

When this remark got back to the unions, they were furious. He was going to let them wear themselves out butting against enraged public opinion, eh?

At the end of his first year in office, Mr. Truman had done several things. He had lost whatever influence he once had over Congress. He had split organized labor and confused the liberals. And he had had his picture taken doing more things than any other man in the White House.

Chapter IV

THE White House cronies, the men who feed Harry Truman opinions and jokes and play poker with him, are some of the most powerful men in downtown Washington. A casual remark, a wisecrack, may change the mood of the President and national policy.

John Snyder, the Secretary of the Treasury, is the best known. He is a small man, about Mr. Truman's height, but with more girth and a slight waddle that has given him the nickname of "Donald Duck." He has small eyes and thin, tight lips in a round face. He dresses conservatively, as behooves a banker, without Mr. Truman's flair for haberdashery.

In public, Secretary Snyder is dull and humorless. His rare press conferences are singularly uninteresting. At these sessions he always appears slightly pained, as if his food did not agree with him. But with Mr. Truman he is a rollicking companion.

The bond between the President and his Secretary of the Treasury is the affection and loyalty Mr. Truman has for the man who helped him when he was just a little fellow in Missouri county politics. The President looks on banker John Snyder as a great financial mind, and nothing can shake this faith. When Snyder was getting hammered from all sides for allegedly making a mess of reconversion, Mr. Truman stuck stubbornly by him.

Snyder was brought in to replace drawling Fred Vinson as Director of the Office of War Mobilization and Reconversion. He was in effect an economic dictator with authority to order and overrule the Civilian Production Administration, OPA, Department of Labor, and other economic agencies on priorities, prices, and wages. He was responsible only to the President.

John Snyder had been on the job only a few weeks when the brilliant young assistants selected by his predecessors, Jimmy Byrnes and Vinson, began walking out. Snyder's views were wholly orthodox – off with the controls stifling business. He lifted L–41, the order restricting building materials to priority housing, a few weeks after V–J Day. Later, it had to be put back on, but the damage was done. Precious building materials had scattered far and wide. He fought with Chester Bowles over steel prices, and then overruled Bowles by lifting steel prices four dollars a ton.

When he came to Washington, Snyder was cheerful and good-hearted. After a few crises and Congressional hearings, he lost his affability and became sullen. During the hectic steel conferences at the White House, Snyder became nervous and irritable. He has never quite recovered.

Mr. Truman was forced reluctantly by Congressional pressure to clip Snyder's wings for a brief period. Chester Bowles was named Director of the Office of Economic Stabilization and given charge of economic policy.

Later, the President found a way to get his friend off the hot seat and into the dignity of the cabinet. Secretary of the Treasury Fred Vinson was sent up the Hill to the Supreme Court, and the little Missouri banker moved across the street from the White House into the dingy Treasury Building.

He still remains close to Mr. Truman. He plays cards with the President, goes on junkets with him, and hustles back across the street every time some new emergency arises. He is there on the spot to give his old friend advice.

The court jester, patronage dispenser, and adviser on high policy was George Allen, a hearty, rollicking Mississippian who tells the best jokes in Washington. He has merry black eyes, handles his weight gracefully, and wears well-tailored suits and loud ties. He has an easy manner with President or cub reporter.

George is the shrewdest of all the White House cronies. He has a highly developed sense of political self-preservation, a penetrating analysis of other men, and all an actor's skill of pace and timing. He knows when to be a buffoon and when to shut up. His own economic and political views are unknown, smoothly covered over by wisecracks.

This gentleman came from Mississippi as a protégé of the late Senator Pat Harrison. As the accommodating, friendly, and entertaining night manager of a Washington hotel, Allen got to know all the best people. He attracted the attention of Harry Hopkins, who, despite his haggard looks, liked good jokes, strong liquor, and a stiff game of poker.

George Allen became the comic relief of the New Deal. He was the man who could make Franklin Roosevelt and Hopkins laugh when they were depressed. He was a perfect host, a first-rate politician, and he knew when not to intrude.

Hopkins installed him in the WPA and gave him a few chores to perform, among them a personal survey of men's hostels. George played the part of a tramp with great enjoyment and publicity.

When he left the government, after a spin as a Commissioner of the District of Columbia, George was ready for big things. He established himself in a suite of rooms in the Carlton Hotel, three blocks from the White House. On the surface, he was the executive of a number of insurance companies. But his major role was as the Washington host and contact man for the mystery man of finance, Victor Emanuel.

In the autumn of 1944, when the White House heard disturbing reports about Harry Truman's campaign, President Roosevelt called in George Allen. He told George to accompany the Vice-Presidential nominee and not let him out of his sight. His job was to keep Harry Truman from making what FDR called "those damnfool statements."

George was by Mr. Truman's side nearly two years, for many months as a Presidential assistant and later as a director of the Reconstruction Finance Corporation. His wide, infectious grin and clowning became a White House stand-by.

He gradually broadened his field, moving his heavy bulk over into the area of Postmaster General Bob Hannegan. While Hannegan was busy trying to hold the Democratic Party together,

George was advising the President on appointments. Allen skimmed off the cream, leaving Bob the patronage of postmasters in second-class cities.

After President Truman sent George's nomination to the Senate to be a director of the RFC, Allen was called before the august Senate Banking and Currency Committee for questioning. This hearing gave Washington a much needed note of comedy.

There was a good audience in the large room with three glittering cut-glass chandeliers. At one side among the spectators was the strong, heavy face of Steve Early, President Roosevelt's press secretary and an old friend of George. Senator Alben Barkley, the Democratic majority leader, had left the Pearl Harbor investigation, which he was directing, to attend the Banking Committee hearing.

George Allen was bowing and smiling like a master of ceremonies.

Another Truman nominee stood unhappily in the room with the self-conscious expression of a sacrificial lamb. He was Commodore James Vardaman, another old Missouri crony, who had been named to be a governor of the Federal Reserve System.

George sat down in the witness chair perfectly composed and at ease. He answered the sharp questions of Republican Senator Bob Taft in a gentle, anxious-to-please manner. Sometimes he smiled or chuckled deeply.

He cheerfully told his life story. Fifteen years before he had been a handshaker for hotels catering to the convention trade. Later he did chores for Harry Hopkins. Among other things, George lived in "flophouses" and "cheap dives" for a few weeks to "find out if the WPA would work." He helped set up a Negro housing project.

Senator Taft asked him dryly what he got out of it. George looked a little shocked at such a rude question. He replied with wounded dignity that he had been made an honorary deacon by the Elder Lightfoot Michaux, a Negro religious leader in Washington.

The story went on. Before George could say Jack Robinson he had become a man of big business . . . vice-president of eleven insurance companies, trustee of another, and a director for twelve corporations.

Senator Taft asked him what he did for the insurance companies.

"Oh," George said vaguely, "I am a kind of public relations man."

The Senator persisted, "At what salary?"

Allen said easily, "Twenty-eight thousand dollars a year."

Did he ever appear before any government agencies hustling business for any of his companies?

George looked hurt. "No, no."

Well, did he ever appear before the Federal Communications Commission in the sale of a radio station? And didn't his presence there tip the scales for a four-to-three decision?

George grinned. "I doubt it, Senator. In fact, I think I was a little bit of a liability."

(Senator Taft was referring to the sale of the big WLW station in Cincinnati to the Victor Emanuel interests.)

The Senator came to another point. He asked in that smooth tone that is supposed to dispel all suspicion, "How did you happen to become a director of Aviation Corporation?"

George wore the innocent look of a schoolboy. He answered simply, "Through my friend Victor Emanuel."

Senator Taft looked startled. A voice at the press table said in an awed tone, "Well, I'll be a son-of-a-gun. I thought that was supposed to be a dark secret."

Taft, still surprised, asked slowly, "Mr. Emanuel is a friend of yours?"

George replied cheerfully, "Yes, he suggested me as a director."

Senator Taft ran down the list of corporation dictatorships. He asked the witness, "What are your duties?"

George grinned, leaned back in his chair to chuckle, and said, "I can understand that might baffle you. I think they really wanted my opinion. They seem to think so."

Senator Barkley smiled contentedly. Brother Allen was taking care of himself ALL RIGHT.

Taft plunged on. "Did Republic Steel want your advice on the steel strike?"

George's eyes twinkled. He said, "You know, Senator, they wouldn't care about my views. Why, *you* would enjoy those meetings."

The committee Democrats smiled at this thrust at Senator Taft's conservative views.

The questioning turned to a particular company. George said enthusiastically, "Oh, that's a *great* company."

The Senator inquired, "How much do you get for attending their directors' meetings?"

George replied owlishly, "Forty dollars. They have assets of over a billion dollars."

The committee room broke out into guffaws. George looked happily around him.

He told of another job, and mused, "I wasn't exactly fired. There just wasn't any enthusiasm for me to stay."

Senator Millikin, a cautious Republican, summed up the committee's views – "A most personable man."

George had competition as the official court jester. His wit is sharp and penetrating, although it always ends up with uproarious belly laughter led by the author.

His rival, Major General Harry Vaughan, an old Missouri crony and Battery D buddy, the President's military aide, has a coarser brand. It is the kind tossed off in a police station press room.

These two kept up a heated contest for the Presidential laughs that would make Jack Benny and Fred Allen look like pikers. A whisper, allegedly started by Vaughan, claims that George keeps a couple of men working up gags night and day. There hasn't been anything like the Allen-Vaughan comedy team since the Two Black Crows.

Harry Vaughan is one of the most unmilitary of generals in the service. He slouches around the White House trying out his jokes on reporters, White House assistants, and Secret Service men. He is a reserve officer whom the President raised to Major General as his military aide.

Dave Niles, the cheerful little White House assistant who handles liaison with minority groups, is the only man on record who has ever stopped Harry Vaughan without a comeback.

Niles had arranged for Mr. Truman to see a group of Jewish

leaders about Palestine and a Negro delegation to protest lynchings. General Vaughan stopped Niles on his way out and said with characteristic heavy humor, "Don't you ever let any white folks in your office?"

With a completely straight face, Niles answered, "Oh, I see anyone, with one exception – white Protestants."

General Vaughan's political views are no help to the New Dealers. When Henry Wallace had been kicked out of the Commerce Department, Vaughan told a friend, "That Goddamn Wallace. There hasn't been a good Secretary of Commerce since Herbert Hoover."

The General had one great campaign which started out as a casual conversation in the press room and ended up with typed statements on the bulletin board. By God, he didn't like the way these athletes were leaving West Point after the war. They got out of the draft by being at West Point, didn't they? A bunch of damn ungrateful bums. It took Charley Ross, the white-haired Presidential press secretary, to get the General out of this controversy.

To dignify friend Harry Vaughan, Mr. Truman gave him the title of Co-ordinator of Veterans' Affairs. To the great delight of Veterans' Administrator General Bradley, Vaughan does not take his job very seriously.

Bob Hannegan, one of the early Truman cronies and the man most responsible for his nomination as Vice-President, made two fatal errors and now is on the outer fringe of the White House friends. The bustling Irish boy from Missouri became too busy with the Democratic National Committee and Post Office Department to make daily pilgrimages to the White House to keep his oar in. And, he frequently disagreed with the President.

Hannegan is a politician of the old Democratic tradition . . . a protégé of the big city Pendergast machine, Catholic, normally cheerful and hard-working. But unlike Jim Farley, Hannegan has an emotional side that tugged him over to the New Dealers. He became an ardent disciple of Franklin Roosevelt and, when he died, transferred this feeling to Henry Wallace and the small group of Democratic liberals in Washington. Hannegan was always trying to bring the President and Wallace together. He was the one cabinet officer who called Wallace after his dismissal and said he was sorry.

As Democratic chairman, Bob cultivated the New Deal wing of the party. He was personally convinced the Democrats had to have this support to win elections. George Allen, John Snyder, and Harry Vaughan made fun of him to the President. "Old Bob turned out to be a pinko," they joked heartily.

Another of the President's earlier cronies who is seen less frequently around the White House is Les Biffle, the slim, curly-haired former Secretary of the Senate. "Bif" is one of the most popular men in Washington and is the acknowledged expert on Congress. He knows every Senator intimately – his habits, opinions, and friends.

When Harry Truman came to Washington as an awed, bewildered freshman Senator, Les showed him the ropes, introduced him to the right people, and gave him sound counsel. In those first confused days after Mr. Roosevelt's death Mr. Truman was lonely in the big White House. So he picked up the phone, called Biffle, and said wistfully, "Bif, get some of the boys together. I'm coming up for lunch."

Biffle accompanied the President on a number of his junkets but he always seemed somewhat out of place. He was quiet, reserved, and a trifle embarrassed.

When the White House and Capitol Hill began throwing bricks at each other, Bif discovered he had to make a decision. He could not be a Truman crony and a successful Secretary of the Senate too. So he gradually dropped out of the inner circle of cronies.

Chapter V

ARCHITECTURALLY, the White House is an oasis of beauty and tranquillity in downtown Washington.

The gleaming white building with the graceful lines, big round pillars on the portico, and sweeping driveways is a strange contrast to the grimy old Treasury and State Department buildings on either side. Busy streetcars clang down Pennsylvania Avenue to break up the traffic jams in front of the White House.

Within the grounds are cool green lawns, giant shade trees, fountains and flower gardens. Friendly squirrels jump up to the steel picket fence and beg visitors for peanuts. A robin made her nest on a column.

Inside, the White House is a dignified colonial mansion. It has a large entrance hall with glittering glass chandeliers. On both sides are hospitable reception rooms. The estate seems built for cotillions and receptions and garden parties. The architects apparently did not contemplate that the President would ever have to do much work. They very considerately put in a handsome cabinet room, where he could meet with his Secretaries and receive their reports.

The architects were not men of much vision. Since the present White House was erected, wings have been added on each end. They house offices for the President and his growing staff of assistants. These additions have not been enough. Presidential staff assistants have overflowed into the musty State Department Building and that marble place, the Federal Reserve Building.

Under Franklin Roosevelt the White House became a great central headquarters for vast governmental operations, instead of a mansion for good living. Harry Truman inherited all this elaborate organization and power which had been built up during Roosevelt's regime.

The new President hastened to tell Senators he didn't want all this power. He was going back to the cabinet form of government.

But gradually Harry Truman, too, built up the same complex kind of mechanism for running the government from 1600 Pennsylvania Avenue.

Matt Connelly, who had been an investigator-clerk for the Truman War Investigating Committee of the Senate, was made executive secretary to the President. He took over the key function of making appointments.

Matt is a good-looking young Irishman from Boston. He started out as a sleuth for the WPA and later was an investigator for the House Appropriations Committee, the Senate Campaign Expenditures Committee, and the Truman Committee. He was known on Capitol Hill as something of a playboy. He was never identified with either the New Deal crowd of committee assistants or the studious clerks who have made Congress a lifetime job. His colleagues considered Matt as rather shrewd and affable.

He and Mr. Truman hit it off well, and Matt became one of the spokesmen for the Truman Committee. He made occasional investigations in the field and turned in the report on Willow Run.

After he moved into the White House, Matt became publicity shy. He has managed to stay out of the limelight and sit back in a quiet corner at the night clubs.

Connelly got the executive secretary job originally intended for Hugh Fulton, the chubby lawyer who made the Truman Committee a going concern. Fulton was the "brains" of the committee. He did the hard work the committee took the credit for. But Hugh made one mistake. When Mr. Roosevelt died, Washington assumed that Fulton would be President Truman's assistant. Politicos and bureaucrats went around to him with their problems. Hugh gave advice and made plans. Some of the cronies whispered into Mr. Truman's ear, "Hugh thinks he's going to run the government. You'd think he was the President."

Harry Truman got into one of his angry, stubborn moods. Hugh did not get the job. He was as surprised as Matt Connelly.

For his military adviser, President Truman retained Fleet Admiral William D. Leahy. At the White House news conferences, the Admiral sits behind Mr. Truman. There is rarely any expression on his stony, lined face. He stares with sharp, penetrating eyes at the crowd of reporters. He never makes a public statement. His duties are not defined by any act of Congress or Executive Order.

A White House spokesman says of him, "Admiral Leahy is a very valuable man. President Truman is quite fond of him. He has informed the President on military and naval operations and matters during and since the war."

Actually, the Admiral is a steady powerful pressure on American military and foreign policy. He is the direct pipeline into the White House for the generals and admirals and can usually get Presidential approval for any plan of the professional militarists.

Before moving into the White House under Mr. Roosevelt, Admiral Leahy performed a special mission as Ambassador to unoccupied France. His job was to keep the old Marshal of Vichy, Henri Philippe Pétain, from handing over the rest of France to Germany. FDR with his sly judgment of the men he used thought that Leahy and Pétain would get along well together. Both were elderly, conservative militarists. Both hated Soviet Russia almost as much as they detested the Nazi upstarts. Both thought the world would be a lot better off if it were run by professional military men.

When Harry Truman became President, Admiral Leahy was just what the doctor ordered. With friends, the Admiral is a charming man with a salty sense of humor and a blunt directness. He fills in Mr. Truman's awful gaps of knowledge on world affairs.

Under Mr. Truman, Admiral Leahy enjoys more freedom than he ever had with Franklin Roosevelt. FDR had a string tied and he could jerk it back if he wanted to. There was a clear, though subtle, understanding between the two men. Harry Truman untied the knots and gave the Admiral a comparatively free hand.

Admiral Leahy's personal views are hidden by military secrecy and the role of a Presidential adviser. He is, however, closely identified with Constantine Brown, the *Washington Star* columnist and a vigorous opponent of all things Soviet. It was Brown who broke the story that Jimmy Byrnes was on his way out as Secretary of State and General Marshall was dusting off his chair.

Secretary Byrnes violently denounced this story at a press conference. A reporter asked him directly if he did not know the report came from Admiral Leahy. Byrnes did not use the opportunity to absolve the Admiral.

The glittering young man who suddenly strode out on the stage as the number one assistant in the White House is Clark Clifford, a handsome, matinee idol type and a St. Louis lawyer. When the heavy fog of gloom covering Washington after the elections lifted, there was Clifford as the beautiful white knight who was going to save Harry Truman from a low Gallup Poll rating.

Clifford sang the lead in college musical comedies and looks like one of those exquisite men identified with advertisements featuring stainless steel and chrome. He has light wavy hair, broad shoulders, big brown eyes, just the right mixture of authority and deference in his personality, and faultless manners. He is easily one of the best-groomed men in Washington.

In St. Louis, Clifford was a social lion idolized alike by elderly maiden ladies and young debutantes. The older men spoke approvingly of him, "Damme, there is a fellow that is all right."

Clifford was slipped into the White House circle by the sleepy-eyed Presidential crony from Missouri, "Jake" Vardaman. Jake was not disinterested in St. Louis society. He picked up Lieutenant (j.g.) Clifford, USNR, and brought him into the White House as assistant naval aide in September 1945. Vardaman was a commodore in the Naval Reserve and President Truman's chief naval aide.

Clifford's duties were not arduous. He was the fellow who straightened the ribbon on the medal before it was given to Vardaman to present to the President before he awarded it in a White House ceremony.

When Jake was boosted up by Mr. Truman to the Federal Reserve System, Clifford became the naval aide, with heavier responsibilities. He was assigned the task of redesigning the Presidential seal and flag.

Clifford was in the Navy less than two years when he was

elevated to the rank of captain and awarded a commendation from the Secretary of Navy for "superb administrative ability, tireless and conscientious devotion to duty."

Back in "civvies," Clifford was appointed to Judge Sam Rosenman's old job of legal adviser to the President. All the way up his swift flight to power, Clifford was assisted by the fatherly support of older men flattered by his deference. Judge Rosenman, a Roosevelt New Dealer, is full of cheerful praise for his bright young protégé.

Actually, Clark Clifford's sharp, but not profound mind dazzles like a Christmas tree decoration amid the cheerless mediocrity of the White House advisers. He wrote President Truman's angry denunciation of the railway strike in the spring of 1946, his radio speech withdrawing meat from under price controls, and his message to the Eightieth Congress.

It was not until Harry Truman's prestige sunk to a soggy low in the fall of 1946 that the handsome attorney stepped in to fill a White House need, as civilian chief of staff. From out of the gloom of the White House marched this Sir Galahad. He was well-poised and self-assured. Soon he was giving Harry Truman the kind of firm instruction the President should have had all along. Clifford was polite, even unctuous, but he got results. There were no longer the series of cheerful blunders at press conferences. The phrase "No comment" became a habit.

Clifford deftly slipped major executive duties away from other aides, principally John Steelman. He helped the President select personnel for key positions. Clifford had the good sense to accept competent advice on the Atomic Energy Commission members.

The young man pulled together stray odds and ends of White House administration and, at least, gave the illusion that the chief of staff knew where he was going. With Clifford by the President's side, the White House seemed a little less like a Missouri courthouse.

After a soft policy toward John Lewis failed, Clifford took over the strike strategy. He sided with Secretary of the Interior Krug's "tough" policy, thus winning a behind-the-scenes tilt with John Steelman.

In the housing controversy between George Allen and Wilson Wyatt, the energetic Housing Administrator, Clifford stepped along with Allen. Their side won and Wyatt resigned. The veterans' priority housing program was abandoned.

John Steelman, another one of the White House lieutenants, is quite well practiced, too, in the art of getting along in Washington. This wide-eyed and friendly man came to Washington because of his enthusiastic flattery of Frances Perkins, then Secretary of Labor.

Steelman was an economics professor at small Alabama State College when Miss Perkins came down to make a commencement address. Professor Steelman showed great interest in the "marvelous work" of the Secretary. He said shyly how wonderful it would be to be in Washington working under such a great person as Madame Secretary.

Two years after Secretary Perkins brought her admirer to the long stone building on Constitution Avenue, he was a more important public figure than she was. While New Deal foes were criticizing Miss Perkins as a crackpot woman, John Steelman wore a virtuous smile on his shiny face. He was taking credit for the settlement of all labor disputes as the Director of the Conciliation Service.

This ambitious and hard-working bureaucrat has a device for success that he might have picked up in one of those mail-order "success" courses. It is a card-catalogue file of all the important persons he has ever met. The file contains first names and anecdotes. Too, he has always insisted that he, rather than his staff, sign all letters to bigwigs and Congressmen, whether or not he actually wrote them.

Before the 1944 election Steelman left the Administration in what appeared to some to be unseemly haste. The inference was that he wanted to be "available" in case the Republicans won and were looking for a Secretary of Labor. Before he left the city, Dr. Steelman had time to write flattering farewell letters to every important figure on Capitol Hill. He set up shop in New York as an industrial relations adviser for a number of cushy clients — chain stores, an airline, department stores.

At the start of the Truman Administration, trusting Lew Schwellenbach brought Steelman back to Washington to help him get started. Within a few weeks, Steelman was for all practical purposes the Secretary of Labor. He became the White House labor adviser and then Director of Reconversion.

Steelman looks like a healthy, middle-aged farmer sight-seeing in Washington. He has a round and innocent face, a hearty handshake, a boyish shyness, and a big frame. He lumbers around the White House as if he were stepping out his forty acres. At every official gathering, Steelman wears a breathless and astonished look as though he were pinching himself and asking, "How did I get here?"

He is one of the hardest working and most eager-to-please fellows in Washington, but has never been accused of having the imagination or profundity of a Machiavelli. On all economic questions, Steelman has leaned to the conservative side. He was for lifting the lid slowly but surely on all controls as the pressure fell on him. In the coal strikes of 1946, he sided with John Lewis on several points. Whether this reflected his belief in Lewis's case or his respect for a successful, powerful man has long been debated.

Charley Ross, the White House press secretary, is a former topnotch Washington correspondent who is protected by the stubborn insistence of his former co-workers that he not be criticized publicly. Charley has not looked really cheerful since he gave up his lucrative position as an editorial writer to sit in Steve Early's old office. He has a patient, long face and mournful eyes that are reminiscent of Abraham Lincoln.

He is called in at the last minute to get Mr. Truman out of jams. He does this with a long-suffering air of tolerance. When the President blithely said he favored Henry Wallace's foreign policy views, Charley went to work and wrote out a retreat for Mr. Truman. At the famous Reelfoot Lake press conference when the President blurted out his atomic bomb policy, Charley wore a pained and apologetic look.

If any criticism of Charley is due, it is because he is too much of a gentleman and not enough of the hard-boiled press agent who gives orders to his boss.

The predominant characteristic of the whole White House crew of Presidential cronies and hired hands is small-town philosophy. This was demonstrated after one of the great crises of the Administration. Mr. Truman motored to a small college in Maryland to collect another honorary degree.

The President said wistfully and from a full heart that everyone would be happier and a lot better off if the country could return to an uncomplicated rural life.

During one of the many periods of disagreement in Washington, Harry Truman had a phrase. Someone handed it to him and he read it to his news conference with a happy smile.

It was, "Things seem to be going fairly well. A spirit of pessimism prevails in all departments."

Chapter VI

EVERY President of the United States is engaged in a constant and sometimes stealthy struggle to maintain his power and prestige. He is surrounded by enemies, real and potential, searching for any sign of weakness.

These prowling wolves are:

Congress. In all the history of the United States, the legislative and executive branches have tangled angrily over authority. It is a ceaseless war, with Congress throwing emergency powers at a President during times of war or disaster and trying to recover them in the spaces in between.

The political opposition both within and without the President's party. These political wolves are looking always for some crack to push and prod open which will ultimately destroy the President. Both major political parties employ writers who are artists at destroying reputations. The old past master of this art was Charley Michelson of the Democratic National Committee.

The powerful pressure groups. The lobbyists keep a keen watch for some symptom that would help them gain control of or destroy Executive policy.

Foreign governments. The political and economic competition among nations is so strong that any indication of a weakness in the President of the United States is seized upon and used in both whispered and open propaganda.

The wolves had lean pickings under Roosevelt. They howled a lot, but they got few real bites. When Harry Truman came into office, the wolves lined up with glassy eyes, waiting for the first misstep.

They did not have to wait long. Ten months after his elevation to the Presidency, Harry Truman sent up a nomination to Capitol

Hill that exploded round the world. He asked the Senate to approve the nomination of husky Ed Pauley, the independent California oil operator and treasurer of the Democratic National Committee, to be Undersecretary of the Navy.

The Senate hearings on Ed Pauley were dramatic and revealing. They exposed the character of Harry Truman, forced him to his first defeat, and showed how he could be beaten. The hearings opened a wide split between Democrats and New Dealers. They brought into the headlines the eternal fighting between Capitol Hill and downtown. They told of the grim, beneath-the-surface struggle between business and politics for control of oil resources. These were not the kind of stories taught in high-school civics classes or printed in neat publicity brochures.

The formal issue was whether Ed Pauley had lobbied for the forces trying to grab the tidelands oil resources, estimated as worth billions of dollars, away from the Federal Government.

Mr. Truman, in making the Pauley appointment, was only following an orthodox rule in local politics – reward your friends and destroy your enemies. (This was a part of Harry Truman's political philosophy, and he had inherited it from the Pendergast machine of Missouri.)

Ed Pauley was a big, two-fisted man with all the aggressiveness of a successful self-made character. He fought his way up through the jungles of oil and politics. He had, by some miracle, wiped out a big deficit in the Democratic campaign chest.

The Republicans leaped joyfully. Charles Tobey, the energetic and caustic ranking minority member of the Senate Naval Affairs Committee, demanded a full and open investigation.

Throughout the long hours of the Pauley hearings, the committee became confused and angry. Each Senator knew his own political future had become mixed up somehow in the hearings. During the long hours of constant, almost monotonous questions, Senator Tobey, the chief interrogator, became a changed man. The bald, pink-faced New Englander became taut, excitable, and furiously angry.

He clashed constantly with Senator Tydings, the lean, precise, sarcastic Democrat from Maryland. Tydings had taken over the defense of Pauley and protested what he called "the oral lynching."

Senator Dave Walsh of Massachusetts, the chairman, sat helplessly in the middle. This big man with sagging cheeks, deep-set eyes, and well-manicured hands did not look happy. He lost his benevolence as the days wore on.

Ed Pauley sat grimly through the hearings. Often an uneasy or angry flush reddened his face.

The climax came when Secretary of the Interior Harold Ickes, the Old Curmudgeon, was called to testify. He sat glumly in his chair waiting for the hearing to open. The committee room was jammed. Forty eager reporters were crowded at the press tables with yellow copy paper spread out before them.

Ickes stirred in his chair and addressed the committee. "When I got your summons last night, it was the first I knew this party was going on."

The correspondents grinned. The Old Curmudgeon was in good form.

Senator Tobey asked eagerly, "Did Mr. Pauley ever tell you the filing of the government suit to claim the tidelands was bad politics, that it might cost several hundred thousand dollars in campaign donations?"

There was a long, complete silence.

The Secretary looked unhappy. He answered slowly, "This line of questioning is embarrassing to me. But you are entitled to an answer. . . . My answer is *Yes*."

A faint, sick smile replaced the jaunty look on Pauley's face.

"What was your answer?" Senator Tobey asked in his dry, New England twang.

Ickes answered firmly, "That I would not let that enter into my consideration."

Toward the end of the parrying back and forth, Ickes was asked what he thought of the Pauley nomination. Gloom and misery spread over his face. But his voice was clear, "I am a member of the Cabinet. I don't know why, but I am. This nomination was sent here by the man I'm working for, President Truman."

In the afternoon, Pauley moved into the witness chair. He was confident and undismayed. He and Senator Tobey argued back and forth over the tideland oil suit. It was a contest between a blunt broadsword and a sharp, twisting dagger.

Then Senator Brewster of Maine took over the questioning. There was an eager, friendly smile in his blue eyes. His voice fairly purred. He asked Pauley, "What would you think about a Federal judge soliciting my support for you? A judge who went to Tokyo with you?"

Pauley answered bluffly, "Oh, did he come to you?"

Brewster purred on, "Yes, he said some fine things about you. He said we ought to have an oil man in the Navy Department, because the Navy was interested in oil."

Pauley replied, "That was nice of him."

Brewster's voice rose just a bit. "I thought it was unusual. I was surprised. I hardly knew him. I cannot imagine he came to me without your knowledge."

The witness answered stolidly, "Apparently, I have many eager friends. I am very grateful."

The Senator purred softly again, "You look after your friends?"

The answer was, "I am loyal to my friends."

"And to your business?"

"Yes."

The Senator said kindly, "You use your position as Democratic Treasurer to raise money . . . and then you think the people in Washington should reciprocate."

Pauley tried to wisecrack. "Mr. Ickes shot something of a load."

Brewster looked straight at the witness, still with that paternal look in his eyes. "I would appreciate it if you raised a million dollars for me. . . . You see no conflict of propriety or morality in using political power to further business interests?"

Pauley said stiffly, "I never used either in connection with the other."

Brewster smiled benignly. "Oh, you are two people."

Pauley turned to a subject weighing heavily on his mind. He said, "I am sure Mr. Ickes was very much confused this morning. I only asked him to help raise money for the Democratic Party."

Senator Brewster pounced softly. "You realize, of course, that the Secretary has been in public life a long time, and is very careful of the reputation of others . . . I think we ought to have an idea of your sense of proprieties. Is it proper for you to sell oil to any department of government if you are Undersecretary of the Navy?"

Pauley answered stoutly, "There is no legal reason why not. I would ask my company not to. But it is a large company. If you feel it is necessary for my company to drop all its business with the government, I ask you to vote No on my nomination."

The next witness was a handsome, black-haired young man, Norman Littell, former Assistant Attorney General. This well-poised lawyer had been in charge of government legal efforts to claim the tidelands. He seated himself comfortably in his seat, drumming on the arm with his finger tips.

He said in a smooth voice, "I would prefer not to be involved in this matter. President Truman made the nomination. He is a man of integrity. I tried several times to talk to the President about this, but I couldn't get through the battery of secretaries."

Senator Tobey took over. "When did you know Pauley?"

Littell waved an arm vaguely. "I saw him several times in 1940. He always brought up the tideland case. The pressure wasn't a thing that hits you with a hammer. It was more subtle than that."

The Senator kept after him. "Did he discuss it with you again?"

Littell replied easily, "Yes, a week before the 1940 election. He raised the tideland matter in a somewhat astonishing manner. He asked me up to his room and said, 'Perhaps you know I raise money. A lot of that money came from people interested in tidelands. These people who donated to the campaign expect something for their money.'"

Littell paused to let his words sink in, then went on, "I felt that I was to be the beginning of the pay-off. I thought of that nursery rhyme – ' "You've come into my parlor," said the spider to the fly.' "

Senator Tobey asked, "Mr. Pauley has said he did not discuss this case with Mr. Biddle, the Solicitor General. Is that true?"

The witness answered quietly, "I am afraid that is not true."

Pauley sat stiffly in his chair staring straight ahead.

Littell looked at some notes he pulled out of his pocket. He said, "There was a conference between Biddle and Pauley. I was there. The meeting was at 4 P.M. on Tuesday, November 12, 1940. Mr. Pauley suggested that instead of pressing the suit with the Supreme Court, the Administration pass a compromise joint resolution in Congress."

Once again that faint, ill-at-ease smile flickered briefly over Pauley's strong face. The Senators, smelling blood, leaned forward intently.

There was melodrama and mystery all through the hearings. A man who allegedly had been in the front of an oil lobby in California was discovered in a strategic spot in the Justice Department. He was in the division handling the Federal tideland suit before the Supreme Court, as Assistant Solicitor General.

Two of the three Senators on the subcommittee which approved this man's nomination said they knew nothing about it . . . had not been present at any committee vote.

Pauley was asked about it by Senator Brewster, who said silkily, "It was entirely coincidental that Judson landed here in the Department of Justice to handle this oil case before the Supreme Court?"

Pauley said brusquely, "I knew nothing about it."

Brewster commented, a little question forming in his last word, "It was entirely fortuitous."

A conversation between Senator Tobey and two prospective witnesses in his office had leaked out to Harry March, an oil man. He was called to the stand. Nervously he flexed and unflexed his long fingers and wet his lips.

Senator Tobey said, "I call upon you now to give the name of the man who told you of the conference in my office."

March looked around him and replied in a low voice, "I gave my word that I would not give his name."

Tobey's voice jumped higher and higher. "Why are you afraid?"

The witness said meekly, "I am not afraid."

"Why were you so interested in the meeting at my office?" Tobey asked.

The reply came out slowly and laboriously. "I received word that Standard Oil of California might be brought into these hearings and I wanted to find out. I didn't want certain agreements between my company and Standard to come out."

The questions came hard and fast.

"Have you ever sought to collect money for the oil legislation?"

"Yes."

"Who did you solicit?"

"Ten or fifteen companies."

"Who did you approach?"

"I don't know."

"Who did you talk to in Washington in connection with the tideland legislation besides Pauley?"

Senator Tydings broke in, "Why in the world did you ask that? What has that to do with Pauley?"

Tobey's voice rose to a shriek. "If the Senator from Maryland will just have patience. The confirming power of the Senate is a sacred trust. These interruptions only make the task harder. My mind goes back to the infamous Teapot Dome investigations."

Pauley was called back on the stand. Tobey and Brewster, the two ranking Republicans on the committee, worked in relays. They questioned Pauley about money he was alleged to have spent in California elections for the oil companies. The witness was vague. He had a bad memory. He kept repeating, "I don't know."

The hearings brought immediate results. The man who would be Ed Pauley's boss and who might be succeeded by him, Secretary of the Navy Forrestal, read the committee a statement in an exact, even voice. It was a skillfully worded, devastating testimony. Nothing blunt, all very silken. The last three lines carried the sting: "I am jealous in the highest degree of the good name and integrity of the United States Navy. I do not propose lightly to expose myself or my splendid associates who have helped me in this tremendous task [of waging war] to the risk of blotting the copybook at the end of the record."

On one of the last days of the hearing, a sheet of paper was passed down the press tables. It was a statement by Senator Tom

Stewart of Tennessee, the Senate spokesman for the powerful Democratic boss, Ed Crump of Memphis. The typed words said, "I regret that Mr. Pauley has not withdrawn his nomination, or that Mr. Hannegan has not had him do it. To continue to embarrass the Democratic Party is bad. We have had other Teapot Dome experiences in this country, and I hope we do not have another one. You cannot mix oil, water and politics."

A correspondent showed the release to Ed Pauley. As he looked down the sheet, Pauley's strong, hard face flushed red. A sick smile flickered, then faded away. He said huskily, "No comment."

At the press table, a reporter whispered to his colleagues, "Some of my GI friends were in town and they came up here to watch the hearing. They went home to start a revolution."

Eventually, pressure from Democratic politicos and the oil companies which were tired of having their affairs dragged out across the committee table forced Pauley to ask that his nomination be withdrawn.

The damage, however, was already done.

Chapter VII

THE most dramatic reaction to the Pauley investigation came from the Old Curmudgeon, Harold L. Ickes.

One morning during the hearings every newspaper office in Washington was startled out of its before-noon drowsiness. The bells rang madly on the teletypes. The keys hammered out, FLASH. There was a pause, more bells. Then the keys rushed over the paper, "Truman Accepts Ickes's Resignation."

Reporters threw on their overcoats and trudged sleepily across Washington. They walked past the rear of the White House, out across the busy traffic on Seventeenth Street, and into the hushed halls of the Interior Building.

Up in the press room, the reporters who cover the building every day were mechanically checking the new press releases. Harold Ickes's last handout proudly announced the sale of 900 mules to the United Nations Relief. The anxious and watchful public was informed the mules were sold for $175 each.

An Interior Department secretary kept getting up and looking at the busy news ticker. She watched the keys hammer out their tales and said with irritation, "Imagine getting the weather forecast at a time like this."

No one thought the remark strange.

A half hour before Secretary Ickes's scheduled press conference, the conference room was jammed. Every chair was taken. Correspondents stood two deep along the walls. Men who had not wandered three feet from the Press Club bar in months were there. Columnists who usually meditate in solitary dignity sat primly in their chairs. They looked a little surprised to find themselves rubbing elbows with the masses.

The conference room was like a well-kept shrine – dimly lit, soft-colored walls and curtains, leather-covered doors.

White-haired Joe Fox, the crack White House reporter, looked at the throng in mock surprise. He said to no one in particular, "Is there a story up here this morning?"

Outside in the hall, cub reporters who had hoped to cover the big story were stuck forlornly in telephone booths. They were holding open the lines for the top men.

Occasionally, as the minutes ticked away, the crowded room lapsed into a nervous hush. It was broken by a cough, then a buzz of conversation began.

At eleven-thirty, a voice boomed from the doorway, "Mr. Ickes's press conference moved to the auditorium."

The reporters grumbled, picked up their coats, and plowed down five flights of stairs.

The Old Curmudgeon, with his sense of the theater, could not have chosen a better place to give his last official testament on the Truman Administration. The auditorium is the birthplace of many causes. Harold Ickes always opened the door to anyone who wanted to plead a cause . . . Palestine, racial discrimination, or prevention of cruelty to animals.

The auditorium has an air of respectability and dignity about it unlike most of the halls where causes are passionately pleaded. The gold seals of every state in the Union are along the walls. The rear of the stage is a huge painting of Southwest America. The lights are dim and indirect.

Harold Ickes shambled down the aisle like an old bear. Beside him was his tall, younger wife. He climbed up on the stage with the agility of a man forty years his junior.

The reporters, who, in their time, had seen many men come and go, burst into loud, spontaneous applause.

A famous columnist said with a touch of sadness, "This is the end of the revolution."

It was, at least, the Old Curmudgeon in his last public performance as a cabinet member.

His jaw was thrust forward. His rimless glasses rested halfway down his nose. He looked over them at the crowded auditorium.

There was a gleam of pride in his sharp eyes. These men and women had come to see HIM. It was the biggest darn news conference ever held in Washington.

This was the man whom Franklin Roosevelt had called with affectionate amusement "Harold, the Ick." Others damned him, swore at him for being an irascible old grump and hell raiser, but called him "Honest Harold."

He had fought almost everyone in Washington with a zestful bumptiousness for thirteen years. He had brought thousands of independent voters into the Democratic Party.

He was a maker of phrases. He had called Wendell Willkie "the barefoot boy from Wall Street." He said of Governor Tom Dewey, "He threw his diaper into the ring."

Harold Ickes started out in the roaring Chicago of the turn of the century. He was a reporter in the days before journalism went soft, when every news beat was a knock-down, drag-out fight and not a plant.

In politics, he prided himself on being a mugwump, whom no party could hold down. He campaigned with bare knuckles for the old Progressive Party of Teddy Roosevelt and was the campaign manager for Senator Hiram Johnson's bid for the White House. He was a Republican and jumped the fences in 1932 to support Franklin Roosevelt.

In March 1933, President Roosevelt brought him to Washington as Secretary of the Interior. Mr. Roosevelt had two motives. He wanted to keep his independent Republican support. And he wanted an honest man to sit tightly on the natural resources of the land. Harold did the job with rugged and pugnacious virtue.

He found time to battle for causes and candidates and write seven books. He belongs to a long list of organizations, including the Save the Redwoods League. He was awarded the Louis Brandeis Medal for Service to Humanity. The Secretary leaned over the stand on the stage and opened up. He said, "A man can resign in one of two ways. He can say – I am leaving. Or, he can tell why. I am telling why, and I'll give you the high lights that are compelling to me."

Except for his thinning hair, Secretary Ickes did not look his seventy-one years. His voice had all the punch and force of a Southern filibuster.

He said, "This is not a tentative resignation." He hit the word "tentative" with a roaring blast.

The Old Curmudgeon went on, "My mind was made up. The immediate cause for my resignation was, of course, the Pauley incident. I don't care to stay in an Administration where I am expected to commit perjury for the sake of a party. I never belonged to a party, and I'm too old to start all over again."

Half the reporters were writing furiously, trying to take down every word. The others decided to enjoy, without the diversion of work, the swan song of the stocky, pugnacious figure on the stage.

Honest Harold went on, "As soon as I read the report of the President's last press conference when he said I might be mistaken about Pauley, I knew what I had to do. He knew I was opposed to Pauley. Not once did he ask for my reasons. I gave him opportunities. All he had to do was to ask me."

The Old Curmudgeon was glaring now.

"I didn't like the President's statement that I might be mistaken about Pauley. I couldn't possibly be mistaken. Even the President of the United States has no right to prejudge me on that kind of an issue. He should have ascertained the facts. He should have read the record."

The auditorium was quiet except for the salty voice of the Secretary. The reporters were stiffly attentive.

Ickes said with a touch of bitterness, "I sent the President my letter of resignation yesterday. I haven't heard from him yet. I wanted to stay over until March 31st because of the Anglo-American oil treaty."

He added proudly, "There wouldn't be a treaty like that in the Senate now were it not for my tenacity."

The Secretary said cheerfully, "But I guess a man who has been in office thirteen years ought to be able to get out in two days."

A low laugh moved over the auditorium. The man on the stage had the crowd.

"On the whole," he went on, "I'm glad it's all over. It's been like waiting for an operation. The doctors tell me I'm doing well. After Monday, I'll be a free man. I can do what I please."

A reporter shouted, "What more is there to say?"

Ickes popped back, "That depends on what Pauley says on Monday."

The questions rained on him. "What are your future plans?"

He said flatly, "I ain't got any. I've been propositioned to write a newspaper column. But you know no girl ever takes the first proposal."

"Will you work against Harry Truman politically?"

The Old Curmudgeon thought just the fraction of a second, then hurled back, "I might work for him in 1948. I can think of worse contingencies." He drew out the word "worse."

"Would you withdraw your advice to progressives last fall to support Truman?"

The Secretary glowered. "That was true then. But since then he has sent some nominations up to the Senate. You observe the plural. Some people think I am expected to commit perjury."

A correspondent asked curiously, "Are you thinking of Bob Hannegan, the Democratic National Chairman, by any chance?"

Ickes flung out the retort, "You figure it out. Hannegan's been moving heaven and earth to get Pauley through."

"When did the President ask you to go easy on Pauley?"

The Old Curmudgeon looked down scornfully into the hall. "It was after the special cabinet meeting on the food problem. I showed him the summons from the Senate committee. Mr. Truman told me, 'You must tell the truth, of course. But be as gentle as you can with Ed Pauley.'"

The next question was, "What was your answer?"

Ickes replied owlishly, "I said I would."

The audience snorted with laughter. The Secretary looked down at the correspondents with simulated indignation. He said, "I did, didn't I? I didn't go out of my way to recite details."

Ickes found time in the mass interview to shout down a heckling reporter. He jabbed at him, "Your column is not only psychopathic; it is untrue." The rest of the audience snickered.

The reporter tried again. "Mr. Secretary, we are puzzled about you."

Ickes glared. The reporter lowered his eyes. The Secretary growled, "Don't let me disturb you. Your trouble is that you are always puzzled. I can't think of anyone less able to understand than you."

The questions got back on the track. "Do your differences with Mr. Truman go beyond Pauley?"

Ickes replied quietly, "The President, in principle, tried to give an honest administration in the Roosevelt tradition. But he was unfortunate in the choice of certain appointments. There were some very regrettable appointments."

The photographers' group around him in the half circle caught the pushed-out underlip, the mixed look of anger and sadness in his eyes.

Another inquiry was, "Do you think Truman was responsible for the selections?"

Ickes grinned and answered, "As Cal Coolidge used to say, 'He did 'em, didn't he?' "

"Do you have any more memoranda on Pauley?"

The Secretary replied lustily, "Lots of them."

A reporter asked timidly, "You said you might continue to oppose Pauley?"

Ickes pursed out his lips in the best curmudgeon manner. He grumbled sarcastically, "*Might?* That's a queer choice of a verb. . . . I oppose Hannegan because he is in the oil business."

A correspondent corrected him. "You mean Pauley."

Ickes said reflectively, "Yes, sometimes I get them mixed."

A reporter with a deadline to make tried to end the conference by shouting, "Thank you, Mr. Secretary."

But it did not work. Most of the correspondents were too fascinated by this bluff, blunt interview. The Old Curmudgeon himself was enjoying every minute of it.

"Do you think there has been a change since Mr. Roosevelt died?" he was asked.

Ickes answered humbly, "The greatest man of our generation died. I never hope to see his likes again."

A simple-minded reporter asked, "Is there a chance you will take another job in the government?"

The Secretary laughed hollowly. "Huh, huh. There is just as much possibility as if I were offered one."

Someone brought up a possible investigation of an Interior Department employee proposed by a Congressman.

Ickes scolded the questioner, "Let's keep our minds on a higher plane than the Congressman."

He went into his own political philosophy. "We ought to have men in office not deviated by political or private purposes."

The Old Curmudgeon was asked, "Will you leave the Democratic Party?"

The Secretary smiled smugly. "I'll tell you something. I never was a Democrat." He added with the sad wisdom of one who has been through it all, "But this third-party stuff won't work."

A voice called out, "Thank you, Mr. Secretary."

The auditorium echoed with loud applause. It was the final tribute of the Washington correspondents.

Honest Harold stood in the glare of the floodlights set up by a newsreel cameraman. He waved his arm happily and called, "Good-by."

This was the beginning of the splitting off from the Truman Administration of its New Deal and independent liberal support. Ickes's resignation was followed by a stream of others from men who were in Washington because, as they said, it was "fun" working for Roosevelt. Others gloomily "went underground" or kept their mouths shut on the job.

Ickes was the first major political or public figure to accuse the Truman Administration of being a mine-run, ward-politics Democratic administration.

Secretary of Commerce Henry Wallace sat back in painful silence. He had lots of company: Democrats on Capitol Hill who boiled over in private but decided not to speak out publicly against the titular leader of the Democratic Party. But when Republicans rose in Congress to taunt the Democrats about the Pauley appointment, very few voices rose in defense.

Ickes put his finger on a flaw in the Truman Administration, the religion of reward your friends and punish your enemies, and turned attention to a series of appointments – Jake Vardaman, the sleepy-eyed Presidential naval aide and old Missouri pal to the exalted job of Governor of the Federal Reserve System; George Allen, onetime hotel clerk, professional politician and Washington lobbyist, to be a director of the Reconstruction Finance Corporation; country banker John Snyder to be Secretary of the Treasury.

Roosevelt had somehow kept the three horses of the Democratic Party – the machine politicians, the Southern conservatives, and the liberals – together in harness. Now, they were flying off in different directions.

This was the beginning of the roaring battle coming up in 1948 for control of the Democratic Party.

Chapter VIII

THE glorious exodus of the Old Curmudgeon was just one skirmish in the bitter civil war between the Truman cronies and the small leaderless band of New Dealers.

Many of his friends watched Ickes's departure enviously. He could take a walk. They had to stay. All of the New Dealers in the Administration found themselves smothered by an unhappy dilemma – to openly rebel against the President or suffer in silence in the hope of "being an influence."

Even in the Roosevelt Administration, the New Dealers had been a minority – a small, very vocal and favored group made up largely of men and women in their thirties. The New Dealers were sandwiched in the right places where decisions could be made. They were backed up at the White House. They had a leader who made government an exciting adventure, a place for knights in shining armor to joust with villains of reaction.

They now found themselves surrounded by hostile groups and their support from the White House gone.

The professional bureaucrats had sourly tolerated the New Dealers in about the same way veteran employees look out of the corner of their eyes at the boss's cousin brought in to a lush job. The New Dealers had jauntily disregarded many of the old regulations for advancement. They had passed over the old faithfuls who had ground out a dull existence as bureaucrats for decades and slipped the jobs to brisk young men fresh from a master's degree. Now was the time for the old boys to pay back a few grudges.

The politicians even in the Roosevelt days had a thinly disguised dislike for the New Dealers. They – the men who earned their keep getting the vote out in the Fifth Ward – had to sit back in respectful attention while the guys who brazenly boasted about splitting their tickets gave them lectures on how to win the elections.

There was even a greater gulf between the politicians and the New Dealers. The politicians looked on patronage – jobs, contracts, favors from government – as natural weapons of their trade. Most of the New Dealers considered patronage dishonest and took happy pleasure in frustrating the politicians.

There were some exceptions. Harry Hopkins was one of the keenest politicians to sit in Washington. He saw opportunities for patronage in hitherto uncharted fields. He built a great political organization out of the WPA without fraud or scandal. Some of the politicians even grew to be moderately fond of the New Deal and worked hard for it.

Now, in addition to the professional bureaucrats and the politicians, the New Dealers found another and even more potent force against them. It was the Truman cronies. John Snyder and George Allen regarded the New Dealers as a queer prank of Franklin Roosevelt's that might just as well be forgotten.

Henry A. Wallace, the spiritual leader of the New Dealers, sat mute in his dark, wood-paneled office in the Department of Commerce. He was frustrated at every turn.

Wallace had roused an almost fanatical devotion in his hectic triumphant fights for the Agricultural Adjustment Administration, in his campaign for American intervention in world affairs, and at two steaming, roaring Democratic National Conventions. In the Truman Administration, he sank to the bottom of his influence in Washington.

A little more than a year before, the New Dealers had shouted themselves hoarse for Henry Wallace at the huge Chicago Stadium. Some had cried when he lost the nomination. Now, they looked to Wallace to lead them out of the wilderness into the promised land or give them a signal to attack. But Henry Wallace was writing beautiful speeches and holding his fire, until the summer of 1946.

There were moments when Henry Wallace was sorely tried.

Should he leave, repudiate Harry Truman, and fight openly for control of the Democratic Party? Harry Truman finally decided the issue in a two-minute telephone call.

Will Davis, the tolerant philosopher who had been Chairman of the War Labor Board and Director of the Office of Economic Stabilization for a few months, was less politically-minded than Wallace. He left early.

Bob Nathan, the husky young Roosevelt brain truster who looks like a reformed prize fighter, cleaned out his desk and bid the Truman Administration less than a fond farewell. He had been Deputy Director of the Office of War Mobilization and Reconversion, writing all top reconversion policy. Nathan and John Snyder differed sharply on economic policy.

Within six months after Truman took office, the bright young men of Washington were packing their bags by the scores. One noon that fall, a New Dealer sighed to me at lunch, "There isn't any fun working for the government any more. No inspiration. No one to demand you do the impossible, and giving you confidence you can. No bold adventures."

The one liberal whom Harry Truman had brought in with him, Secretary of Labor Lew Schwellenbach, was having his troubles. The big, mournful ex-Senator from Washington found himself nudged out of influence by John Steelman. He saw his hopes for promotion to the Supreme Court vanishing with the appointments of Senator Burton and Fred Vinson to the Court. Lew Schwellenbach sat back at his desk sadly resigned to an unkind fate.

The New Dealers looked hopefully to three men with whom they had occasionally held hands in the Roosevelt Administration.

Fred Vinson and Jimmy Byrnes, the two former Southern Congressmen and past masters of the art of compromise, were pushed outside the small circle of influence. Fred Vinson, the easy-going Kentuckian, was named Secretary of the Treasury and then Chief Justice of the Supreme Court, both times to make room for John Snyder.

Jimmy Byrnes, named Secretary of State, was led into political warfare with Soviet Russia. He had no time for the New Dealers whom he occasionally helped when President Roosevelt was alive.

Postmaster General Bob Hannegan, the Irish boy from St. Louis who had sold Harry Truman to FDR, was a kind of last resource for the New Dealers. They went to him with their complaints only to find Hannegan loaded down with sorrows of his own.

The big surprise in the Truman Administration was Chester Bowles. An aristocrat (Yale, '24) and successful businessman, Bowles became the rebel and glamour boy of the early Truman Administration. Doleful New Dealers looked up in surprise, then joy.

Bowles was the one who talked back zestfully and with a salty tang. He scrapped happily for price controls. Bowles operated with all the enthusiasm of a small boy digging a hole.

Bowles looks more like a faithful college alumnus than an economist or politician. That is a part of his disarming, engaging personality. He has a long face that, when relaxed, droops into the friendly melancholy of a great Dane. He has a boyish crooked smile. His lips curve up on the left side. He dresses in careless good taste and wears his hair clipped short.

In his appearance before Congressional committees, Chester Bowles had the eager, appealing manner of a schoolboy trying so hard to make a good impression on the new teacher. He speaks with a soft, youthful eagerness. It is an informal manner with frequent use of slang. Answering questions, he will say, "Yeah," or "Okay."

To many of the wistful New Dealers, Chester Bowles's features began to blur and take on some of the characteristics of Franklin D. Roosevelt.

They saw in Bowles the same lusty appetite for public affairs. He took it as a Senator takes to long speeches.

At the darkest moments for price control, when his colleagues were moping in their offices, Chester Bowles was happily slugging back through radio addresses and press conferences. He thrived on opposition. During the war – when price control was accepted with grumbling resignation – Bowles did not act like a man who was having fun. That came when the fight grew hot.

This taste for public affairs, which, once acquired, is worse than alcoholism, developed in Bowles after he had won a reputation as a wonder of the advertising world. He had no experience in the rough-and-tumble of public life when he became OPA Director of Connecticut more on a dare than anything else. He came to Washington as a lamb in a den of wolves, a little innocent from the business world. He wound up showing a few new tricks to the wise boys.

Price control would have been a dead duck mutilated by pressures and carved up by the politicians long before if Bowles had not stuck stubbornly by it. There was always a question in the minds of some of his friends whether price control developed the flair for public administration in Bowles, or whether the enthusiasm for public life won a convert to price control.

He was Director of OPA when Mr. Roosevelt died. He was popular then both on Capitol Hill and downtown because of his competent and cheerful administration of the price control agency.

Judge John Collet, a Truman crony from Missouri, was fumbling along amiably at the job of Director of Economic Stabilization. The swift disintegration of the Administration's economic policy was so disturbing that the President had strong pressure from the Hill and his economic advisory board. Collet was conveniently allowed to resign. Bowles took his place.

For a short time, Bowles enjoyed a glorious honeymoon. President Truman introduced him to a cabinet meeting, saying, "Chet has a tough job. Let's give him all our support."

Not many days later, Bowles and John Snyder disagreed on basic issues. The Economic Director was boycotted and excluded from White House conferences. He was not invited to cabinet meetings. Snyder pigeonholed his recommendations.

These setbacks did not discourage Bowles. He looked on them as a challenge.

Like Roosevelt, Bowles showed an uncanny ability to dramatize himself and his side of the issue. He turned a dull and somewhat obscure argument over economic controls into a roaring campaign for the consumer.

Bowles always attracted large audiences in his sessions with Congressional committees. Reporters, who are, in effect, the critics of the hearings on Capitol Hill, liked to watch Bowles. He always put on a good show.

He had, for one thing, a knack of making his opponents look foolish. At one hearing he was being heckled at every turn by Jessie Sumner, the shrill Congresswoman from Illinois.

While he was explaining his policy on food prices, Miss Sumner's high voice called out sarcastically, "Did it ever occur to you that you could expand production and get more butter if you let prices go up?"

Bowles let her remark sink in. Then he answered sweetly, "That's some feat. You have to have cows first."

The audience roared.

Another time, Senator Wherry of Nebraska, the Republican whip, stopped Bowles at every sentence with sharp criticism. Bowles finally asked with a disarming naïveness, "May I read this statement I have here?"

Wherry snapped, "I'm going to interrupt you and ask questions."

Bowles smiled slyly and replied, "No extra charge, Senator."

The Senator growled, "I've got to congratulate the witness. We have the best salesman in the United States as head of the Office of Price Administration."

The witness flipped back, "But I haven't sold you yet, Senator." The audience in the committee room applauded loudly.

At still another hearing, Bowles led Senator Taft, one of the sharpest minds on the Hill, into a trap.

Taft – arguing with Bowles over food subsidies – said irritably, "Why don't you use wage increases to pay for higher food prices?"

The witness answered calmly, "You don't buy groceries on wage rates. You buy with earnings, and they have gone down since V–J Day."

Without stopping to think, the angry Senator flung back, "I don't need any subsidy to pay my food bills."

In all of the heated hearings on price control, none of the Congressmen or Senators were able to best Bowles in the hard catch-as-catch-can of debate. He sat back with a vaguely benign calmness waiting for his openings, and deftly sliding in.

Senator Bankhead, the champion of high-priced cotton, grew so stirred that his hands shook and his eyes beneath his bushy brows glared spitefully.

Bowles's press conferences were as fully covered as President Truman's. The reporters went because they enjoyed Bowles's use of words. Senator Taft will never live down a phrase Bowles tacked on his profit amendment to the price control bill. Bowles called it "a delayed-action bomb" and "a booby-trap amendment."

Bowles used a very simple formula he brought with him from advertising – simplify your argument in the most favorable terms. He reduced the whole complicated debate over economic control to, "The enemies of price control are conspiring to raise your cost of living. If they are successful, prices will go way up out of reach and then there will be a crash and depression."

The farm lobby, which had always managed to appear on the respectable side of every argument in Washington, could not understand how it was jockeyed around into looking like an evil dragon. The National Association of Manufacturers bought newspaper space and radio time recklessly to protest its virtue. Many Congressmen who honestly believed no price controls would promote full production and low prices were furious at the way Bowles was able to tar them. It was just like the old days. Only Roosevelt could have gotten away with a campaign like that.

Bowles had a keen sense of timing. He let his opponents roar themselves into hoarseness and work themselves into a frenzy. Then he struck. In the hot early summer of 1946, Congress was tired, worried over the elections, and confused. It wanted to get home and was certainly not concerned over passing a strong OPA bill.

At a strategic moment, after Congress had carelessly written a grotesque price control bill, Bowles hit. He made a strategic radio speech after purposely jerking off the price pressure on several common household items. Prices went up. Worried housewives turning on their radios heard Chester Bowles talk about spiraling costs. The mail that followed changed a few minds on Capitol Hill.

Bowles brought to his job as head of the OPA and as Economic Stabilization Director a talent for organization. He developed and used not only the sprawling empire of OPA-paid officials but its advisory boards in his campaigns to enforce price control and finally to save it.

His counterattack to keep OPA alive and healthy was a job of organization. It was aimed both at Congress and at the White House. His strategy was to build up solid pressure for his side.

He combed over official Washington looking for help. The State Department sent its sharpest operator, Will Clayton, up the Hill. Acting Secretary of State Dean Acheson told his press conference that amendments passed in the House and Senate would destroy the program of relief feeding for Europe. Secretary of Commerce Henry Wallace and the other New Dealer in the Cabinet, Lew Schwellenbach, issued statements. So did the chairman of the Wage Stabilization Board.

For its psychological effect, Bowles let a story slip out that he had been bargaining with organized labor for a no-strike pledge during the reconversion months in return for guaranteed price control.

He lined up all the organizations – consumer, veterans, labor groups – to join him in the counterattack. It was the kind of job Franklin Roosevelt used to do. Bowles, too, thoroughly enjoyed himself during that crowded week.

He was able to attract the same kind of hero worship that followed the late President. One cute, red-haired girl reporter who covered all of Bowles's appearances on the Hill would sigh as he strolled nonchalantly into the committee room. Then she would whisper, "Isn't he wonderful!"

Housewives who had never left their kitchens and their nurseries before stood on street corners circulating petitions to keep OPA and banged on Congressmen's doors.

The men who worked with Bowles became his ardent disciples. They shouted his praises all over Washington. One of Bowles's most valuable converts was Paul Porter, the tall young

New Deal politician and administrator. Unlike Bowles, Porter had an in with Democratic politicos and top-flight government administrators. This lanky, genial Kentuckian had been publicity director of the Democratic National Committee and chairman of the Federal Communications Commission before he was persuaded to take the unhappy job of running OPA.

Paul became Chester Bowles's lieutenant, political ally, and advance man.

At the height of his bitterest battles over price control – a fight he was losing – Chester Bowles was being whispered as a comer for the 1948 or 1952 Presidential nomination. This tribute to a good operator was not displeasing to Bowles. Nor did it run against his own ambitions. Chester Bowles was bitten by the political bug. He ran a fever and a bad one.

He had one sobering setback after he left Washington. His strategy was all mapped out. He would be elected Governor of Connecticut, and from there spring to the White House.

But this amateur politician ran up against professionals. Young Senator Brien McMahon of Connecticut had no intention of letting Bowles grab control of the state machine. Bowles went to the Democratic convention in Connecticut full of confidence. The professionals took him to the cleaner's. He lost the nomination to a college professor with no private ambitions.

Chester Bowles is not through. He wrote off the Connecticut fiasco as good experience, and looked around for other stepping-stones. He began casting about for a program long before he had a stump to climb on. He tried to think out a long-range economic program for Americans. He worried over the problems of diversifying farming and industry in the South. He made a trip around the world to learn firsthand of the issues and prejudices that divided men, and the hopes that might bring them together.

A man with that much bounce and ambition is hard to keep down.

Chapter IX

THE gray dome of the Capitol rises like a proud and lovely lady on the sloping hill at the end of Constitution Avenue. The first glimpse of the Capitol as one looks up the green sweep of the Mall is breathtaking. There, aloof and beautiful, the Capitol stands solidly looking over the acres of government offices. A statue of Freedom towers on the dome. At night, giant searchlights turn the dome dazzling white. It is a landmark from across the Potomac River and from the hills running down into Washington.

Long lines of tourists tramp through the gray halls. They sit on the hard benches of the House and Senate galleries staring curiously at the unfamiliar scenes down below. On warm summer nights, people rest on the Capitol steps listening to the brave music of the Marine Band. Lovers loll under the spreading trees on the lawn.

Much of the time, the men and women down below in the government offices imagine they see a derisive smile on the statue topping the dome. And Congress fancies it hears the babel of revolt down below. The eternal struggle for power in Washington is between the Hill and downtown. The battle is never won or lost. It flows back and forth. All the agencies sprawling out below the Capitol look up to the Hill for policy, for money, for some clue to the voice of America. The shouting inside the Capitol echoes in every office.

Franklin D. Roosevelt at the height of his power forced a sullen Congress to pass his bills and create the New Deal. Toward the end this authority was slowly ebbing away as waves recede after crashing against the beach.

One spring afternoon a frightened man was driven down from Capitol Hill to the quiet mansion at 1600 Pennsylvania Avenue, there to become President of the United States.

From that moment the great power that lies in Washington began surging back up the Hill with a fearful undertow. In the succeeding months the confused clamor from the Capitol was Congress speaking its mind on every subject from the new form of death – atomic energy – to taxes. The stiff creaking downtown was the bureaucrats giving unaccustomed salaams to the mighty men of the Hill.

Under the dome of the Capitol is a world all its own. It is a world that lives close to make-believe and drama. The shadows of the past and future move steadily over the skylights. The pageant is exciting and exhausting, for, one climax having been reached, another starts building up.

Inside, the Capitol is an ancient gray stone building with long corridors bulging out into halls cluttered with statues and paintings, the catacombs in the basement, high-ceilinged offices, the two legislative chambers, and the correspondents' rooms perched up on the gallery floors.

The actors of the continuous story are the Congressmen who move out of their cloakrooms to strut on the stages. The drones are the hundreds of scurrying clerks and secretaries who set the stage and, quite often, even write the lines. The lobbyists and correspondents are everywhere, leaning curiously over the galleries, in the offices, lounging possessively in the cloakrooms, and in the lunchrooms. The only difference in appearance between the two is that the lobbyists are more affluent and convivial. Correspondents after long experience develop a lean, hungry, and saturnine look.

The strangers in this world are the constant procession of tourists. They are the backers of this show. They help pay for it. They stare into the dim and dusty room that used to be the original Senate chamber, and they climb up the narrow winding stairs to the dome. But they see only a blurred glimpse of the real show.

In the last angry days of the Seventy-ninth Congress, a caravan of tourists plodded patiently down a narrow stretch of corridor. They squeezed apologetically past a knot of reporters gathered around a door. Behind that door was the people's business. The weary men inside – the Congressional Conference Committee on Price Control – were wondering desperately just what did the people want. The voices from outside could not penetrate the thick walls and be heard over the din of lobbyist pressure and political slogans.

The first experience of watching the show is a shock. Neither the history books nor lectures by eminent authorities on government are any preparation for the scenes below the galleries.

The House chamber looks like a railroad station half an hour before time for the coaches to pull out. The hall is long, narrow, and dark. Rows of benches padded with black leather line the floor. There is an atmosphere of faded and now dingy grandeur. There is the same aimless confusion as in a station. Several dozen Congressmen lean over the rail at the back of the chamber smoking, talking, and laughing. Others swing through the doors of the cloakrooms at a brisk trot.

Except on rare occasions half of the benches are empty. Many of the Congressmen on the floor listen indifferently. They read newspapers, clean their fingernails, or huddle together in private conversations.

Most of the women members of the House look as if they had come to the station an hour before train time and were wondering uneasily if they were in the right place. They sit with a dignity that is out of place in the restless House.

A loud undertone of conversation is the background for debate. The Speaker pounds his gavel at regular intervals to say, without much conviction, "There will be order in the chamber." For a few seconds the noise dies down a little, then turns up again.

This does not disturb the speakers. They stand in the well of the House before the Speaker's throne. They shout with terrifying vigor if only thirty or forty colleagues are listening instead of an enthusiastic throng of thousands of cheering voters.

There is an unreal atmosphere about House debates. They are a mixture of the artificial language of lawyers, the old-fashioned and insincere phrases of Congressional courtesy, and the uninhibited anger of a barroom brawl.

There are moments of sheer burlesque, such as the time when Dewey Short, the one-time ministerial student, minced on the floor in an imitation of a toe dance. His ridicule defeated the fine-arts bill. The tall man with a balding head kicked his heels and pirouetted while the House roared.

There are moments of old-fashioned melodrammer . . . when stocky Representative Hook called John Rankin "a damned liar" and the little, gray-haired man swung at him with both fists flying.

There are times of complete incoherence. The final speech is being made for or against a bill. The chief actor is trying to shout his lines above the roar. Minor characters on the floor are yelling back at him. And, from all over the chamber comes the booming chant, "Vote. Vote."

There are intelligent speeches by conscientious men, but their memory is drowned out by the sheer volume of noise expended by demagogues, fools, and politicians. It is like the crash of thunder and the vivid streaks of lightning obscuring for a moment the beneficial effects of the rain.

The House is in a continual state of war. It is always angry . . . at the bureaucrats, the New Dealers, Wall Street, big business, Russia, England, the Communists, the brass hats, and the CIO. The same words and slogans run through all the debates.

Representative Willie Gallagher, the philosophical old handy man, said, "The trouble with Congress is there's too much talkin' and not enough votin'."

All the crosscurrents of American life blow across the stage. . . . Midwestern isolationism, hate and fear of labor bosses and government controls from the farms and small towns, breaths of liberalism, respect for civil liberties from New England, red-baiting. . . .

Labels, a little ragged and worn, are attached to men and causes. Liberalism means devotion to the New Deal policies; conservatism, the old guard; isolationism, votes against lend-lease, extension of the draft, the British loan, world control of atomic energy; interventionism, support of the FDR foreign policy. The labels are tattered, because there are factions within factions, the Taft conservatives or Wherry conservatives, the Rankin ultraconservatives.

The House of Representatives is run like an Indian tribe, by a few elders. These men reach the pinnacle of power by accident of residence (they come from districts where they have virtually no political opposition and are able to climb the slow ladder of seniority) or by ability to talk or think faster than their colleagues.

Even before Mr. Roosevelt died, the House was dominated much of the time by a small bipartisan combination of conservatives, Democrats Gene Cox of Georgia and Howard Smith of Virginia, who ran the all-powerful Rules Committee, and Republicans Joseph Martin and Charles Halleck. This clique was responsible for House passage of the Case labor bill and the death of the OPA.

The most powerful man in the House is the Speaker. He sits inscrutable, the symbol of authority, on his throne at the front of the House. A huge American flag hangs down the wall behind him. He sits on the third tier of the Speaker's stand, a white marble throne with bright blue blotters on the desks. Below the Speaker are his parliamentarian and clerks and stenographers.

The Speaker holds tremendous power. He can steer the course of debate and bang through bills by recognizing the right people at the right time, and by his rulings on parliamentary questions. He is chosen carefully by the party controlling the House. He should be an expert parliamentarian, a shrewd politician, and have intimate knowledge of the restless crowd before him.

Sam Rayburn of Texas, the Speaker when Democrats controlled the House, is a professional politician and one of the best. He looks like one of the old Caesars. He is not a tall man but his erect, proud carriage and heavy shoulders give the impression of height. He has a strong, impassive face and a completely bald, polished head. His black eyes, usually cold, change quickly to good humor when he quips or tells a funny story. Like most good politicians, Rayburn has a cupboard full of stories.

The Speaker had limited amiability and on the floor he looked like a monarch either surveying or moving among his subjects. He had such power he was treated with deference on all sides. His rulings were fair. Besides, Sam Rayburn was a bad man to cross. He could make life in the House very unhappy for an enemy.

Rayburn was a great help to Franklin Roosevelt. FDR gave the orders and in most cases Rayburn carried them out efficiently. In the early New Deal, Rayburn was billed as a liberal himself. He worked for many of the banking and stock market reforms of the first term. As the New Deal branched out into other lines he became less active.

Rayburn was so respected in the House that his speeches carried great weight. He could change a close vote on almost any subject. With Truman as President, however, Rayburn only rarely moved off his throne to go onto the floor.

One of Rayburn's little vanities was a small metal sign on the desk in his private office. It said simply, "The Speaker."

His Republican successor, Joseph W. Martin, Jr., of Massachusetts, has an engaging personality that disarms his opponents. He appears to be that familiar American, the benevolent and friendly small-town merchant, who presides at Fourth of July picnics and teaches a Sunday-school class. His broad face relaxes easily into a harmless smile. A lock of black hair falls boyishly over his forehead. He dresses plainly.

At Joe Martin's rare press conferences, his attitude is, "Shucks, fellows, I don't know all the answers." These meetings are as productive as an interview with a circus elephant. His answers are amiably vague. On the House floor Joe Martin putters around like an old man in his garden.

The Congressman, like Harry Truman, is proof of the argument that anyone can win political eminence given enough time, party regularity, and luck. Reporters in need of space fillers write lyrical stories of his rise from a poor blacksmith's son to GOP chieftain in Congress.

Martin is a party hack who has given loyal obedience to the Old Guard for twenty-four years. His official biography, which every Representative writes with a deep sense of pride, is a dull history of a wheelhorse. It lists all the Republican Party posts he has held from chairman of the Massachusetts Republican Legislative Committee to delegate at large to the GOP National Convention, to National Chairman.

There is nothing flamboyant or daring about him. He is a dull speaker and is not a brilliant strategist. No great pieces of legislation bear his name. That is not Joe Martin's role. He is the classic example of the willing party worker. He takes orders and is not a prima donna. He does dirty jobs without complaint and keeps his mouth shut. He is a tactician, an old dog who has learned all the tricks.

If Martin has any political philosophy, it is a conservatism that would have delighted Rutherford B. Hayes or William Howard Taft. He has consistently supported legislation which labor thought was aimed against it. He is opposed to Federal handouts and voted to weaken such New Deal agricultural programs as Commodity Credit Corporation, parity payments, and rural electrification. He was for reducing the funds of the WPA and the school lunch program. He wanted to cut the appropriation for OPA as early as 1943, and opposed price ceilings on homes and the veterans' emergency housing program. Joe Martin voted to exempt railroads and insurance companies from antitrust laws. He worked diligently to have the House Un-American Activities Committee made a permanent body. He punished Republicans who opposed him in this by keeping them off major committees.

This friendly New Englander voted against fortifying Guam, against a world trade bill, against Lend-Lease and extension of Selective Service. He favored decreasing the number of military aircraft. In March 1940, Martin spoke out, "The third-term movement floats on a cloud of internationalism. The American people have a right to ask again and again whether the conduct of our foreign relations conforms to a policy of peace to which the American people are overwhelmingly committed. We had one bitter experience in 1916. . . . Our people will not be deceived again."

The field generals of the House are the floor leaders. They rally their forces together to do battle and call the plays.

The Democratic floor leader, John W. McCormack, is a lean, gray man from Dorchester, Massachusetts. He is a harassed and overworked Irish practical politician without imagination. He looks like a schoolmaster – a tall man with black hair, strong features, and wearing a gray suit. He speaks crisply and impatiently as he scurries from one errand to another.

McCormack's job is to schedule legislation, select committee members, and organize the divided Democrats behind the Administration must bills. He spends much of his time buttonholing members in the cloakrooms while keeping half an eye on the floor. He never seems relaxed as he hurries from one chore to another.

The Democratic leader is a routine orator who substitutes political phrases for profundity in debate. He speaks with equal enthusiasm for whatever Administration bill he has orders to shove through. He loyally followed the twisting of the Truman policy without regard to its effect on him or his own convictions. He worked for the British loan, which was unpopular among the Irish in and around Boston. He steered the Truman labor bill through the House.

McCormack is not a master strategist, nor does he have a compensating warmth of personality. He lacks any real profound understanding of the mass of legislation surging over the House. His slogan is, "For Pete's sake, let's get it over with." His virtue is that he is a tirelessly hard worker.

Representative McCormack has an impossible job. Without Roosevelt's inspiration, the Democrats have sagged into little groups. There are no great phrases like, "All we have to fear is fear," to give the Democrats zeal and drive. At times the only difference between the two parties in the House is that one is in and the other out.

The chief Republican strategist is a youthful-looking and vigorous follower of the Old Guard, Charley Halleck of Indiana. He is a familiar American type, the well-to-do small-town smart aleck. Halleck has a sharp mind, physical vitality, and cockiness. He is good-looking – slim, dark curly hair, an aggressive and commanding face.

An illustrative story is told by fellow Republicans of a meeting in Halleck's honor at Logansport, Indiana. He rose and is widely reported to have said, "Not so long ago, I had dinner with a big American industrialist, a very big industrialist. He said to me, 'Charley' – they all call me Charley down there. He said, 'Charley, do the people of Indiana believe in free enterprise?' I said, 'Joe, of course they do.' "

The "Joe" of the story is supposed to be Joseph Pew, one of the main financial backers of the GOP.

One of Halleck's party assignments, chairman of the Republican Congressional Campaign Committee, brings him in touch with all the major Republican sugar daddies. In this capacity, Halleck received campaign funds and allocated them to Congressmen.

Charley was selected for leadership in the very low moments of GOP influence in Washington, in 1934, and has never failed the ultraconservatives of his party. He is belligerently anti-New Deal and for the *status quo*. He was against the trade agreements bill, British loan, price controls, civilian control of atomic energy, livestock subsidies, and school lunches. Halleck plays around with Southern Democrats on the right wing of their party. He and Congressman Smith of Virginia worked out the strategy for getting the Case labor bill on the floor and passed.

The Congressman has a fondness for high society. He and his wife entertain in their big home in Northwest Washington and they are frequent entries in the social columns.

His job in the House is to work out the strategy with the GOP leadership, call the shots and see that the votes are counted. I have seen him during price control and labor legislation pull Republican votes out of the cloakroom and office buildings by a great show of authority and energy.

Congressman Brazilla Carroll Reece of Tennessee's freak Republican district, a banker and teacher by trade, was the GOP National Chairman during the 1945–1946 period. He is a cautious, mousy man who browses around in the dim and quiet rooms of Washington's Metropolitan Club.

One of the lighter explanations for Reece's selection as National Chairman is that he looks so unlike the popular idea of a

Republican leader – the big man with thick jowls, a bass voice, and glaring eyes. Reece is a slim, inconspicuous man with a soft voice and mild eyes. His thin graying hair is parted in the middle.

Reece held a press conference in national headquarters after his appointment as GOP front man. The morning papers that day carried comments from Harold Stassen and Senator Wayne Morse criticizing the selection.

A reporter asked Reece for comment. The new chairman hemmed, "Governor Stassen does not approve of all my record. I do not know of anyone whose record I fully approve of. He did not point out anything specific. The chairman does not set the policy. He just organizes for victory."

Another question whammed across the table. "Do you consider yourself an isolationist?"

Reece looked around the room as if he were searching for the nearest exit. He answered, "It is pretty hard for a man to describe himself. I am generally regarded as not an extremist one way or another. I am not an extreme isolationist nor an extreme internationalist."

The hunting instinct of every reporter there was sharpened by that reply. The hunt was on to smoke the GOP National Chairman out of his hole. It is a chase the hunted brings on himself, for correspondents generally have a "live and let live" philosophy.

The next question was: "Do you call yourself a moderate isolationist?"

Reece pursed his lips. "First you will have to define the word. I am not in favor of isolating the country entirely from the rest of the world. We all recognize that nations must co-operate to advance the interests of peace."

Another correspondent drew a bead and fired, "I assume you are still a Taft man."

Reece answered with a slight quiver of asperity, "I assumed you would ask that."

"Well," the reporter inquired casually, "how about it?"

"I am not anyone's man. I am not sharpening the ax for anyone."

"Do you think you can beat Truman with anyone?"

"I am confident the party will select an able man."

"How are you going to get the labor vote?"

"I have not had time to develop the details of party organization."

"How do you expect to get labor support in view of the Case labor bill?"

That was a sore point and Reece replied primly, "I see no conflict."

"Will you gain control of the House of Representatives in the next election?"

"Quite definitely."

"Do you intend to co-operate with Governor Stassen's open forums?"

"They are an interesting idea."

"Will you embrace them formally?"

"The national committee will tend to continue its work."

He was handed a clipping of Senator Morse's blast. Reece smiled brightly. "This is just one man's opinion."

"Do you think there is any rift in the Republican Party?"

"No."

"Do you care to comment on the inference that the Young Republicans are opposed to you?"

"I do not so construe."

"Do you approve all of Stassen's record?"

"I think he made a good record as Governor. I am not familiar with all the details."

"How do you like his record on world affairs?"

"It is difficult to express one's own opinion."

"Some people say all is not melodious in the party. Can you coalesce all groups?"

"Yes, by all means."

"Can you comment on the British loan?"

"There is no party policy on it."

"How will you vote?"

"That is difficult to project."

Reece said good-by to the reporters with a smile of relief. That was the last time the press galleries took him seriously.

Martin, Halleck, and Reece, representing the right wing, are facing a widening split in the Republican Party. On one side is the Old Guard which is convinced that the way to make a party record and win elections is to oppose anything offered by the Administration. This is the old "one-hoss shay" the Republicans have been trying to ride to victory since 1934.

The Old Guard is still in control of the party. It was badly frightened by Wendell Willkie, regards Harold Stassen as a sinister influence, and looks suspiciously at Bob Taft. The greatest threat to the Old Guard is coming from a growing number of moderate conservatives.

The big issues on which the split occurred in the Seventy-ninth Congress were foreign policy, British loan, extension of the draft, atomic energy, and price control. Enough Republicans crossed party lines to put these bills over despite the defection of Southern conservatives. Fifty-two Republicans in the House joined a majority of Democrats to resurrect OPA from the dead.

The Republican split will grow instead of diminish, because the rebellion is new, the GOP has the responsibility in Congress, and the various Presidential aspirants are jockeying for position. Lusty battles for party control in 1948 are already developing between the Old Guard, moderates, and liberals. Joe Martin watches this coming struggle sadly. It was so much more pleasant in the old days when all Republicans except a few heretics who didn't count stood firmly against the intrusion of New Deal ideas.

A few weeks after the 1946 elections, Henry P. Fletcher, one time GOP chairman and a confirmed Old Guard member, pleaded at the national committee meeting, "Don't rock the boat, boys. We're coming into port!"

Chapter X

THE little Caesars of the House are the old men who run those separate domains, the committees. They have life-and-death power over the hopeful bills parceled out to them.

All of the chairmen reached their authority through the accident of political longevity, not because they were wiser than the rest. All of the Democrats heading the eleven most important committees in the Seventy-ninth Congress were elders. Half of them were over seventy. Six were from the South. Four were confirmed conservatives. The Republicans who succeeded them are younger, from small-town and rural constituencies and uniformly conservative.

One of the most potent of all these autocrats was Clarence Cannon, the fussy little man from rural Missouri. As chairman of the Appropriations Committee in the Seventy-ninth Congress, he had almost absolute control over the purse strings of every government department. His whisper was the law downtown. Any department which for some reason or other incurred his displeasure might just as well resign itself to penury. Cannon, however, was always considered fair and never cut off any department because of personal whim. Over the long years of Democratic control, Cannon developed into an expert on government.

He was succeeded by Republican John Taber, a stubborn old man from upstate New York with a mania against government press agents. He considered the Office of War Information a creation of the devil and spent much of his time harassing gentle Elmer Davis and searching suspiciously for "Communist agents" or "fourth term agents," who, to him, were very much alike. The Congressman is no favorite of the press corps. He once suggested that reporters were getting fat and lazy from reading mimeographed handouts instead of chasing down facts.

Brent Spence, the Democratic chairman of the Banking and Currency Committee, is a kindly Kentuckian who had the job of trying to nurse the OPA through the House. He is a tall, stooped man with friendly, blinking eyes and a fringe of gray hair. He does not have an enemy in the world, but his tolerant persuasions were no match for the tough and determined pressure groups and their friends in the House.

The current and Republican chairman of the same committee, Jesse Wolcott of Michigan, is one of the toughest strategists on the Hill. He called the shots to defeat price control and housing legislation. He is a master of destruction by amendment.

Sol Bloom, Democrat, of the Foreign Relations Committee, has the pompousness of many physically small men. This impression is aided by a pince-nez on a black cloth cord and the way he ordered his committee around. As chairman, he was impatient at hearing anyone but Congressman Bloom. He took his position seriously, insisted on the protocol associated with it, and enjoyed having his picture taken with visiting statesmen.

Bloom is a firm disciple of American intervention in world affairs, but he does not have much influence in the House because he is regarded, somewhat unjustly, as rather an absurd little man. His self-importance and vanity obscure the fact that Bloom worked hard for the Roosevelt foreign policy. His Republican successor, Dr. Charles Eaton of New Jersey, is a dignified, white-haired man who says little and follows closely the policies of Arthur Vandenberg.

Robert L. Doughton of North Carolina, ranking Democrat on Ways and Means, is a tall, very old man who totters around the Capitol and is easily one of Washington's greatest authorities on taxation. He has written more tax laws than any other man now alive. His character is indicated by his nickname of "Muley." The leading GOP member, Harold Knutson of Minnesota, is a grumpy, bald isolationist who reciprocates the dislike Harold Stassen has for him. His contribution to the nation's fiscal problems, shared by John Taber, was to suggest after the GOP victory a 20 per cent across-the-board cut in personal income taxes.

Democrat Adolph Sabath of the Rules Committee looks like one of those exquisitely made European dolls. He is a small, stocky man with snow-white hair, a neat little mustache, pink cheeks, and sparkling eyes. He dresses impeccably and speaks with a thick accent. He has a shrewd and lively mind amazing in a man of his more than eighty years.

Sabath is an enthusiastic New Dealer. He loses his witty good humor and steams into a fit of cholera when a liberal measure is attacked. He sputters and chokes and pounds the stand with the vigor of a man many years his junior.

The Congressman was born in Czechoslovakia and has been a fixture in Chicago politics and Congress for more than a generation. He served in the House under eight Presidents, beginning with Teddy Roosevelt. As the foreign language groups in his district changed, Sabath cheerfully learned to speak new languages. He speaks so many he was used by the government during the war to broadcast to Europe.

Sabath confesses to one weakness – he loves to play pinochle. He plays with President Truman and admitted with disarming innocence that he had played a few hands with Murray Garsson, the lobbyist and munitions promoter under Congressional investigation.

The Congressman's great cross was that his committee members were almost uniformly anti-New Deal. Gene Cox, Howard Smith, and Roger Slaughter, who was so anti-Administration he was purged by the Missouri Pendergast machine at President Truman's request, ganged up with Republican Charley Halleck and Clarence Brown.

The prize package was Andrew Jackson "Jack" May, the blustering former chairman of the Military Affairs Committee. He is a big bald man, handsome in a bluff kind of way. He has the aggressive cheerfulness of a shoe salesman and the animal cunning of a politician. But most of all Andy May is simple, crude, and vain. Had he not had his exalted position as chairman of the Military Affairs Committee in the Seventy-ninth Congress, May might have been a mill-of-the-run politician and Congressman. Certainly no one in his right senses would have gone to plain

Representative Andrew J. May for influence in winning $78,000,-000 worth of war contracts.

May came from a poor, mountainous district of Kentucky. The bluff man with his easy familiarity was something of a hero to his constituency. Old Andy had showed those city fellers up in Washington a thing or two.

As a committee chairman, May was a bully. In the atomic energy hearings, May badgered and cut short the eminent scientists who argued for civilian control. He accepted the simple explanation that scientists were some kind of dangerous radicals. Andy's friends in the War Department didn't like the scientists and wanted military control of atomic energy. That was enough for him. He treated the military witnesses, principally General Groves, with exaggerated courtesy.

When the question of civilian versus military control of the atom came before his committee, May voted the proxies of absent members for military control. During the House debate on the issue, which he controlled because of his position, the Congressman cut short or would not recognize many who wished to speak for civilian control. He was responsible for the complete confusion in the House on atomic energy.

May was a pain in the neck to those sticklers for convention, the two Secretaries of War, Stimson and Patterson. At one time friends of the War Department went to President Roosevelt and pleaded with him to appoint May to a Federal Judgeship. The President was sympathetic but did not exalt Andy to the bench.

Representative May is not by any stretch of the imagination a great intellect. The chairmanship of the Military Committee in a time of all-out war was too much for him. He was given too much power and it went to his head like three stiff snorts of Kentucky mountain whiskey. He got the confused idea that he was just about the most powerful guy on Capitol Hill and could do what he damned well pleased.

The most obvious members of the House are a small group who dominate every debate. You will find them, or men like them, in every session of Congress howling and waving their arms. The leader of this clique of chronic "aginers" is a restless bundle of energy, John Rankin of Mississippi. He is a small man with an unruly mop of gray hair and a constant look of impatience. He prowls instead of walking. He roams through the Capitol with his shoulders hunched over and his eyes as sharp as a cat's.

He bubbles over with words and motions when he has the floor. He manages to bark and rattle along at a swift pace in a Southern drawl. Rankin is an actor whose first performance is a hit. It is a flailing tumult of denunciation. He crouches. He throws his arms in all directions. He bangs the flat of his hand down violently on the stand. He speaks his lines passionately. He is a caricature of the oratorical Southern Democrats.

But the later performances pall. There is no variety. He packs all he has into the one show repeated at the drop of a hat.

John Rankin sees a Communist under every bed except his own. As he looks out of the Capitol down the Hill toward the rows of government buildings, he sees Communists crawling like ants. He is against almost every Administration bill because he darkly imagines it will give the New Dealers a chance to employ thousands of men in the pay of Moscow.

He broke into the debate on the atomic energy bill, which he tried to kill, with this angry statement, "Everybody knows that when you permitted the commissioning of Communists, you packed them in the War Department over the protest of our military leaders. They are packed into every department of this government, if you want to know the truth of it. Let us try to get rid of these subversive elements that are trying to undermine and destroy America."

Rankin is the burning spirit behind the House un-American Activities Committee and sends its investigators out like witches on a broom to discover some new seat of Communism. When atomic energy became popular, Rankin shoved one of his investigators off to the big atomic plant at Oak Ridge, Tennessee. He announced that scientists are Communists, too.

Rankin is a fanatic who must have some cause to consume his restless energy. In his earlier days, he fought and clawed for the TVA.

Rankin has no serious influence within the House. It has all worn out. He does perform a useful service for the House conservatives. He provides them with an excuse to vote against bills they oppose but for which they cannot find a satisfactory reason. Rankin brings up the Communist issue. There it is. He is an annoying and disrupting influence on the administrative agencies with his threats of star chamber investigations.

The Congressman lives in the Methodist Building a few steps from the Capitol. It is a place where gentle old ladies and a few Congressmen live. Over the door of the excellent cafeteria are the flags of the Allies. Rankin must pass under the hammer and sickle every time he has dinner.

Rankin does not enter the social swim of Washington. He is the wild hermit who comes out of his cave to mumble angry warnings into the heedless winds.

One of his foremost companions in the brass section of the House was a woman, Miss Jessie Sumner of Illinois, who qualified as having the loudest voice in the Capitol. It was a curiously high, shrill scream. This gentlewoman who graduated from Smith College and studied at the University of Chicago, Columbia, and Oxford was an isolationist and economic conservative. She stood at the extreme right wing of the Republican Representatives.

Miss Sumner has a comfortably broad figure and blond hair. Her eyes have the same restless scorn as Rankin's. She was the clown of the group, bawling out her jibes to the guffaws of the Republican benches.

In all major debates, Miss Sumner would sit impatiently waiting for the first opening. Then she would jump to her feet, crying, "Mr. Speaker." She was a constant source of annoyance to the Administration, because she was quick to turn its bumbling errors into broad jokes.

Another lieutenant is Dewey Short, the tall, dapper Republican from Missouri. He is highly emotional and easily works himself into a fever of anger. All during a debate in which he is interested, Short will sit in his bench making loud remarks to those around him. Then he will pop to his feet and bellow like a bull.

During the House debate on atomic energy, Chairman May of the House Military Affairs Committee was piously defending himself against charges of obstructing atomic legislation. The Missouri Congressman across the aisle grew more and more restless. His remarks to his neighbors could be heard in the gallery.

Suddenly he was on his feet, waving his arm and shouting, "And I was charged with you, and it is a dirty lie, a dirty lie." His face contorted with anger.

Off the floor and away from the arena of politics, Short has a pleasant, likable personality. The heated atmosphere of the House works on him like a fever.

Short climbed up the seniority ladder to be second ranking Republican on the House Military Committee, much to the annoyance of the generals. He argued against extending the draft and led the cry, "Bring the boys home." Except for his vote for the United Nations Charter, his record is isolationist.

An ally of Short on the Military Committee and of Rankin on the Un-American Committee is J. Parnell Thomas, a New Jersey Republican. He is a short, stocky man with a red face and bald head. He spells them on the floor but has neither the style of Rankin nor the wit of Short. But he is more discreet and shrewd than either. With the Republican sweep in the 1946 elections, Thomas fell heir to the Un-American Committee chairmanship. At several hearings he actually silenced Rankin just as he was at the point of erupting and spewing words over the room.

Clare (No Pockets) Hoffman, a Republican from a rural Michigan district, joins the noise makers when a labor bill is up for debate. He is called "No Pockets" because his pet eccentricity is not to have any pockets in his clothing. Hoffman fancies his resemblance to Will Rogers, and lets a thick lock of hair dangle on his forehead. He has also developed the same twangy drawl. But the Congressman has none of Will Rogers's easy friendliness. Hoffman's eyes are narrow and dissatisfied.

On summer evenings, after the flag has been hauled down for the night over the House, Hoffman and Rankin walk restlessly up and down before the Methodist Building together. The old ladies have become so accustomed to this odd pair that they no longer glance at them.

At the other extreme, the end of the left wing, is Vito Marcantonio, the American Labor Party Congressman from New

York City. He is a small, thin man with a dark intense face and black hair. He sits with his shoulders hunched over and a cold, skeptical look on his face. When he is aroused, his eyes blaze with fury and he spits out his words.

Marcantonio has a sharp mind and coined a phrase that will probably long outlast his stay in Congress. He called the Southern Democrats "Rankin Republicans." The Congressman is no little innocent in politics. He was for some time Fiorello La Guardia's campaign manager in Harlem, where rough political fights are the rule rather than the exception.

Marcantonio is a marked man in the House. His usefulness is impaired by his reputation. Many Congressmen are reluctant to vote for anything he sponsors for fear his name will be linked with theirs at campaign time. Marcantonio is rumored to be a "fellow traveler" and some enemies suspect he may be a Communist. Marcantonio realizes his unusual position in the House and employs it as a nuisance value.

In the closing days of the Seventy-ninth Congress, when everyone was yearning to go home, Marcantonio got back at his archenemy, Rankin, with a vengeance. The Mississippian rose to ask a contempt citation against several persons who had defied the House Un-American Activities Committee.

Marcantonio calmly arose with a point of order. There was no quorum in the House. The clerk went through the weary process of calling the roll. Rankin tried again. Another point of order was raised. This farce continued for six roll calls. Rankin was furious. He demanded that the Speaker rule Marcantonio's quorum calls "a dilatory motion."

Sam Rayburn, obviously enjoying the situation, ruled the motion was not dilatory. He looked at the sprinkling of members on the floor and remarked that it was quite clear there was not a quorum present.

Marcantonio sat directly across the aisle from Rankin. He did not so much as look at him. He merely stared ahead with a sardonic smile.

Chapter XI

ONCE upon a time, the term "New Dealer" was popular on Capitol Hill. Men wore it with a kind of cocky defiance or embraced it with the warmth of a politician who knows a good thing when he sees it.

These days if you call a man a New Dealer you had better smile or know your man. The 100 per cent New Dealers declined in membership to about twenty-five or thirty in the House in the Seventy-ninth Congress and this number was cut in half by the 1946 elections.

A few of them were:

Frank E. Hook, the stocky, black-haired Representative from Ironwood, Michigan. He has the solid, earthy look of a village blacksmith and is respected in the House as a sincere and honest man. He has the quality known as "guts," which makes him some kind of rare bird in Washington. He comes from the northern tip of Michigan, the first Democrat ever to represent his district, but he has fought consistently for New Deal policies.

Hook is no great shakes as an orator and is known chiefly for two words he spoke in defiance of Congressional courtesy. He called John Rankin a "damn liar" on the floor of the House. Hook has none of the finesse of the Southern politicians or the organizing talents of a Jim Farley, but he fell heir to the leadership of the 100 per cent New Dealers.

Jerry Voorhis, the passionate idealist from California. One of his colleagues said of him that Voorhis was too far above the level of the House to be appreciated. The Congressman looks much younger than he is. He has a long intelligent face, a high forehead, and a manner so earnest that it often irritates his more earth-bound colleagues. But he has the same boyish appeal as Van Johnson and is a great favorite at women's clubs.

Voorhis is one of the few men who can speak lucidly, and without heating up like a steam-cracked engine. Instead of steaming into anger, he grows more and more earnest.

He came by his liberalism through curiosity. After graduating from Yale, young Voorhis decided to find out what the world was really like. He became a factory worker, a ranch hand, a freight handler, and worked in an automobile assembly plant. He traveled in Germany for the Y.M.C.A. and was the headmaster of a boys' school.

Voorhis believes passionately in one world. Like the missionary, he believes we are all brothers under the skin and should live together in peace and prosperity. He is a follower of the theory of the greatest good for the greatest number.

Voorhis is one of the many New Dealers from the West Coast. Some of his associates from the Coast are liberals by expediency, or are the fashionable liberals whose New Dealism is exhibited at Hollywood parties and New York teas. They run about the country bellowing about Franco and leaving it to men like Congressman Andy May to worry over atomic energy control bills.

Adam Clayton Powell, Jr., the tall striking Negro from New York City. He is a handsome, well-dressed, light-skinned man with a good mind, a dramatic oratorical style, and ambition. He stands between two worlds. He has gone beyond the rank and file of his race and the path into the white world is blocked off to him. The only doors left open are those to the radical soirees.

Adam Powell is smarter, better educated, and more successful than a large per cent of the men around him on the floor. He knows it. Powell has degrees from three universities and has studied abroad. He has a tremendous talent for organization. As a minister, he built up his church. He organized a credit union, a co-operative store, and a co-operative insurance system, all for Negroes. He led a movement, including a successful strike, to get employment for Negroes.

Powell is one of the few Congressmen to associate with Marcantonio. He does it defiantly and under the noses of his Democratic colleagues from the South. He has none of the humility of the professional Negro politician. He wants to be recognized as a leader regardless of color.

The New Deal ranks were thinned and their leaders defeated in the 1946 elections. Frank Hook was beaten. So was Jerry Voorhis. Some of the other vigorous young liberals replaced in the Eightieth Congress are John Tolan, Herman Kopplemann, Andy Biemiller, Charley LaFollette, and Emily Taft Douglas.

Of the 135 Representatives who voted to sustain the Presidential veto on the Case labor bill, 55 were defeated in the conservative landslide.

The 90 per cent New Dealers are a group of younger men who have come through the school of practical politics and are being trained by their elders for leadership. They are the most effective of the liberal groups, because they have political know-how and savvy.

A good many of them are Southerners, who like to be referred to as the "new statesmen" of Dixie. They are fiercely jealous of the reputation of the South and hold a deeper grudge against the Rankins and Bilbos than those who huff and puff at them from the safe distance of the North. A few of these Southerners are John Sparkman, now Senator of Alabama; tall Mike Monroney, a Phi Beta Kappa, and former political writer for the *Oklahoma News;* Albert Gore and Percy Priest of Tennessee, and Brooks Hays of Arkansas.

The 90 per cent New Dealers are the largest of the liberal groups in the House and form the backbone for Administration strength in the House. There are many able and conscientious men and women in these ranks, such as Wright Patman, the hard-working Texan.

Then there are the liberals by association. They are men who say defensively, "I knew Roosevelt when." Lyndon Johnson of Texas was one of the fair-haired boys when FDR was alive. Since then he has become little more than another Texas politician.

The smallest niche in the liberal hall is reserved for the frustrated Republican liberals. They are given the cold shoulder by the GOP leaders and are watched suspiciously by the Democrats. The Democrats think there must be a catch somewhere. These guys are spies.

Joseph Clark Baldwin, aristocrat of the bluest blood, is one of these. He is a member of the Porcellian and of the Racquet and Tennis Club, a vice-president of a corporation on Park Avenue, and a one-time reporter for the august and conservative *New York Herald Tribune*. Every time his cultured voice registers a quiet "Aye" for a progressive bill, the Old Guard hissed, "That turncoat." The Republican Party has now brushed its hands of him indignantly.

Every time the Old Guard looks at Baldwin, it thinks of Roosevelt and shudders again. Both were aristocrats who turned to politics. The GOP does not want anyone LIKE THAT around. The party turned against Baldwin in the 1946 elections. He was not re-elected.

The House of Representatives is no sanctum for the male. It has been invaded by a steadily growing number of women Congressmen. As a whole, they have done such a good job at lawmaking that some alarmists shake their heads sadly and predict that one day there will be more women than men in the black benches.

The Congresswomen, with some few exceptions, have been a credit to Congress. They work hard. They make an effort to study legislation. They have an idealism that goes well with lawmaking in these advanced days of atomic energy and the United Nations.

Mrs. Mary Teresa Norton, dean of the Congressional ladies, is a motherly-looking woman – the prototype of the older woman who transfers her energies to civic affairs when her children grow up.

Actually, Mrs. Norton is an experienced practical politician and a graduate emeritus of the Hague machine of New Jersey. She was vice-chairman and chairman of the Democratic State Committee of New Jersey.

Mrs. Norton was advanced from an efficient and intelligent

Congresswoman to a position of power and leadership in the New Deal by the President and Mrs. Roosevelt. The idealism of the New Deal, a little guidance and support from the White House, made her a crusader for labor legislation. As chairman of the House Labor Committee, she pulled through some of the most fundamental labor laws of this country.

She has missed the Roosevelts and the added inspiration they gave her to try the impossible. When, under the Truman Administration, liberals were trying to broaden the coverage of the minimum wage law, and increase the minimum, she compromised for a small increase in the minimum. Her attitude was that "half a loaf is better than none." She also knew that without a strong figure in the White House, Congress was not going to be anxious to go to work on further reforms.

Mrs. Norton's junior by a few months is Mrs. Edith Nourse Rogers, Republican, of Massachusetts. She has carved out a field for herself and is the recognized champion of disabled veterans. She lobbies energetically and effectively for them. She fills the Capitol with disabled veterans and ceaselessly buttonholes her colleagues in their behalf.

It is impossible for the Representatives to put these boys and their problems out of their minds when they see young men with sleeves and trouser legs pinned up clumping awkwardly down the corridor.

Mrs. Rogers first became interested in disabled soldiers when she was working with the American Red Cross in this field in 1918. She was appointed by three Presidents – Harding, Coolidge, and Hoover – as their personal representative in dealing with the problems of disabled veterans.

She made a tour of the European battlefront in this war during the great smashing drive on Germany. She was shocked at the extravagance with which human lives were thrown away. She was appalled to see American men killed because of lack of ammunition or ill-considered orders.

Mrs. Rogers was so disturbed by what she saw that upon her return she unburdened her concern to the higher brass in the War Department. She said she thought Congress ought to know about it. The Congresswoman was asked not to say anything about it for fear it would unsettle national morale at a very crucial moment. A month or so later, a British correspondent broke the story and she made her report to the House.

The figure of Mrs. Rogers, a conscientious, elderly lady with gray hair hanging down on her forehead and the inevitable red rose on her lapel, is linked forever with the cheerful boy in khaki moving slowly and painfully by her side on metal crutches. These boys are her cause.

Mrs. Rogers, like three of the women Representatives in the Seventy-ninth Congress, is a member of the House Foreign Affairs Committee, where she is a cautious internationalist with many fears about Russia.

The other women members were Mrs. Emily Taft Douglas, Illinois Democrat; Mrs. Frances P. Bolton, Republican from a suburb of Cleveland; and Mrs. Helen Gahagan Douglas, the California Democrat and glamour girl.

Mrs. Bolton is a quiet, well-poised woman who says little either on the floor or in committee. She has been active in Republican politics and in public health and educational fields. Mrs. Bolton is typical of most of the other women in her interest in some fields other than politics.

Mrs. Emily Taft Douglas was one of the best prepared lawmakers on the Hill. She is the wife of Professor Paul H. Douglas of the University of Chicago, who, early in the war, wanted to make an issue of isolationism versus intervention in Illinois politics.

Professor Douglas ran for the Democratic nomination for U. S. Senator, hoping to oppose the isolationist Curly Brooks, the Republican nominee. Douglas did not have the support of Chicago's Kelly-Nash machine and lost the primary. A few weeks later, to prove his sincerity, Douglas enlisted in the Marines as a private. He served in the Pacific, was wounded twice in action, and rose to be a major.

While her husband was in the Pacific, Mrs. Douglas ran for Congresswoman at large from Illinois on much the same issues. Her constituency is the largest in the House, 8,000,000 people.

Mrs. Douglas was trained in public affairs as an organizer for the Illinois League of Women Voters and as chairman of its sections on government and foreign policy.

Helen Gahagan Douglas is a dramatic and impulsive woman who has become the darling of the New Dealers. She brings into Congress a breath of Hollywood and the New York stage. She lists her profession as "stage star and opera singer." Mrs. Douglas is the wife of Melvyn Douglas, the actor.

She is attractive and enthusiastic, with a clear voice that projects well above the din of the House. She dresses rather girlishly and wears her hair up so that she appears much younger than her forty-odd years.

Mrs. Douglas is one of those people endowed by temperament and training for the spotlight. I first remember her on a stifling hot afternoon at the Democratic National Convention of 1944. She was bravely singing "The Star-Spangled Banner" in glorious oblivion of the noise. She is conspicuous on the House floor, either sitting wide-eyed in a bench, in busy consultation with the New Dealers, or lifting her voice into the galleries. She will speak energetically and dramatically on almost any subject in which the liberals are interested. She enjoys a scrap.

Helen Gahagan Douglas has copied many of the oratorical tricks of Franklin Roosevelt and addresses her appeals to the nobler emotions. This rarely fails to leave the House quite cold, but it is effective with less cynical audiences. She takes herself very seriously, as though she were responsible for saving the world.

She definitely is not the student of government, as is Mrs. Douglas of Illinois. Rather she is a saleswoman for the New Dealers and is rushed from platform to platform to hawk their wares. She picks up information easily and speaks with a glibness and flair.

Mrs. Douglas was deliberately chosen for national prominence by the Democrats to counteract the glamour of the Republican *grande dame*, Clare Boothe Luce. They watch each other warily.

After Mrs. Luce's sparkling lecture to the House on atomic energy, Helen Gahagan Douglas arose with an earnest but not as learned address. Mrs. Luce was witty and intellectual and played on fear. Mrs. Douglas was calling for attention to the healing powers of atomic energy. Clare Boothe Luce glanced across the aisle with a mixture of curiosity and amusement. It was not lost on Mrs. Douglas.

Mrs. Chase Going Woodhouse, Democrat, of Connecticut, has been trained for government service. She is a handsome, white-haired woman who wears pince-nez. She had one of the best minds in Congress. Her remarks on the British loan were one of the high points of the debate – clear, logical, and as filled with facts as a Ph.D. thesis.

Mrs. Woodhouse has studied in the universities of three nations, taught economics in five colleges, been an economist for the Department of Agriculture's Bureau of Home Economics and a consultant to the War Manpower Commission. She was an effective member of the House Banking and Currency Committee, which considers basic economic issues.

She was not conspicuous from the gallery. She spoke rarely and only when she believed she could make an effective contribution to the debate. Mrs. Woodhouse was defeated in the 1946 GOP sweep.

Mrs. Margaret Chase Smith, the widow and secretary of a former Republican Congressman from Maine, is the most charming and gracious of all the women. She is a very lovely woman with white hair and the gentle manner that makes others want to do things for her.

Mrs. Smith is a successful business executive in her own right and served as a technical adviser to the International Labor Organization Conference in 1944.

Whenever the Republican elders chide her for her liberal voting record, she smiles gently at them and their wrath falls apart. She is one of those people toward whom it is impossible, at least for a man, to hold a grudge.

The deep South was surprised and a little startled by the voting strength of a mere woman, Miss Eliza Jane Pratt, from the Eighth District of North Carolina.

Miss Pratt is a professional public servant who served as secretary to Congressmen from her district for twenty-two years.

When the incumbent Representative died, the menfolks in charge of politics thought it would be a nice gesture to let "Liza Jane" run for the seat. The males were a little startled at the result. Miss Pratt not only carried all the Democratic counties, but even ran ahead in a traditionally Republican county.

From the generous distance of the gallery, Clare Boothe Luce looked like a demure schoolgirl – a trim, lithe figure, wavy golden hair falling down almost to her shoulders.

Mrs. Luce is a curious paradox. In some moments, she appeared to be a mysteriously dreamy schoolgirl. At these times, she floated instead of walked. She bestowed gentle, faraway glances on her colleagues.

But when she began to speak on the floor, Mrs. Luce became a clever, shrewd woman fighting with dramatic oratory, cutting satire, feminine charm, and stunning denunciation. She appeared to be cold, intellectual, and an actress. There often was no warmth in her appeals, only the fascinating glitter of a keen mind.

Mrs. Luce had a personal dislike for Franklin D. Roosevelt that was almost an obsession. With the intuition of a worldly and ambitious woman, Mrs. Luce recognized Roosevelt's ruthlessness and his deliberate dramatizations.

According to a story she tells, Mrs. Luce was trying to decide whether to run for the United States Senate. A friend told her to be patient and wait for a sign. If she were not to run, she would be handed a white rose.

The next day, when Mrs. Luce entered the House, a strange young man handed her a white rose. She was startled and asked him who he was and why he gave her a rose.

The young man explained that he was passing out roses because the House was holding memorial services for the late President.

In telling the story, Mrs. Luce remarks, "I guess he didn't want any of us to run."

Mrs. Luce's great weakness in debate is that she must be witty. During the House debate on atomic energy, Mrs. Luce made a masterly and effective stand for the civilian atomic control bill. She had obviously taken time and effort to acquaint herself with the subject.

But toward the close of the debate, she said she had heard that atomic energy might be used to breed new creatures. Mrs. Luce added, "I suddenly imagined myself many years from now confronted by a commission that had gotten rather bored, as it might well, with the follies and futilities of man. . . . They might decide the time had come to treat human beings with these radioactive particles in order to get a new type with a very large head, one eye, one ear bent permanently to hold a telephone, one arm with only a forefinger and thumb for signing documents and checks, no legs, and an anatomy constructed to fit most comfortably in a swivel chair. In other words, they might decide to make a human species – the Bureaucrat."

There was a great roar of laughter. The members nudged each other appreciatively.

Helen Gahagan Douglas was on her feet a few minutes later. She said sweetly, "In the field of atomic energy there is a great deal of hysteria. The gentlewoman from Connecticut has given us her playfully imaginative conception of what atomic energy may mean in one instance to mankind."

It might have been a scene from *The Women.*

Chapter XII

THE floor of the House of Representatives is a big, noisy stage where the actors have their hour or two of glamour. Almost every kind of occupation is represented in the House. There were such exotic creatures as an opera singer, an Indiana high school basketball coach, the editor of a woman's fashion magazine, and a diplomat in the Seventy-ninth Congress.

The average Congressman is a small-town lawyer. Before coming to Washington he labored over such problems as getting a divorce for Mrs. Jones, electing a sheriff, and getting an appropriation of seventy-five dollars a month for a night watchman to scare the town drunks. In Congress, he is called upon to decide on international control of atomic energy, billions of dollars of expenditures, and price controls.

The new Representative comes bouncing up the Hill with a spirit of adventure and flushed with success. He figures that passing laws is a mighty easy way to earn $12,500 a year, and he secretly believes there just might be a chance for him to land in the White House one of these days. He also has some stern ideas on how Washington ought to be run. He'll show these bureaucrats and politicians a thing or two.

After several months, the chronic complaint of Capitol Hill settles over the new Congressman. It is a mood of painful frustration. He does not have the time or energy to make even a pretense of intelligent judgment on all the issues thrown at him. He is beset with job seekers and constituents with all kinds of errands, from getting a million-dollar contract to advice to the lovelorn. His lofty ideas of remaking the world or even of getting money for a new post office at the county seat are smothered by the vastness of government and the stern seniority rules in Congress.

Still, there are those brief tantalizing moments of power and importance that keep Congressmen running for office. It may be the moment when the local newspaper runs a big headline, "Congressman Scatterhorn Denounces New Deal Bureaucrats," the time when General Eisenhower offered him a cigarette at a reception, or when, at a committee hearing, he snapped at a cabinet member.

One Congressman kept himself in a happy glow for weeks by figuring out just how much money the British loan would cost each county in the district. His hour of fame came when the county-seat newspaper threw a headline clear across the front page, "Rep. Landis Says British Loan to Cost Brazil [the county-seat town] $250,000." He received a condescending pat on the back from his Republican elders for this neat trick.

There is, too, a fascination about Washington that makes the home town seem pretty tame.

Actually, the separation from the Congressional payroll is not as dreadful as the defeated Representative may imagine. A former Senator of many years' standing tells of returning to Washington with a heavy heart after his election defeat.

He met one of the ever-present job seekers in the hall. The Senator snapped at him, "I don't know of any jobs and I'm not going to look for any."

Telling the story later, the former Senator said, "Right then, I suddenly realized I was a free man."

The life of the average Congressman is dull and confused. He is on the treadmill most of the time. When he arrives at his office in the morning, there is the mail waiting for him like an uneasy conscience. Congressmen get so they dread looking at it. A good share of the letter writers look upon their Representative as a four-flusher, a glorified errand boy, or a wealthy uncle.

In the closing days of the Seventy-ninth Congress, when Representatives and Senators were running back and forth from committees to night sessions and worrying over their primaries, Senator McClellan of Arkansas received a letter from an unknown constituent. The writer said his son, age ten, was not in school and he thought it would be a good time for him to see Washington. The Senator replied cheerfully, but perfunctorily, that yes, he did believe a visit to Washington would be most educational.

Several days later, the Senator received a telegram: young Johnny was arriving on the train and he was expecting the Senator to meet him. As it turned out, not only did McClellan have to meet the young Arkansas traveler but he had to put him up in his crowded Washington home.

Lonely women look to their Congressmen to scare up a good providing husband. One Representative received a letter from a female constituent advising him in the warmest personal phrases that she was now a widow, still in the prime of her life, and would like a man to share her bed and board. She added coyly, "Of course, you are my first choice, but I heard tell you were married."

There are other personal requests. An Indiana woman wrote her Congressman in the days of clothing shortages. She was indignant. She wore a size fifty-two but could not buy dresses large enough. Couldn't the Representative do something about it?

Or the farmer who wrote, "Ples send me yur bulletin on bedbugs. I met yu at the county fair. I bot Hank Brown's place. It's got bedbugs. P.S. Ples send Arthur Hill ur bulletin. He's got bedbugs, too."

There is a tremendous volume of mail involving details of paper work and telephone calls . . . veterans who have mislaid papers entitling them to unemployment benefits, mothers who want to get their boys out of the Army, priorities for housing, GI loans, tax refunds, government contractors wanting to hustle up the settlements.

Old-timers can fondly remember way back in the dim past when the constituents did not bother their Congressmen with views on pending legislation. The New Deal changed that. Congressmen are now engulfed by letters, telegrams, and telephone calls. The OPA bill brought an all-time high. They were mostly letters from individual constituents and required more than the routine, "I have received your letter and noted the contents therein."

On every bill of major importance, the Congressmen are besieged by lobbyists . . . manufacturers, farmers, labor unions, wool growers, veterans' organizations, chain-store interests, cattlemen, and hundreds of others. The lobbyists are persistent. They wait outside the Congressman's door or lurk in the subway as he marches over to the floor. They call on him at home. All these varying and strong pressures give the average Congressman the dizziness of a child who rides too long on the merry-go-round.

The conscientious Congressman has a long day. One Congressman, a member of the busy Appropriations Committee, gets to his office at seven-thirty in the morning. He reads the first of the four mail deliveries of the day to get a cross section of his constituency. He pecks out answers on a battered typewriter and makes notes for his secretary.

At nine o'clock, he is ready to see visitors and make the numerous telephone calls around the government required of him to help his callers. Forty-five minutes later he is hurrying to his committee for a two-hour session.

Between lunch and two o'clock, he goes on the House floor. From two to five, he is back in the committee room again. Then he plods wearily through the subway to his office, dictates letters, and signs them. A tired man, he leaves for home at seven o'clock in the evening.

The wise and fortunate Congressman is armed with a competent secretary to handle the heavy load of mail and requests. The jewels of Capitol Hill are the secretaries who know how to answer letters, pair the boss's vote when he is absent, find the right Federal agency to handle a constituent's request, and who should be polished and who brushed off.

A few secretaries have spent most of their adult life on Capitol Hill and are passed from Congressman to Congressman like heirlooms. The moment the votes are counted and Congressman Jones, who has an excellent secretary, is defeated, this jewel will receive many ardent proposals. I know of secretaries who have worked for both Senators and Congressmen, Republicans and Democrats.

One of the real experts on government in Congress, Senator Bob La Follette, was the secretary of his famous father.

Some Congressmen indulge in the more lucrative but less successful practice of putting wives, sons, or daughters on the payroll as secretaries and clerks. They do not usually work out as well as Senator La Follette.

No Congressman ever has the opportunity to study intelligently even a fraction of the bills upon which he must vote. A very few hire outside experts to make reports on bills for them. A generation ago, a Congressman had a much easier time making up his mind. Government was infinitely smaller. The main issues were taxes and tariff. Party positions were clear. If a Congressman was in doubt, he could just ask his floor leader for advice. Now, who is to advise him on the control of atomic energy?

The voices from home are confused. In the old days, a Representative could get guidance from the local political boss, the banker or leading farmer. Now he has demanding petitions from the National Association of Manufacturers, the Farm Bureau, CIO and A.F. of L., American Legion, and a hundred other organizations. During the price control fight, the Congressmen received so many and conflicting pressures that they gave up trying to figure out what the home folks wanted. They struck out blindly.

The Congressman cannot even rely on his party leadership these days. Both the Republican and the Democratic Parties have split so widely on major issues that the leadership has walked away from laying down a party line. They feared the result would be to spread revolt and split the factions further apart.

Almost every Congressman is faced with a painful fact. He may lose his job in two years. Every two years he must take off weeks or months to convince the folks back home that he ought to remain their Congressman. This takes time, money, energy, and influence.

There are a few political freaks who rise from nowhere without money, organization support, or a large personal following and get elected to Congress. One was Willie Gallagher, the kindly old street sweeper from Minneapolis.

Congressmen, especially from urban districts, are continually harassed by the necessity of raising funds for their campaigns. They spend thousands of dollars in the primary and election. One

Congressman from a combination city-rural district spent $7500 in his last election. He declared for the official record $2500. The remainder was "soft money," or cash distributed around where it would help the most. This is a usual practice.

The Congressman must buy radio time, newspaper advertisements, billboard space, hire halls, pay for picnics and barbecues, employ workers, kick in to the party's war chest, and, occasionally, buy off "nuisance" candidates.

The continual search for campaign funds is a harassing ordeal. In the process, the Congressman is constantly giving away pieces of his independence. He gets $600 from a group of merchants with the understanding that he will seek exemptions for them in price controls and minimum wages. A high-pressure promoter on the prowl for a lucrative government contract kicks in $2000 to the campaign chest. The inference is that the Congressman will talk to officials in the right places.

The strain of the hunt for contributions was shown in some remarkably frank letters written by Representative John Coffee of Washington and his former secretary, Paul A. Olson, to a contractor whom they had assisted in getting a war contract. The contractor sent Olson a check for $2500, which Coffee said was a campaign contribution.

Olson wrote the benefactor: "You have no idea how gratified John is, and how much mental relief and worry has been lifted by reason of the assurances you gave at the foot of the stairs over in the Capitol Building. If a few more people in the world would show the same sense of appreciation and understanding of this gigantic problem that snows him under every two years, then the going for John as a member of Congress would be a lot easier.

"However, this financial strain and burden of putting on a campaign every two years, plus meeting all the demands headed on a public official by way of tickets, donations, etc., along with the terrific cost of maintaining a family in the National Capitol, does not deter any of us from making at all times the best fight we can in the interests of the Sixth District and the individual citizens like yourself who live in it."

Congressman Coffee wrote, "A considerable share of my worries over the situation Paul described to you have been dispelled."

Despite the great pretense of rugged independence on Capitol Hill a large share of the bills originate from outside sources . . . a lobbyist, or governmental official.

These bill writers ignore the rank and file of Congressmen as unimportant. They go to the key men, the chairmen or ranking minority members of committees, or Congressmen with a strong personal following on the Hill.

The caller will explain chummily, "Look, Joe, we've got a problem that will interest you. Now, it's this way . . ." He will wind up amiably, "To save you all the trouble, we've had the bill written. I know you are pressed for time. Here it is."

The source of these bills is a deep, dark secret never referred to on the floor, although it may be common knowledge in the press gallery that the legal section of the War Department wrote SB 0054. The scowling looks cast downtown and the fierce cries of independence on the Hill are an act and a tradition.

This is no reflection on Congress. It has neither the time nor the facilities to originate legislation dealing with broad sweeping policy, or involved and technical subjects.

When a bill is introduced, it is referred to one of the powerful Congressional committees. The committees have broad and dictatorial power over all bills in their field, for the committee report is normally adopted.

Most of the committees are run, sometimes benevolently and more often with a heavy hand, by the chairmen. The chairmen hire the help (the men and women who do the real work), they decide who will appear before the committee and give testimony. They can bottle a bill up in the committee. They control debate in the House.

These chairmen are political freaks – men who have been so long in Congress they have slowly moved up the seniority ladder to the top job. Out of the twenty most important committees in the House, fourteen have chairmen from the South.

The real work of the committees is done by the unsung heroes of Capitol Hill. They are the hundreds of committee assistants who labor without praise or publicity at difficult tasks. The credit must always go to the Congressmen. The assistants are supposed not to be seen or heard, except off the record.

In major debates these committee assistants sit by the side of the committee chairman as he roars into action. When the chairman gets stuck, he leans down, whispers to his assistant, gets more ammunition, and then thunders forth into battle again.

Washington correspondents learn after futile experiences in badgering Congressmen with questions about committee actions to slip around to the committee room and talk to the assistants. If anyone knows, they do. But the assistants are cursed with anonymity. They must not be quoted.

A good many of the committee assistants are disillusioned bureaucrats who have climbed the Hill. They do not get any more money. But they are exhilarated by their sense of independence and the thought they are doing something where they can see the results. Some of the most competent officials in all Washington are Congressional committee employees.

The assistants check the bill with other legislation, search through it for trick clauses, make sure the policy is what it is supposed to be, and investigate downtown to find out what the actual effect of the bill would be. They confer with the so-called "author" and line up the witnesses for the committee hearings.

The hearings are good for the ego of the Congressmen. The committee members are both judge and prosecutor. A little frustrated man from Smithville who cowers when his wife snaps at him can glower at a bank president, a union leader, or a cabinet member and call him such choice names as "crook . . . Communist . . . pip-squeak . . . bureaucrat." There is nothing the witness can do but make a mental note to break the guy's neck if he ever gets out of Congress.

The hearings, if exhaustive enough, will bring out all the issues, the facts and prejudices, and the many differing points of view. Then the hard work begins. The committee closes the doors, sits around the table, and tries to mold a compromise. This is the test of statesmanship.

Day after day and into the night, the elected representatives of the people wearily search each other, the heavy pressures building up, and the public interest.

The bill is then reported to the House for action, often with a majority and minority report. The Senate Atomic Energy Committee published ten thick books on its hearings, in addition to its short report. These committee reports are the law in the lower House, for they are usually followed in the voting.

The most powerful committee in Congress is the House Appropriations Committee. It controls the purse strings for every dollar spent downtown. It can block any Federal program or cripple any agency by the simple method of pauperizing it. All appropriations originate in the House.

Strong men downtown will blanch and tremble over a rumor that chairman John Taber of the Appropriations Committee is looking crossly in their direction. Gruff administrators who have a reputation of being tough cookies will open the door and bow and scrape to a member of the House Appropriations Committee.

The committee guards its reputation for penury jealously. It made General George C. Marshall, the wartime Chief of Staff, come up to the Hill and explain in a secret session why he needed billions of dollars for the mysterious Manhattan Project. To compensate for blank-check allotments given the War and Navy Departments, the committee would reassert its independence by taking a minor officeholder over the coals for an appropriation of a hundred thousand dollars.

The older members of the committee, Clarence Cannon, John Taber, and Louis Ludlow, the tall, ambling, shy, second-ranking Democrat on the committee, actually dictate governmental appropriations. Ludlow, for example, has devoted his Congressional life to studying government. He rarely takes the floor, but one of his infrequent talks will assure passage of an appropriation. So well versed are these committee leaders that when the ponderous appropriations bills come on the floor, the House gratefully accepts their recommendations.

Appropriations are an example of the compromise that is the life of Washington. The agencies always ask for more than they know they can get. They pad out vacant jobs and launch into detailed explanations of projected programs.

Then, when the Appropriations Committee with a cold and fishy eye scratches them out, there is a terrible howl. But inwardly the bureaucrats are patting themselves on the back for not being skinned.

The real passion of the Appropriations Committee is the scribblers or publicity men downtown. They are known on the Hill ungenerously as "propagandists." The Office of War Information was always filled with Appropriations Committee investigators prowling around for signs that Elmer Davis was promoting himself for President, or FDR for a fourth term.

Any hint that an agency has set aside a tidy sum for "public relations" is pounced upon excitedly by the committee. The boys downtown have found a way of getting around this. The publicists are quietly listed as "assistants to the Director," or "Congressional liaison."

In this constant game, all the agencies downtown have men who are supposed to sit up nights figuring out ways to outwit the House Appropriations Committee. Actually, the committee is not nearly as omnipotent as the bureaucrats fear. The members do not have the time to go into all the appropriations and study them. Instead, they are like the policeman on the beat whose mere presence prevents crime.

Another committee way on top of the heap in power is the Rules Committee. It is like a traffic signal – giving the green light to some bills, stopping others.

So many bills are introduced in Congress that only a fraction are ever considered seriously. From June 1 to July 13, 1946, a heaping total of 575 bills were thrown in the Congressional hopper. Nine out of ten will die in committee.

But there are still too many bills on the calendar to be acted upon. If the Administration, minority, or any strong group wants action on a bill buried on the calendar, it must get unanimous consent to have the bill called up out of turn.

If this is not forthcoming, the supporters of the bill must go to the Rules Committee. This committee has power to recommend bringing any bill, wherever it is buried, up for action. Many times, the committee members are subject to terrific pressure because of their power. President Truman asked that his Congressman, Roger Slaughter of Kansas City, be beaten in the Democratic primary, because Slaughter, as a member of the Rules Committee, obstructed Administration measures.

The committees are sprawled all over Capitol Hill, in basements and faraway corners of the Capitol Building, there are so many of them. In the Seventy-ninth Congress there were thirty-two regular and eleven special committees in the Senate and forty-eight regular and seven special committees in the House.

The first faint beginnings of reform of the crumbling old Congressional system broke over Capitol Hill in the Seventy-ninth Congress.

It passed the La Follette-Monroney Bill for the reorganization of Congress with great enthusiasm.

Under the act, Congressional committees were cut down to size, fifteen in the Senate and nineteen in the House. Salaries were raised so that committees can be staffed by top-flight experts and technicians instead of bumbling political leftovers. Lobbyists must file detailed financial reports every quarter. The heavy and exhausting burden of private and special bills is removed from Congress. Members who have served long beyond their time of ability can retire on a pension and make way for younger men.

The bill would have gone further, but Sam Rayburn demanded as the price for House action that several portions be removed. The deleted parts would have cut down his power.

These sections would have created an over-all Congressional policy committee, established a joint legislative and executive council to eliminate the wearing feuds between the Hill and downtown, and provided for a broad legislative budget.

Self-reform in this fantastic little world has begun!

Chapter XIII

THE Senate, in comparison with the noisy and restless House, seems like a slumbering men's club still lost in the dreams of Rip Van Winkle's day.

Two painted tin boxes tucked away in a niche of the back wall contain snuff. The boxes are freshened every day with a few drops of water. When the snuff gets stale and moldy, it is changed.

The ivory gavel resting on the heavy green cloth top of the Presiding Officer's desk is one hundred and fifty years old. There is one small crack in it brought on by the vigor of an enthusiastic New Dealer.

The reading clerk of the Senate, John Crockett, looks like a figure from a musical comedy of the Civil War period. His white hair droops over the back of his high starched collar and tumbles down his forehead. He wears a long, gray frock coat. Old John rattles off the titles of the bills in the loud hurry of a tobacco auctioneer.

Stoop-shouldered Senator Clyde Hoey of North Carolina, who often sat above Crockett presiding over debate, looks something like a twin. There are the same frock-coat suit and white hair. The only difference is that Hoey has a gentle, resigned look on his wrinkled face and wears a red rose in his buttonhole.

Out on the floor, Tom Connally of Texas looks like a faded and yellowed newspaper clipping. He wears his long and curly white hair in the manner of William Jennings Bryan. He dresses deliberately in the style of a generation ago with his pants legs narrowing down to small cuffs.

Old Arthur Capper of Kansas totters in and out of the chamber as if each trip might be his last. His face is drawn and gaunt with the cheekbones standing out. He has to cup his hand over his ear to hear the debates.

The page boys swinging in and out of the doors are dressed like reform-school boys of a generation ago in their Sunday best. They must wear dark blue serge knickers, black cotton stockings, a white shirt and black tie.

The Senators sit at small, mahogany, school-type desks. These appear so fragile that a big wind from a filibuster might collapse them. The skylight up above is supported by steel girders to keep it from falling in.

The difference between the House and Senate is recognized in an old joke involving the names of identical committees, the House Foreign Affairs Committee and the Senate Foreign Relations Committee. As the story goes, the Senate is too old to have "affairs"; it has "relations."

Many Senate debates have a timeless quality – as if the same subjects had been argued a hundred years ago and would be talked over on this selfsame spot generations hence.

There is an intimate, personal air about the Senate debates. The ninety-odd men know each other so well there is none of the House atmosphere of strangers pulled together on the last day of the world.

Each Senator has a sharp personality, as seen from the gallery. Down there, on the left, the long man sprawling out with a cellophane-covered cigar in his mouth is Bill Langer of North Dakota, one of the last of the stormy independents of the twenties, now the dean of the Senate isolationists.

A few seats from him, the man with the great bald head and large dark eyes is Eugene Millikin of Colorado, the legal authority of the Senate. The boys in the press gallery call him "the Wizard of Oz" because of his shiny head and air of great wisdom. The large man slouched down in his seat with a gloomy stare on his face is Joe Ball of Minnesota. Across the aisle, the good-looking younger man dressed like a college boy is Warren Magnuson of Washington. The dour old man with white hair is Elmer Thomas of Oklahoma.

The high priest of the United States Senate sits on the front row by the aisle. He is Alben Barkley of Kentucky, the Democratic leader, seventy years old. He has a ruggedly plain face and a big, solid frame. His are the most tolerant eyes in Washington. They have seen so much they are rarely moved to anger and then only when someone profanes the dignity and good name of the Senate.

Alben Barkley believes the United States Senate is the greatest deliberative body in the world. He knows its weaknesses and flaws better than most men, but he would regard it as something just short of treason for a writer or politician to ridicule this exclusive body.

With the death of Franklin Roosevelt, Senator Barkley, whose two great gifts are infinite patience and a sense of humor, became the most important Administration leader in Washington. Day after day and into the night, Alben Barkley stood by his desk in the Senate like a rock outlasting the angry waves of opposition.

This man might be President today. He was on Franklin Roosevelt's list of acceptables for Vice-President. But the party leaders scornfully crossed him off. "Too old," they said. He accepted the verdict without anger.

Senator Barkley, sitting calmly in his seat during a furious whirlwind of debate, is a familiar sight. Then when the voices are tired and the tempers cooled to sullenness, Barkley is on his feet squinting with his nearsighted eyes and saying, "Mr. President, I move . . ."

One afternoon, in the final spring of the Seventy-ninth Congress, voices rose and fell monotonously in the Senate. A mild glow of sunlight filtered into the gloomy chamber. Outside, men and women lay sprawled out on the grass, their faces turned to the warm, satisfying sun. On the other side of the Capitol the halls were deserted. The House of Representatives was on vacation.

Hour after hour, Alben Barkley was on his feet. He was answering questions, patiently steering the debate. Other Senators wandered in and out. Late in the day, Barkley rose wearily and in his slow, courteous voice said, "To be perfectly frank, it is very discouraging to try and legislate all these matters with Senators not in the chamber. The Easter season is over. Senators are due back in the Senate. I do not say this with any pique but because it will be in the interests of good legislation."

The whole burden of the Administration program had fallen on Barkley. The Senate had been angry, tired, and divided. It was in no mood to pass on bills loaded with controversy . . . the three and a quarter billion dollar loan to Britain, price control, extension of the draft, civilian control of atomic energy.

But when a husky young clerk pulled down the flag over the Senate and the Seventy-ninth Congress, almost all the Administration program was through, signed and sealed. The learned editorial writers spoke of how "President Truman pushed through the main planks of his program." But it was not Harry Truman. Alben Barkley, the man too old to be President, did the job.

Barkley forced the Senate to act when it was obviously sullen and reluctant by the simple strategy of outlasting his opponents. He prevented adjournment and forced the Senate to work on through the night. He could stand a day and night of continuous session but the enemy cooled off in the long, dreary hours of early evening. Many times I have seen the opposition leader walk across the green carpet of the Senate, pause at Alben Barkley's crowded desk, and ask for a compromise.

The Senator is a master of compromise. He enjoys it fully as much as Franklin Roosevelt relished a victory. To Barkley, compromise is an ancient art far more useful to civilization than war, victory, or defeat. He and his opponents will sit down in Barkley's antique, high-ceilinged office a few feet from the Senate floor and there explore each other. Each one has a line from which he cannot retreat. Somewhere in the middle areas, Barkley builds his compromise. The other Senators are willing to sit down with Barkley because he never embarrasses them by forcing them to go behind their final line.

When the Senate is about to crack from anger and tension, it is Alben Barkley who moves in smoothly with a comforting joke. When the witticisms are read in the cold black type of the *Con-*

gressional Record the next morning, they may not seem funny. But, somehow, they were just what the Senate needed, and Barkley knew it.

I have seen the black mood of anger hanging over the Senate dissipate into a chortle of laughter after Barkley drawled out a mild joke. He knows exactly when to drop them in. A minute or so later or earlier might have drawn all the anger in the Senate on him.

Despite his great power and prestige, Barkley refuses to take himself seriously. At the time of the furious fighting on price controls within the conference committee in Barkley's office, the reporters caught him as he left the meeting and walked down the hall to open the Senate.

They asked him eagerly, "Are your prayers on the OPA going to be answered?"

Barkley looked them over serenely and said, "The prayers of the righteous availeth much." He paused. There was a twinkle in his eye. "I guess I am not righteous enough."

The Senator is a very tolerant man. He has no bitter enemies or pet hatreds. He supported the anti-poll-tax bill and the FEPC. He made an earnest speech in which he set out his philosophy. "The United States should be setting an example for the rest of the world. Until every man who fights for his country, regardless of race, religion or creed, or what part of the country he lives in, has equal employment and voting rights with his fellow men, we are failing in our duty as leaders."

Senator Barkley has an exceptional thoroughness in debate. He is not as quick or as penetrating as Bob Taft or Wayne Morse, but he covers the ground more thoroughly. When Barkley addresses the Senate on any subject, whether it is war contracts or atomic energy, the main points are carefully explained.

He is one of the most liberal and world-minded men on the Hill and were it not for his personal prestige would probably be labeled a "left winger." While many other Democrats lost their enthusiasm for liberalism when Roosevelt died, Alben Barkley plodded steadily ahead along the left fork. He quietly and calmly selected the road himself.

Barkley has a strange menagerie under him, as the Democratic leader. The seat next to him is filled by the Senator from Tennessee, Kenneth McKellar. The sharp political mind of McKellar is blurring into absent-mindedness but he still is a tremendous power in the Senate.

McKellar looks like an old black crow blinking on a limb. He is an elderly man with a spreading nose and dim peering eyes, and he is deaf. He dresses in black suits of an ancient style and black bow ties.

He has clung fiercely to every bit of power he ever had and reached out for more. As acting chairman of the Appropriations Committee, he had the hex so fixed on the Administration downtown that patronage from Tennessee is way above its normal. This endeared him to Ed Crump, his friend, sponsor, and boss. Crump is the political chief of Memphis. In the final hours of the Seventy-ninth Congress, McKellar arose to make one of his few speeches – a defense of Ed Crump.

During Mr. Roosevelt's last year, McKellar – a little rudely and impetuously – asked the Senate to elect him Presiding Officer. This office is purely honorary except when a President dies and the Vice-President moves downtown. Then the Officer presides over the Senate.

Some of the Senators thought McKellar was being a little hasty, but they voted it to him indifferently. When Truman moved off the Hill, McKellar climbed up in the chair and inherited the Vice-President's shiny long limousine.

His position was of great value to the Southern conservatives. During the debate on the fair employment bill and the anti-poll-tax bill, McKellar shuttled Southerners into the chair when he grew tired and went out for a nap. As one awed Northern freshman Senator put it, "McKellar and his friends parceled out the talking time."

McKellar is an unreconstructed rebel who looked upon Roosevelt benignly only when Crump told him to. But with Harry Truman in the White House, McKellar has been an enthusiastic Administration supporter. The reason is that President Truman dropped in on a Tennessee State Society party in Washington and spoke a few cheerful words about the "great man and good friend, Kenneth McKellar." The Senator glowed with appreciation and has been right ever since.

The man sitting next to McKellar is the cold and able leader of the Southern conservative bloc, Walter George, whom FDR tried unsuccessfully to purge. He has a strong, even distinguished face, dark eyes behind thick glasses, white hair, a wide forehead, and a stubborn chin. He wrote the taxes and Social Security laws as chairman of the Finance Committee.

He is too old now to go looking for a fight, but Walter George never ducks one coming his way. A few days before the Senate was to adjourn, Wayne Morse, the independent Republican, blocked unanimous consent to bring the Social Security amendments up ahead of the anti-poll-tax bill.

Senator George's temper flared up like a rocket. He growled, "All right, let the filibuster start right now. We'll just stay here all summer then."

Strong men all over the Senate grew pale and pleaded with Morse to go along. They knew Walter George was quite capable of carrying out his threat.

Another powerful and conservative Southerner is "Ole Tawm" Connally of Texas, former chairman of the Foreign Relations Committee. After the debate on the World Court, one of the girl reporters screamed of the Senator, "That made-over isolationist." It was not a bad description. It caused secret delight that night among many of the more world-minded Senators.

Connally weakened the World Court resolution by offering an amendment which would give the United States the right to decide when a case was domestic and the Court could not consider it.

Speaking for his amendment, Ole Tawm beat the drums like the Southern politician he is. He beat his fist on the desk. He waved his arms wildly. He shouted, "I don't want any world court telling us what to do with the Panama Canal. We bought and paid for it. And I don't want any court telling how many foreigners we've got to take in. There are a lot of hungry people who think we would feed them better."

The Southerners are far from being of one stripe.

There could hardly be any greater range of views than those held by "Pappy" O'Daniel of Texas and Theodore Bilbo of Mississippi, on one hand, and scholarly young Bill Fulbright of Arkansas, on the other.

O'Daniel looks more like a professional at a wealthy and swank golf club than a friend of the poor and downtrodden. He is handsome, solidly built, middle-aged, and dresses in sports clothes. He is the anchor at the extreme right of the Democratic Party. O'Daniel is an isolationist and economic conservative.

Bilbo is one of the last persons a Capitol sight-seer would suspect of being a United States Senator. He looks more like the janitor at the fire department or county jail. Although the Senator is well educated, he speaks a drawling mixture of slang and profanity. His common appearance and way of talking are among his best political assets.

Bilbo is a scrawny, hammered-down fellow with pale and squinting eyes. He walks with a bowlegged, rolling gait. The stringy hair on his large and partially bald head is plastered down with some kind of greasy hair oil. An operation has twisted his lips into a perpetual leer and his cheeks are sunken. The Senator puffs on a series of foul-smelling black cigars. On "dress up" occasions, Bilbo wears a small diamond-studded horseshoe in his figured necktie.

On Capitol Hill, he followed a familiar routine. Each noon Bilbo ordered a huge meal in the Senate restaurant, usually a thick juicy steak and a gigantic salad. He tucked a napkin in his shirt collar and dug in with great relish. Then he would go to the Democratic cloakroom, select a comfortable black leather couch, and take a two-hour nap punctuated by loud snores.

The record of the Senate War Investigating Committee hearings on Bilbo is a sorry chapter in American political life. The Mississippi Senator was accused of accepting thousands of dollars and lavish gifts from war contractors, and of accepting $1500 from an elderly drug addict who wanted Federal permission to get two grains of morphine a day.

Through most of the hearings, Bilbo was jaunty and indifferent.

He cocked his feet up on the table in front of him, puffed his cigar, and flung jibes at the press table.

Chairman Jim Mead gravely opened the hearing. "The allegations will be treated in the same manner as any other charges made to this committee. We approach the hearing with an open mind and no prejudices. . . . All men are equal before the law in a democracy."

In a loud whisper, Bilbo flippantly told the reporters, "Much ado about nothing."

Later Senator Ferguson was questioning Bilbo about the gift of a Cadillac and furniture for his "Dream House" one Christmas. The interrogator remarked dryly, "That was a pretty good Christmas." Bilbo answered lightly, "I've had better." He dismissed the donation of the Cadillac by a war contractor as "just an old Southern custom."

When the Mississippi Senator was asked about $25,000 received from contractor "Big Boy" Newton, allegedly for campaign purposes, Bilbo said proudly, "Ah'm a good collector."

Bilbo treated the whole investigation as an unwarranted bit of scandalmongering by busybodies who had nothing else to do. He told the committee these accusations were of no concern to it. After all, Bilbo drawled, they had been aired in the 1946 campaign and the Mississippi voters had re-elected him.

Bill Fulbright is the kind of person about whom mothers would nod their heads approvingly and say, "A mighty promising young man." He is handsome and well poised, with a gentle and engaging personality. He is independently wealthy and one of the best-educated men in Congress.

His father built one of the great economic empires of the South. He wanted his son to be a gentleman. Bill was a Phi Beta Kappa and halfback at the University of Arkansas. Later he was a Rhodes Scholar at Oxford. His world was broadened further by a journey through the Balkans with a famous foreign correspondent, M. W. Fodor. After he returned to America he became an assistant in the Department of Justice and helped prosecute the test "sick chicken" case in the old NRA.

Then he went back to the University of Arkansas as president.

The governor, Homer Adkins, fired him, so Fulbright went into politics to get even. He was elected to Congress.

In the lower House, young Fulbright gathered together a number of the more serious-minded juniors every Friday to talk about world affairs. Foreign correspondents and diplomats met with them.

Franklin Roosevelt heard of these meetings and called Congressman Fulbright to the White House. He had some chores for such a bright young man. Fulbright became a sounding board for advances in American foreign policy. It was the famous Fulbright resolution which paved the way for the Atlantic Charter.

When he came to the Senate in 1945, Fulbright organized support among his fellow freshmen for the United Nations. He and ten others met regularly for a while to hear men from the State Department and Embassy Row.

When FDR left for Yalta to meet Churchill and Stalin he had with him a letter from sixteen freshman Senators who pledged their support of international organization. This was Bill Fulbright's work.

Then Franklin D. Roosevelt died. Young Bill Fulbright, coming up fast, was shocked and stopped in his tracks. His inspiration was gone. The man who resolved his doubts and gave him little pushes on the way was dead.

Fulbright has spoken out since the President's death only occasionally. Once, in the bleak winter following Roosevelt's death, the Senator could no longer hold back his concern over the wandering steps of American foreign policy.

He told the Senate, with an apologetic air, "Our actions and policies in foreign affairs seem to be improvised on the spur of the moment. We play by ear without the slightest regard for the harmony of the composition. Such a method can only lead to disaster."

Ole Tawm Connally glared at the young whippersnapper over his horn-rimmed glasses. But Fulbright went on stubbornly, "We must make known to the world our intentions and purposes. We have a choice between armed might and imperialism, and the rules of law enforceable by the United Nations."

Senator Fulbright's great cross is his lack of aggressive self-confidence. He feels himself hemmed in by the tight ring of Senatorial elders and frustrated by the indifference the Senate gives to most speeches.

But the promise is there. He has moments of rebellion and independence. He was the only Democrat to vote against jovial George Allen, President Truman's crony and storyteller, to be a member of the RFC. He was one of the twelve Senators who voted against the Connally amendment weakening the World Court. He made a learned speech against repeal of the excess profits tax. He was the only Southerner to vote against seating Bilbo.

Scattered around the right side of the floor are the elder liberals, the men who carried much of the burden of the New Deal in its twelve hurried years . . . Barkley, tired old Robert Wagner, little Joe O'Mahoney, gentle Elbert Thomas of Utah with his fine and scholarly radical mind, and Jim Murray of Montana.

These men have faded gradually into the background. Younger and stronger voices are beginning to be heard.

Chapter XIV

IN the hot and troubled summer, the usually stodgy *Washington Star* published on its front page a cartoon that brought chuckles to the capital.

The cartoon had two figures, Secretary of State Byrnes in a frock coat and President Truman. Byrnes was saying, "You ought to hear that fellow Molotov argue."

Mr. Truman was replying with a smile, "Shucks, Jimmy, you ought to hear Senator Taft."

All over Capitol Hill, the cartoon pulled faces into grins. Through the days and nights of the OPA debates, the dry-as-dust voice of Bob Taft had rasped in the ears of the Senate.

Robert Alphonso Taft, Republican, of Ohio, son of a former President, is the strategist and assault commander of the Old Guard in the Senate.

When he comes strolling down the Senate aisle in a benign mood after a good lunch, Senator Taft has a curiously misleading appearance. He looks as if he must have been a very cute and well-behaved baby. On those occasions Bob Taft has a happy, satisfied smile in his active eyes. There is a trace of a dimple on his smooth cheeks. His head, shining and bald halfway to the back, completes the cherubic infant appearance.

A minute or two later, the Senator's dark eyes may be flashing with anger or his smile may have widened into his Cheshire-cat look.

As soon as he begins talking, Taft loses all resemblance to a happy baby. His speech is the dry, slightly twangy, scornful voice of a frustrated professor lecturing to a class of not very bright athletes in a small, Midwestern college. He looks disapprovingly over steel-rimmed spectacles. His dark and conservative suit hangs on him limply.

Bob Taft is a powerful force in the Senate but it is not because he is a hail fellow or can tell good jokes. He is distinctly not the kind of man anyone but a drunk would slap on the back. His sense of humor, if any, is saved for less public occasions than Senate debate.

The Senator is a leader because he has one of the quickest minds in Washington, is tireless, knows the Capitol like a book, and has a crisp air of authority.

On the Senate floor or at a committee meeting, Taft's mind works like one of those fascinating mechanical gadgets manufacturing doughnuts in store windows. An opposing point is fed into him. His mind pulls it in, picks it apart, and fashions a sharp rejoinder. His replies give the impression of being neat, logical, evenly painted and polished. The dry voice contributes to this impression.

He manages to hopelessly frustrate many of his opponents by irritating them so much they scream at him, or stand shaking in cold fury. Then the large Cheshire-cat grin spreads over his face. He plainly enjoys this.

Bob Taft is not invulnerable himself. He has a temper that rises like a Roman candle. The trick is for his opponent to remain cheerful and calm and to throw in barbed remarks with an innocent air. This so infuriates the Senator that he loses his normal caution. He hates to be played with this way. Chester Bowles was one of the few public officials who could infuriate Taft, much to the obvious pleasure of Bowles.

The Senator has boundless energy and just cannot be run down. He is active on all his committees, including the Special Committee for the Reconstruction of the Senate Roof and Skylights.

He dominates GOP policy in the Senate as chairman of the Republican Strategy Committee. He is the most influential member of the party group that selects Senate committee members. Bob Taft has a controlling weight in economic policy by his membership on such key committees as Banking and Currency,

Education and Labor, Finance, and Postwar Economic Policy and Planning.

Taft is in almost every major Senate debate. He will discuss thoroughly and at some length any subject involving profits, even if only a half-dozen Senators are nodding drowsily at their desks. He is a man who loves to poke and argue.

Senator Taft practically grew up in Washington and in politics. His father was that jovial and hearty man, President William Howard Taft. The son took to politics with a predatory curiosity. He was in Washington as a young man lawyering for the U. S. Food Administration. This experience opened his eyes to the eternal secrets of bureaucracy.

With all his energy, curiosity, and special knowledge, Bob Taft could probably be a great discoverer of juicy scandals, except that they don't happen to interest him.

Senator Taft instead is the most effective and energetic conservative in Congress. His eyes are focused on economic matters. He had more fun in the OPA fight than Congressman Rankin does chasing a suspected radical off the Federal payroll.

Robert Taft is an infallible conservative. A liberal Senator remarked, half facetiously, half seriously, "Sometimes, when I just can't figure out how to vote on a bill, I watch Taft. Then, I vote the other way. He hasn't failed me yet."

The Ohio Senator's philosophy is upper middle class economics garnished with a benevolent paternalism. To less shrewd politicians of the right, Taft sometimes appears to be a menace right out of the pages of the *Daily Worker*. Naïve John Bricker once said in all seriousness he was afraid Bob Taft had been consorting with Socialists.

Actually, Taft believes the system he supports will endure without serious change only if lower income groups are given enough to keep them quiet. This is nothing more than the traditional philanthropy of the wealthy, "Society should take care of the poor."

This is the basis of Senator Taft's vigorous support of the Wagner-Ellender-Taft housing bill which the real-estate lobby considers an import from Moscow. The Senator's analysis is quite simple; the capitalist system is unable to provide the cheap mass housing needed to prevent a wave of dissatisfaction. The government with all its resources must step in. Taft feels the same way about medical care for the poor.

After the 1946 elections, Bob Taft was asked if he still backed the W–E–T housing bill. The Senator shrugged his shoulders and a dry smile brushed over his face. He commented, "You've got to be liberal about something. I still support the bill."

Although Taft is considered a spokesman for "Big Business" on the Hill, he is not a stubborn or noisy reactionary. He considers that type stupid. The Ohio Senator feels that he knows better than the National Association of Manufacturers what is good for it, and he has no false modesty about saying so. He is a champion of strong profits for manufacturing and is candid enough to admit it.

But he does not indulge in slam-bang denunciations of labor unions or of liberal measures which have become well established, such as social security and Federal aid to education. Bob Taft was the fellow who stopped the Truman labor bill, with its drastic penalties on striking union members, when it reached the Senate.

Taft's strategy in the Seventy-ninth Congress eventually won the grudging admiration of his fellow Republicans. Some of them had wanted to tear him to bits when he coldly held them back from grabbing the Administration's program and jumping up and down on it.

His tactic was far more subtle. Let Harry Truman and his boys make the mistakes. Let them alienate labor and other politically important groups while the Republicans sat back virtuously. Senator Taft probably did as much as any man to destroy effective price control, but his strategy managed to spread blame mainly on the blithe little man in the White House.

Bob Taft let the Southern Democrats lead the way with amendments slicing up the OPA and then agilely inserted those he favored as the bill swung by. He voted for the patched and torn compromise price control bill and defended it against the brawling attack of some of the less inhibited men on his side of the aisle.

The Senator has never shown much more than a mild interest

in world affairs, except when economic factors enter in. He was a sharp antagonist of the British loan.

For two Republican National Conventions, Senator Taft has been the choice of business interest in the "grand old party" for the Presidential nomination. But his personality just isn't showy enough for the rank and file.

The Senator's ambitions to live in the White House have not infected him with the usual coyness of candidates. It may be an odd way to enjoy yourself, but Robert Taft is having the time of his life leading the Old Guard into the victories in Congress they dreamed about during the dark, dark days of "That Man in the White House."

Senator Taft's chief lieutenant is a noisy Nebraska undertaker, Ken Wherry. It is always a source of intense pain to the liberals to be reminded that Wherry defeated the late George Norris for his Senate seat.

Unlike Taft, Wherry is a flashy personality and inveterate Rotarian. A big ring gleams like a headlight on one finger. His suits are bright and well pressed. In spring and summer he wears two-toned shoes. His curly graying hair is carefully brushed.

Senator Wherry rushes into the fray with the joyful bellow of a bull and his arms waving. He never seems relaxed on the floor or at a committee meeting. In those rare moments when he is not talking, he appears like a lion crouched for a spring. An impatient scowl spreads over his face. He chews gum furiously.

Even in conversation, Wherry's voice is never soft. There is a harsh, commanding note to it.

When Wherry is whipping his Republican colleagues into the right emotional pitch for the battle, he is much like a football coach . . . the same back slapping, pep talk, and sharp orders.

Although he is a newcomer – elected to the Senate in 1942 – Wherry is already a darling of the GOP Old Guard and something of a pain in the neck to his Midwestern neighbor, Harold Stassen. As a freshman, Wherry was elected Republican whip of the Senate.

His talent is as an organizer. In Nebraska, before he jumped into politics, Wherry organized automobile, farm implement, furniture, undertaking, and farming businesses. He promoted county fairs. He is an enthusiastic joiner, Shriner, and Legionnaire.

In the lonesome years of the great New Deal strength, Wherry was a boon to the Republicans. He energetically campaigned for both the Governorship of Nebraska (1933) and the Senate (in 1935) and was defeated. In 1941–1942, the GOP high command turned over to him the job of organizing states west of the Mississippi.

Wherry is a less discriminate and profound conservative than Taft. Anything with the glow of the New Deal on it is like a trigger setting off some explosive within him. He is not one of those Republicans who believe in occasionally siding with the Democratic majority. He is an Old Guard partisan and proud of it.

While Taft is supposed to represent large industries, in his thinking, Wherry reflects the interests of retailers and wholesalers. He tried to jam into the OPA bill an escalator system for raising their profits.

Wherry's method of attack is a hard right to the chin, no boxing. He throws his whole heart into the punch and when the opposition fails to fall, he sometimes grows confused and splutters with anger.

In the last days of the OPA fight, Wherry was trying unsuccessfully to persuade Senator Barkley to support his profit raise for merchants. He had already spoken on it for some minutes when Barkley had the floor.

Wherry impatiently interrupted Barkley. The majority leader, obviously irritated at Wherry's buzzing insistence, tried to brush him off.

Wherry snapped, "We have a right to establish our case here."

Barkley wearily replied, "The Senator established it in his time. Does he want to establish it in my time, too?"

Wherry shouted, "I can certainly ask all the questions I want to."

The majority leader, who has learned that indifference is often fatal to the Wherrys of Congress, yawned. "What did the Senator say?"

From there on, the dialogue went like this:

Wherry – "There is no limit on debate here."

Barkley – "No."

Wherry – "Very well then. We can establish our case in the Senator's time or my time."

Barkley – "Mr. President, I have tried to be courteous to the Senator."

Wherry – "And I have tried to be courteous to the distinguished majority leader."

Barkley – "I did not ask the Senator to yield to me while he was speaking. He has already taken up more of my time than I have myself."

Wherry, sulkily – "If the Senator does not want to yield to me, very well."

Barkley, patiently – "I have not done anything but yield."

Wherry – "I ask the Senator to yield right now."

Barkley – "Very well, I yield right now; right now; right now."

At this the Senate broke out into sympathetic laughter. After a few more sentences of legislative horseplay, Barkley said again, "I am yielding."

Wherry, flustered, asked, "Will the Senator yield?"

Barkley – "I said I am yielding. I am still yielding."

A few minutes later, Wherry got so involved in his explanation that Taft had to jump in and give him a hand.

One of the little feuds in the Senate is between Wherry and Claude Pepper, who is just as vociferously liberal as Wherry is conservative. The two heartily dislike each other.

After President Truman had vetoed the compromise OPA bill, Wherry would rise each day and read off figures showing that cattle were pouring into the markets. As soon as he sat down, Pepper would get up and coolly read statistics allegedly showing a sharp rise in the cost of living. Wherry would glare furiously at him, while Pepper stared back coldly.

The press gallery has learned that Senator Wherry is quite a guy to help out in a pinch.

Newspapers frequently get complaints from readers, advertisers, and professional complainers alleging scandal, fraud, and all variety of bad situations. Occasionally, a bored editor will send one to his Washington correspondent to see if he is on his toes, with a curt note, "Get someone to investigate this."

The reporters have learned they can call Senator Wherry and ask, "Will you investigate this for us, Senator?"

He will reply cheerfully, "Oh, sure."

The next day he will make a speech or give an interview angrily demanding an investigation into deplorable conditions at Pago Pago. The newspaper will run a bold, black headline, "Senator Wherry to Investigate."

That is the last heard of it. But the newspaper, the correspondent, and the Senator are happy. The newspaper got its headline. The correspondent disposed of an irritating chore. The Senator got his name in heavy type.

Despite the way Wherry and Taft have run away with the Republican leadership in the Senate, there is a nominal GOP leader. He is a gentle, sweet little man, Wallace H. White, Jr., of Maine. When Taft, Wherry, and some of the other more belligerent Republicans go trampling into the battle, White sits at his desk in the front row looking very much like a bewildered white rabbit watching a herd of elephants trumpeting past him.

White is beloved on both sides of the aisle. He is regarded as a sincere and conscientious gentleman. In debate his voice is never raised into shouts. He does not thump his desk. His arguments are never bitter.

Wallace White lives in a little private world of his own, a world very much shadowed by the past, by his expert knowledge of communications, and by his reverence for the Senate.

His grandfather was a Senator, and White was his secretary. He takes more pride in this than he does in his own position. The Senator has been in Congress since 1917.

His election as minority leader is accidental. It is a result of the acute factionalism within the Republican ranks.

The former GOP Senate leader was the late Charley McNary. He held his forces together with an iron hand, marshaling them together for every vote. He dreamed of the day when the Republicans would again be in control of the Senate.

His assistant was Warren Austin of Vermont, who attracted

the lusty dislike of the dominant isolationist crowd on his side of the aisle, because he spoke out forcefully for intervention in world affairs.

As a compromise, mild-mannered Wallace White was named minority leader. Austin was placed on the Foreign Affairs Committee, but balanced by the isolationist, Wiley of Wisconsin, on the same committee.

When McNary died, the little white-haired man from Maine took his title. Senator Taft, the real leader, did not want the title. Wherry was unacceptable to the non-isolationists and liberals in the GOP seats.

As master of the impasse, Wallace White sits meekly and cheerfully on the aisle.

The "statesman" of the Republican Party, and very jealous of that reputation, is Senator Arthur Vandenberg of Michigan. He is known variously in the press gallery as a stuffed shirt, a cynic, an actor, and a great Senator. One correspondent who watched Vandenberg operate at world conferences impishly calls him "the varnished vacuum."

He looks like one of those "men of distinction" in the whiskey advertisements – a tall, sturdy, well-dressed man with an imposing manner. He has a broad intelligent face with rather stern eyes, white hair brushed meticulously across his head. He dresses in well-tailored double-breasted suits and wears a bow tie.

Senator Vandenberg's manner is somewhat cold, but impressive. His deep voice rumbles out lofty phrases in dramatic fashion – pauses for emphasis, voice lowered and raised at exactly the right time. After you have heard the Senator make his fifth or sixth speech on foreign affairs, you are bothered by the thought that you have heard and seen this performance before.

His audience on the Senate floor is usually attentive, for most of his colleagues – with little time and opportunity to investigate the twists and turns of world affairs – look upon him as *the* expert on foreign policy.

He knows that by a combination of acting, real knowledge, and influence on the State Department, and balancing his views adroitly so as not to arouse the angry shouts of the isolationists or the wrath of the Administration, he can maintain his position with no difficulty. There is no one in the Senate or House to challenge him.

Arthur Vandenberg was a newspaperman, writer, and lawyer – all good training for his role as a Congressional leader. As a newspaperman, he learned the tiresome art of separating fact from fiction, the trick of deceptive phrasing, and the knack of attracting attention by key words. As a writer, he polished up his rolling sentences. As a lawyer, he learned to dramatize himself and his subjects.

These abilities developed within the Senator, perhaps unconsciously, something amounting to scorn for his colleagues, the Washington correspondents, and the public.

His speeches are a combination of good reporting, observations, prejudices, and acting.

When he rises to make one of his periodic reports on world affairs, Senator Vandenberg waits for the hush to fall over the chamber. Then he proceeds in a bold, positive manner.

As an actor, the Senator cannot refrain from a little Fourth of July oratory. He ended his report on the Paris foreign ministers' conference – after a blistering attack on Russia – in hushed piety, "Lord God of hosts, be with us yet, lest we forget, lest we forget."

Senator Vandenberg enjoys the world conferences. He likes to match wits and obstinacy with shrewd men while he holds the high cards. He glows in the spotlight.

He was converted to the United Nations, not born to this philosophy. In the prewar years when Franklin Roosevelt was trying to pull the nation out of its isolationist mood, one of his strongest and craftiest opponents was Arthur Vandenberg.

The Senator was not a noisy isolationist. The very bitterness and rancor of those men lost them influence in Congress. Vandenberg was cold and deliberate, cautioning the Senate against going too far. He worked effectively behind the scenes in the Foreign Relations Committee, controlling enough votes to keep the Administration from moving swiftly.

Mr. Roosevelt, although he disliked Vandenberg intensely, saw he was an opponent he could not beat in an open fight. The only way to win Vandenberg's great influence was to convince him.

The President invited the ranking Democratic and Republican members of the House and Senate Foreign Affairs Committees to represent Congress at the birth of the United Nations in San Francisco.

It was this conference and the others which Vandenberg attended that convinced the Senator that the United States must take a leading role in world affairs. He is no longer an isolationist. There is no label yet invented to aptly describe his position. His views reflect the struggle in the minds and emotions of most average Americans between national sovereignty and pride, suspicion of "foreigners," and the desperate need for world unity in the atomic age.

He comes back to these points again and again in his speeches, as if he thought by saying them he could find some answer.

In one report to the Senate, he said, "Peace with justice is the supreme necessity for America and for the world. Peace is indivisible in the atomic age. The pursuit of effective, dependable peace with justice takes priority over every other human need."

Senator Vandenberg despises the Soviet, its socialism, its truculence, its "iron curtain," its spread throughout eastern Europe, its brooding suspicion of American motives. Most of his speeches are filled with this bitterness.

Yet he comes back uneasily to say, "War between us [the United States and U.S.S.R.] would be an unthinkable calamity, which I am certain they, as well as we, abhor. . . . Given patience, fair play, tenacity, and firmness in American attitudes, it is possible for Eastern Communism and Western democracy to find friendly common ground."

Arthur Vandenberg exercises tremendous influence on American foreign policy, not only on the Hill, but in the gray old State Department Building. Secretary Byrnes knew that without Vandenberg's support, the Administration might have rough going in Congress. So the Secretary of State tailored his policies to those of the Senator.

The Senator takes himself very seriously as a man of destiny. He can even see himself in the White House. But he would settle for the job of Secretary of State.

Chapter XV

THE oil lobbyists were sitting like keen-eyed hawks in the Senate gallery. They watched intently as the Senate moved step by step toward passage of the tidelands bill. This bill would turn over the tidelands and their rich oil deposits to the states.

The Administration's fight against the oil grab was losing. Not even Alben Barkley could stop the bill. The Senate threw aside his amendment. The oil men allowed a smirk to spread over their faces. They relaxed and sat back more comfortably in the hard gallery benches.

Right below them, on the Senate floor, a stiff, slim man with black hair and a small bristling mustache pulled a bill out of his desk. He wrote swiftly on it in pencil and snapped his fingers. A black-stockinged page ran to the clerk's desk with the bill.

Then the author, Senator Wayne Morse, independent Republican from Oregon, rose to his feet and said tersely, "Mr. President, I offer the amendment which I sent to the desk and ask to have it stated."

Old John Crockett began to read in his loud singsong. The oil lobbyists leaned forward and stared at each other with their mouths open. All over the floor, Senators were popping out of their chairs and angrily waving their arms.

Republican William Knowland of California, one of the tidelands sponsors, strode over to Morse. This husky young man towered over Morse like a giant and glared furiously at him. Wayne Morse sat with cool indifference. He leaned back in his chair and touched his finger tips together.

Morse had tacked the anti-poll-tax bill to the tidelands bill.

Up in the gallery, an oil lobbyist stopped a Senate official he knew and said, "How can we get to this Morse?"

The clerk flung back, "That's one guy you can't get to, brother."

Southern Senators were shouting at the presiding officer, demanding that he rule Morse's amendment out of order. Senators who planned the strategy to ease the oil grab through rushed out into the cloakrooms for a new huddle. The oil men clambered out of the gallery.

One after the other, Republican and Democratic leaders pleaded with Morse to withdraw his amendment. They spoke feelingly of party loyalty, of patriotism, of respect for Senate rules. The Senator listened stonily.

Claude Pepper of Florida, often teamed up with Morse on liberal battles, argued piously with Morse to back down. Why, Pepper said almost tearfully, no one was more anxious to have the poll-tax bill passed than he. He was in charge of the strategy. But, Pepper said sadly across the chamber to Morse, this was no way to get the anti-poll-tax bill passed.

The press gallery had filled up rapidly. The reporters were standing up watching the scene down below. They smiled broadly at each other. Morse had pulled the slickest trick of the session.

He was either going to force a vote on the poll-tax issue, which neither the Democratic nor the Republican leaders wanted, or kill the tidelands bill. The Southerners, much as they might be tempted by the persuasion of the oil lobbyists, would not vote for the bill if it had the poll-tax rider tacked on.

The Southerners seized control of the floor in case they had to filibuster. Dick Russell, the lean and balding junior Senator from Georgia, was standing defiantly by his desk. He would not let anyone else talk unless he promised to return the floor to Russell.

At the height of this commotion, Wayne Morse rose quietly. He was a trim figure with a rigidly straight back and expressionless, deep-set eyes. The Senate quieted down as he started to speak.

Looking directly at the anguished Mr. Pepper, Morse said, "If the Senator from Florida is really interested in getting the anti-poll-tax issue before the Senate, I should like to inform him it is now before us. But if the Senator is concerned with playing politics on this issue, then I can understand his suggestion that I withdraw the amendment."

Morse spoke crisply, much like a professor delivering a lecture. At these words, the Democrats looked uneasily at each other. The Senator bore on icily, "I know of no amendment more vitally concerned with the preservation of this thing we call the American system of government. It is basic to the liberties of free men. Is it possible that some of our fellow citizens are to be allowed to enjoy the freedom only in the abstract?"

Morse was not quite through yet. He bore down another line: "We know that getting this bill before the Senate in this session demands parliamentary strategy. Was the junior Senator from Oregon the first one ever to use strategy? He is a babe in the woods compared to some of the strategists who have attached riders to bills, filibustered, and demonstrated their mastery of strategy."

Wayne Morse was thoroughly enjoying himself. He was the author of an unexpected satire. He went on, "If I am learning a little bit about Senate strategy, why criticize me? I will not withdraw the amendment."

For a moment when he finished there was a deep silence over the Senate. Once again a brash freshman, Wayne Morse, had made the United States Senate look foolish, like a group of smudgy children caught in a naughty act. He won his point. The tidelands bill was dropped.

Morse has become the conscience of the Senate, sometimes an impudent conscience. When the Senate begins speaking the lines in one of its solemn political farces, it is Wayne Morse who interrupts with the cry, "Fraud." When the Senate bows to the lobbies or to political expediency, Wayne Morse is up in his seat pointing his finger and saying sharply, "Now, now."

Morse was elected as a Republican but he does not let that bother him. He is one of those rare birds in Washington, a pure liberal. He came by it honestly, by conviction.

The Senator blithely ignores the GOP leadership and is a member of the loosely knit coalition of the left wing. He is also an ardent internationalist. He has offered to form an independent liberal coalition of Republicans and Democrats, but has had no takers.

Being a nominal Republican does not inhibit Morse from publicly lecturing the Democrats or President Truman. He was the first one to recommend to Mr. Truman that he withdraw the nomination of Ed Pauley and avoid a political scandal.

Morse scolds his own party like a virtuous spinster. He tells it the GOP will never be popular until it takes off the old conservative clothes.

The Senator's professional manner comes naturally. He was dean of the University of Oregon Law School before he came to Washington as a public member of the War Labor Board. Very few people can recall the names of any other WLB members, Morse so dominated the board.

When he first hit the Senate and bounced out of his seat often, his elders looked down on him with lofty severity – a youngster who would have to be disciplined. But gradually this attitude became infiltrated with a wavering doubt.

In one heated Senate session, Morse was up and down firing at will with sharp accuracy.

A veteran Senator leaned over to a neighbor and growled, "That damn fool talks all the time. He must think he knows everything."

His colleague, who had been following the debate closely, smiled mysteriously and answered, "Maybe he does. Maybe he does."

Morse has won the respect of the Senate by his complete thoroughness and lack of demagoguery. He saw, after a few weeks, that the men who controlled the Senate were those who knew the rules so well they could play tricks with them. Morse learned the rules, and no one is more expert in parliamentary strategy than he. He can cross up the Southerners and tie them in knots.

Morse was able to force out the World Court bill in the last hours of Congress, despite the opposition of Old Tom Connally and Arthur Vandenberg, and get it passed. He did the job almost alone – by strategy, by calm and dispassionate debate.

Wayne Morse — one of the ablest men to sit in the United States Senate — may never be a great popular leader. He lacks the warmth of personality that made George Norris such an influence on American thinking. Morse is a rugged individualist with a cold and even abrupt personality.

A few desks from Senator Morse is a small man with curly white hair that tumbles over his forehead. He is George Aiken, the honest and friendly liberal from Vermont. He represents the sturdily independent farmers and factory workers of his state against the few powerful families who have so long controlled Vermont politics.

Senator Aiken looks like one of the farmers who voted for him. He listens to the endless hours of debate with the half smile of a man who knows it is mostly buncombe. Then he will move over and whisper some of that inward laughter to Wayne Morse. Until Morse came to the Senate, Aiken was a lonely man on the Republican side of the aisle.

Aiken's record is consistently liberal. He fights for civil liberties, and against bills restricting the rights of any minority — Negro, labor, Jew. He has worked hard but vainly for the St. Lawrence Seaway and carries on a constant campaign for rural electrification and education bills.

Some months after Mr. Roosevelt died, Senator Aiken was invited to take part in a debate. The question was — should liberals join the Republican or the Democratic Party?

The Senator said in his pleasant New England drawl, "The independent voter ought to come to the Republican Party, because the Democratic Party is no longer the party of Franklin D. Roosevelt. It is now the party of reaction. The only chance of the liberals is not only to join the GOP but to *control* it. This is the only way the policies laid down by Franklin D. Roosevelt can be continued."

The Republican National Committee offices on Connecticut Avenue were, to put it mildly, aghast. A radical was boring from within.

Joe Ball came out of the Northwest with the reputation of a rugged liberal. That reputation was short-lived. He ended the

Seventy-ninth session as a rather sullen and morose conservative. Ball looks as if he ought to be an independent grass-roots liberal of the Abraham Lincoln variety. He is a big strong man with dark hair now turning gray. Locks fall over his forehead, giving him a boyish look.

Across the aisle, the Administration's very own problem child is Senator Claude Pepper of Florida. He is the *enfant terrible* who refuses to stay in line. He wants to lead the procession and is the self-appointed champion of the New Deal. Since the death of Mr. Roosevelt, other Roosevelt New Dealers have either "gone underground" or been reconverted, but Pepper is bolder and brasher than ever.

He is a homely man with a long and sad face like that of an old horse. He generally wears black double-breasted suits and ties to match his thick clump of hair. His dark eyes can look as gloomy as prophecies of hell or flame with the passion of a zealot.

The Senator looks and sounds a good deal like a hell-fire and damnation evangelist. He is one of the most fluent and passionate orators to come to the Capitol in many years. As he speaks, it is plain there are only two roads to follow – one leading to the true glory and the other to damnation.

To politicians looking for a speaker to liven up a dull campaign, Claude Pepper is just what the doctor ordered. The Senator can make a large audience sing and kneel down to pray. This somber black figure can lay a spell over a crowded hall, but the Senate, used to all kinds of actors, is only irritated.

Claude Pepper is an oddity in the Senate. He comes from the deep South, but offends the old tradition of the mint-julep, frock-coated politician. He has none of the cold logic of Wayne Morse or the friendliness of George Aiken.

Depending on one's view of him, Claude Pepper has an abundance of "guts" or "gall." He is not afraid to take an unpopular cause in Washington and beat the woods with it. He was one of the few Democrats in public office to show a complete lack of reverence for Harry Truman and say so. He spoke up loudly for Russia when official Washington was drawing back distastefully from all things Soviet. Throughout the Seventy-ninth Congress, he was the darling of the New Dealish bureaucrats, Congressional clerks, and lobbyists.

Senator Pepper hammers stoutly at the walls of "special privilege," and storms after the Old Guard with the enthusiasm of a country preacher attacking sin.

The White House and Democratic National Committee are afraid of Claude Pepper. Mr. Truman would dearly love to read him out of the party, but he is afraid that the Senator would not be so meek a martyr as Henry Wallace. The Democratic National Committee, which wrote him off the speakers' list for 1946 and then hurriedly put him back on again, fears that the Senator would love nothing better than a lusty, brawling battle. Pepper would enjoy being the crusading white knight of the New Deal tilting lances with the politicians, and the Democratic high command knows it. It does not want to give him that chance.

The Senator is a shrewd practical politician himself. He knows that the Democrats are going to find out they cannot stay in power without liberal support. If he can tie up that following, Pepper can sit back and let the politicos come to him. When the New Deal chuffed and faltered in the Truman Administration, Senator Pepper rushed in to snatch the fallen flag. His eagerness to be the New Deal standard-bearer was not entirely popular. Other New Dealers who are less aggressive wish Pepper were not quite so conspicuous.

The Senator is a confusing personality, even to those who agree with him seven eighths of the time. They cannot quite decide whether he really is a sincere crusader, just loves a scrap, or enjoys the headlines.

Some answer may be found in his background. He was a poor farmer's boy in Alabama. He worked his way through college stoking furnaces, waiting on table, and working in a steel mill during the summer. He has no reason to love the *status quo* of the old South.

There is no question about Claude Pepper's vigor. He throws all his energy into the causes that interest him. He likes a fight and will pick an argument. He is a bad guy to have for an opponent and a hard man to team with.

When Glen Taylor walked into the Senate in January of 1945 he was shrugged off as a political accident. A cowboy strumming a guitar for votes! Hmpff.

But this handsome young man sitting in the back row neither looks nor acts like a ham actor in a grade B Western. He looks more like a Hamlet. He has a pale, dramatic face and dark alive eyes. He sits quietly in the Senate. He listens closely to the words falling all around him, like a man trying to make sense out of a language he is just learning to understand.

When he rises to speak, there is a passionate ring in his voice, and idealism in his words. He is not angry, as Pepper, nor does he try all the trickery of oratory. He speaks with simple eloquence.

The politicians? Glen Taylor ignores them. Senator Morse fought the politicians and tried to outwit them. But Taylor just doesn't pay any attention to them. They do not interest him.

Glen Taylor is one of the most world-minded of the Senators. He introduced a resolution instructing American delegates to the United Nations to work for an eventual world republic. Tom Connally promptly put it in a dusty pigeonhole of the Foreign Relations Committee and forgot about it. Taylor is not discouraged. He is going to take his campaign to the public.

He is a devoted supporter of organized labor and carries these convictions over into his personal affairs. Taylor refused to sign the Senate payroll because he would have been required to sign an affidavit saying he was not a member of any organization which approved striking against the government. Taylor still holds a card in an A.F. of L. union. The Senate clerk finally ruled that Taylor would not have to sign this affidavit.

Many Senators have less than affection for their colleague from the same state. But they ordinarily do nothing about it. Too much trouble. But not for Glen Taylor. He thought his fellow Democrat from Idaho, Charley Gossett, was too conservative. So Taylor pulled out his sound truck and stumped the state against him in the primary. Gossett lost.

Taylor's stock in the Senate went up. A man with that much energy and conviction was too dangerous to ignore.

Chapter XVI

WASHINGTON's grimy slums stretch for dreary blocks of sagging red brick and frame buildings only a few steps from the dignified Capitol.

Incongruously mixed in between the taverns smelling of sweat and stale beer, the untidy groceries, and the tattered rooming houses are three government buildings. They are the gleaming Social Security Building with its sterile halls, air conditioning, and indirect lighting; the handsome Railroad Retirement Building, and the big, warehouselike Census Building.

On that sleepy afternoon in April, 1945, these were the anthills of economic control for the nation. They were overflowing with officials, clerks, and stacks of regulations. From these buildings price controls, rationing, and priorities over the life of the nation – raw materials, food, transportation, manpower – were tightened and relaxed like the throbbing of a huge heart. They housed the OPA, the War Production Board, the War Manpower Commission.

Men like Big Bill Knudsen, Don Nelson, Leon Henderson, Paul McNutt, and Chester Bowles had restlessly paced the cool halls while children played noisily across the street and men drowsed in the slum doorways. This whole parade of men brought in to keep a nation at war working and producing and the vast, complicated machinery they operated took orders from the quiet offices in the White House.

Four weeks after Franklin Roosevelt died, the war agencies moved mechanically without hard-and-fast orders or broad policy from 1600 Pennsylvania Avenue. The big presses went ahead printing ration stamps. Mimeographed regulations flowed regularly from the busy machines.

A few days before his death, Mr. Roosevelt had moved Fred Vinson, the big former Congressman from Kentucky with a drawl thick enough to cut, into the top economic job of the nation — Director of the Office of War Mobilization and Reconversion. Vinson looked out of his large, sleepy eyes at the pressures pumping up all around him and warily played a game of wait and see.

The plain-spoken men from the A.F. of L., CIO, and railway brotherhoods told Washington bluntly they were on the hot seat. The rank-and-file members of labor were grumbling loudly over wage and job controls. The nonstrike pledge was hanging by a thread.

The National Association of Manufacturers was whispering to Congressmen and WPB officials that the sooner they got rid of priorities and allocations, the quicker the United States would be humming back to good old normalcy again. The farm lobbies were loading their guns for price control.

Only one thing held back a swift disintegration of economic controls. The war was not over yet. While men were still dying, it hardly seemed proper to start the bitter battles over reconversion.

On V–J afternoon and night, crowds were shouting, dancing, laughing, and crying in front of the White House. In many of the economic control offices in the slum area, men who had been clamped down at their desks worrying over regulations kissed their secretaries and tore up mimeographed sheets of orders. Thank God, it was all over.

By this time John Snyder, the little Missouri banker, was Director of War Mobilization and Reconversion. He was still in a jovial mood. He said carelessly, "What the hell, we don't need all the controls any more. The war's over."

J. A. Krug, the husky head of the WPB who had been brought in from TVA, was out to make a good showing that he wasn't one of these damned Washington bureaucrats. He recommended tossing out priorities and allocations. All steam ahead for reconversion!

On Capitol Hill, Congressmen who had endured regulations

over which they had no control added an extra shove. War had been no fun for Congress. It had been prodded into voting for controls. When constituents complained about regulations, Congressmen had trotted down to the war agencies like meek messenger boys and been given a polite brush-off. They had, in fact, been sternly lectured by officials, who obviously enjoyed it, that war was no time to play politics.

In the conferences that took place every day, only two voices spoke out against lifting of all controls. They belonged to Will Davis, the friendly man with unruly hair, tolerant eyes, and an amazing record as a labor conciliator and economist, and to Chester Bowles.

Davis, then Director of Economic Stabilization, warned, "The dinner is not over until the dishes are washed."

But within a few days after the end of the war, the whole intricate machinery for economic control was being dismantled. Wage and manpower controls were pounded loose and discarded. Allocations and priorities were ripped off hundreds of basic items. The L–41 order giving the government control over building materials was junked. Later, the pent-up demands for new construction and veterans' housing forced it back on. Not, however, in time to prevent race tracks, movie theaters, and bars from grabbing precious lumber, steel, and masonry. By mid-autumn rationing was discarded. Price controls were being loosened. The men and women who had rushed to Washington to run the economic machinery were pouring back to their jobs in industry.

Congress was swept along without protest. The House and Senate virtuously tore up the excess profits tax. This tax had been designed to drain off the immense purchasing power jingling in American pockets and to help pay the cost of the war.

In the great winds of haste, the few voices that did speak up in Congress were drowned out. The race back to normalcy was on.

Price control alone was left. The items on which price controls had been lifted were climbing steadily, and the cost-of-living indexes began to creep up. Congress sighed and voted in 1945 to continue price control for another year.

All the pent-up pressures then fell on the sole economic weapon left – price control. A battle, often bitter and even violent, raged over Washington in the winter, spring, and summer of 1946.

The issue was the same one that came up again and again in the New Deal – free enterprise to operate in its own rugged and unrestricted way versus government controls. All the forces that had battled Franklin Roosevelt united for the war against price control.

The forces were never evenly divided. The farm lobby – the American Farm Bureau Federation with its smooth-talking, politically expert president Ed O'Neal – was the battering-ram. It led the fight because of its potent political power and its contacts all over Capitol Hill. The farm lobby could count on the solid backing of the cotton bloc and most of the delegations from the cattle and corn-hog states.

The National Association of Manufacturers went in for full-page newspaper advertisements and a campaign of agitation among businessmen. The NAM snatched a Washington correspondent from his newspaper job to cover every hearing and every session of Congress where price control was debated. He usually knew a good deal more about what was going on behind closed doors than his former colleagues of the pencil and copy paper.

The retailers and real-estate people flagellated themselves into spasms of anger. They wrote, phoned, and buttonholed their local Congressmen.

On the other side were an indifferent President Truman and his economic adviser, John Snyder. At no press conference did Mr. Truman ever exhibit any real enthusiasm for price control. In private conversations Snyder said it was all a lot of hogwash dished up by the fellow Bowles to keep his name in the paper.

Organized labor was too busy with strikes and wage policies to give its full attention to price control.

About the only consistent organized support price control received on Capitol Hill was from enthusiastic amateurs, the women's organizations. Many women who had politely sat back studying and reporting to their memberships now got into the battle with both arms swinging. Such organizations as the League of Women Voters, General Federation of Women's Clubs, the P–T–A, Business and Professional Women, and the Y.W.C.A. did the most effective work day in and day out to save price control. They dramatized the issue of price control to hundreds of thousands of women whose interest in public affairs had never advanced far beyond the need for a new school building and toilet facilities in the park.

Six months after the Truman Administration came to office, the supporters of price control were fighting a rear-guard action. It was gloomy fall weather in Washington. For days the sky was the color of lead. Rain dripped ceaselessly from the towering trees on the Capitol lawn. The fallen leaves scattered on the grass were turning from gold and red to a dull, burnt brown.

The mood was one of pessimism. The Administration was sagging apart on the economic issue. The first hint of the split over price control came at a hearing of the Senate Small Business Committee.

Senator Kenneth Wherry, the flashy, sharp-tongued Republican whip, arranged the hearings as a club to beat price control to death. He looked around the crowded committee room like a circus ringmaster. A smile of triumph was on his face and his big ring flashed on his right hand.

John Snyder was sitting quietly and unobtrusively in one corner. He looked like a merchant Wherry might have called in from his home state of Nebraska. Sitting near him was Chester Bowles, looking more than ever like a cocky college boy.

The room was as jammed as a movie theater on bank night. This was to be the first statement by the Administration on its basic economic policy for reconversion. The lobbyists were all there . . . reporters, with sheets of yellow copy paper scattered before them . . . some of the regular Washington characters who use committee hearings as a place to rest in a warm room.

Snyder began by reading a prepared statement in a flat, monotonous voice. He read without enthusiasm of the need for controls against an inflationary boom.

Senator Wherry started firing questions at him. What did he

think of the Bowles housing program? The Senator gave a sarcastic twist to the word "Bowles." (Wherry was referring to a program worked out by Bowles and the National Housing Administration to put price ceilings on new and used dwellings.)

Snyder blinked and answered timidly that well, he didn't understand the proposal thoroughly. He had not had the time to study it thoroughly.

"But I will assure the Senator," he added, "nothing will be done to hamper construction."

One of the OPA men standing near the press table stared angrily at Snyder. He whispered loudly to the reporters that Snyder had too studied the program.

Senator Wherry smiled triumphantly and moved ahead to exploit this unexpected bonus. He jabbed his finger at Snyder and snapped, "If this Bowles bill is passed, do you think it would help build houses?"

Snyder turned his eyes down and said meekly, "I would have to read it carefully."

The Senator adopted a friendly manner. He said soothingly, "Don't you think price controls should be lifted on all building materials? The builders I talk to say the Bowles plan would stop housing. Don't you think that controls over materials and homes slows production?"

President Truman's buddy repeated, "I would have to study the bill."

Bowles was leaning forward thoughtfully. He was carefully studying Snyder's reaction. Senator Wherry was smiling in anticipation.

A committee investigator friendly to the price control side took over the questioning. He asked Snyder with just the right amount of respect, "The Administration then might approve controls on the prices of homes and building materials?"

Snyder replied in a low monotone, "If the controls would not stifle production."

The committee officer tried again. He asked sympathetically, "Do you see any resistance by builders to price controls and to starting new construction?"

Snyder pursed his lips nervously, then opened them to reply, "I hardly know. The reaction to price controls is varied."

Senator Wherry moved back in. "I get the impression," he said, "that you hesitate in this price control program.

"By the way," the Senator added loftily, "just what committee cleared this policy?"

Snyder answered apologetically that the White House economic advisory committee had approved it. He did not explain that the committee was representative of business, labor, farming, and the public.

Senator Wherry attacked again. "I see by the papers that the Administration has okayed a 15 per cent wage increase. Will *that* be figured in these price ceilings for builders?"

Snyder said unhappily, "I don't know about any 15 per cent being the policy."

The Senator spoke again in that professionally kind voice. "It seems to me that the plans of Bowles were not studied adequately by Mr. Snyder."

The Reconversion Director murmured, "I have only a small staff. In our meetings with the OPA we ask questions. But we have to take OPA's word."

Senator Wherry's technique changed with Bowles just as a prosecuting attorney switches tactics in cross-examining key witnesses and then the man on trial for murder. He let Bowles read a few lines until the OPA chief said, "I think there is a tremendous need for housing."

Senator Wherry snapped at him, "You assume so. It is your opinion."

Bowles said sweetly, "Oh, so you say there is no need?"

The Senator almost shouted, "It's up to you to prove there is a need."

The exchange subsided, then Bowles read on, "There is need for housing for veterans."

Wherry challenged this. "How do you know? Talk, talk, talk!"

The hearing turned into a personal argument between Wherry and Bowles over the need for price controls, and Bowles's own integrity. Sitting over at one side, Snyder looked sourly at Bowles.

From the beginning, it was evident that the crucial battle would be won or lost in the Senate. Each of the major figures in this drama stood out sharply against the dull background of the Senate floor. From the gallery, they looked like gladiators as they rose in the countless hours of debate.

On the one extreme of opposition to any form of price controls were:

Kenneth Wherry.

Old John Bankhead of Alabama, a tall, stooped man with eyebrows as thick as caterpillars. He never made a pretense of patience with witnesses before the committee or other Senators supporting price controls. Bankhead had one single purpose – higher prices for cotton. He was such a potent ally of the farm lobby that he was awarded the Farm Bureau Federation's award for "distinguished and meritorious service in the interest of organized agriculture" in 1941.

Pappy O'Daniel, who tried to filibuster price controls to death. The heavy-set Texan was so personally unpopular in the Senate that his campaign to talk the OPA out of existence flopped for lack of support.

Pitted against them in support of strong price controls were:

Bob Wagner of New York, the tired and aging hero of the early New Deal, father of social security legislation and the Wagner Labor Act. Wagner was ill and never able to drive and lead the fight to keep OPA.

Sheridan Downey of California, whose angry and passionate speeches on the floor frequently led to applause from the gallery and caustic remarks from his opponents on the floor. He was joined by Glen Taylor of Idaho.

The majority of the Senate was bunched into two in-between groups. One was led by Senator Bob Taft of Ohio, whose dry voice, pedantic manner, and sharp mind made him the ideal spokesman for the Senate's conservatives.

Taft was philosophically opposed to government control. But he recognized that if price controls were suddenly lifted and prices shot sky high into an inflation, the reaction might defeat conservatives in the fall elections and force the imposition of tougher controls. His formula was to smother the kind of controls Bowles wanted by amendments setting up a profit equation.

The other middle group was led by Alben Barkley, the patient, tireless majority leader. He wanted strong price controls but was willing to settle for what he could get.

Senator Barkley's doctrine was spoken gravely on a hot June afternoon in the Senate. He said, "We present to the Senate a bill which does not altogether satisfy anyone, but which, in the democratic process of give-and-take, is the best bill possible."

Chapter XVII

A BLACK mood drifted over Capitol Hill in mid-spring. The weather turned cool overnight. A sharp wind tugged at the Congressmen as they walked up the stone steps to their offices. A gray sky glowered overhead.

The elevator boy on the Senate side of the Capitol was the first to notice something was wrong. He grumbled, "Everyone's mad around here. You can't do anything right."

From the back of the car, a passenger commented, "This is going to be a bad week in Congress."

This was Monday, April 15 — the day that Chester Bowles began his drive to keep price controls. He sat in a Senate hearing room, across the table from a cold audience.

The chairs for spectators were filled . . . a few lobbyists carefully watching the faces of the Senators, some curious soldiers, and a number of women peering over the heads of those in front of them to get a glimpse of Bowles.

There was Senator Robert Taft staring coldly at Bowles. Senator Bankhead of Alabama, the leader of the cotton bloc, glowered. Bald Senator Millikin of Colorado looked skeptically across the table. Senator Capehart, an Indiana manufacturer, puffed at the stub of a cigar and smiled in anticipation. He was all primed with questions.

Bowles, now the Economic Director of the Truman Administration, took a long last drag at his cigarette and began: "We are in the same stage of conversion to peace that we were in 1942 in our conversion to war. The pipelines were full of war goods then, but they had not showed up on the battle fronts. Now, our pipelines are filling up with consumer goods."

Bowles did not get far in his statement. Senator Capehart, who looks like a middle-aged kewpie doll – a flat face and a red lock of hair curling over his forehead – broke in, "Why don't you satisfy the demands of the manufacturers and increase prices 10 per cent?"

Senator Taft said dryly, "How can you hold prices down when wages go up?"

The witness asked patiently, "Can I answer?" There was a roguish, schoolboy look on his face.

Democratic Senator Murdock said angrily, "Give the man a chance to answer."

Bowles explained, "All through the thirties wages were increased. Costs went down and profits went up."

Senator Taft stopped him sharply. "Lots of people are going out of business these days."

Bowles argued back, "There are fewer bankruptcies now than ever before."

Taft bit off his words impatiently. "Bankruptcy is going out of style. They just quit. . . . You did not answer my question."

Bowles replied good-naturedly, "Obviously, I am never going to satisfy you."

Senator Bob Wagner of New York, the old progressive fighter, was slumped in his chair. He watched the exchange through partly closed eyelids. He was sick and tired.

Senator Taft pounced in again, "You've got to increase prices 30 per cent if you let wages climb."

That afternoon, on the Senate floor, the cotton bloc rose in wrath against the OPA.

Round-faced Senator Eastland of Mississippi led off. "Mr. President," he said, "the attempt by Mr. Bowles to mislead the American people into believing that increased cotton prices would cause an increase in the price of clothing is not only false. It is absurd."

He waved his arms vigorously. "Who is responsible for the shortages? It is officials in OPA." His voice grew into a roar. "The qualification for a job in OPA is to know Professor Frankfurter. The only thing I know to do today is to abolish the agency."

Downstairs in the gloomy statue-lined hall below the dome of the Capitol several hundred clubwomen were gathering to buttonhole their Congressmen. The OPA bill was coming up for a vote in the House in a few days. There were dignified dowagers, enthusiastic housewives, and wide-eyed college girls in the delegation.

A pretty brunette was clutching a big bundle of papers. She explained eagerly to reporters, "This is a petition from five hundred thousand people in Illinois."

A gruff Capitol police lieutenant strode into the hall. He shouted to the chattering women, "You'll have to move on." Another policeman began pushing the women and grunting, "Move on. You can't meet in here."

The women looked helplessly around and then thronged down the long hall toward the House of Representatives. They clustered around a doorkeeper, who told them, "Ladies, you're not going to get any of those Congressmen off the floor."

He whispered an aside to a friend, "These amatoors never get anywhere."

The next morning – Tuesday – Chester Bowles came back to the sunlit committee room for more heckling. He started off hopefully, "Rising prices would mean a higher cost of living and a paralysis of strikes to raise wages."

He spread out his arms and asked, "What more could you expect?"

Senator Capehart started to speak. Bowles said, "If you will just let me finish, I'll stay here all month to answer questions."

Senator Taft pounded the table with his hand, saying, "The first and most indispensable step is not price controls. It is to stop government spending."

Bowles swung back, "Congress took off the excess profits tax. Is that inflation?"

For once, Senator Taft was caught without words. He paused, then replied lamely, "Oh, I don't know."

The witness followed through, "It didn't help balance the budget any."

Senator Taft started off on another tack. "We need wage controls. There is nothing to keep an employer from paying wages as high as the sky. The government deliberately stimulated wage increases."

Bowles drove in quickly. "Profits, too, are up. They are two or three times what they were before the war."

All through the morning the voices crossed in disagreement. Bowles would read one, two paragraphs, then he would be struck by sharp questions. There was no letup.

Taft criticized the food subsidies. He said irritably, "Why don't you use wage increases to pay for higher food prices? Then you won't need subsidies."

Bowles explained, like a father talking to a small child, "You don't buy groceries on wage rates. You buy on earnings, and earnings have gone down since V–J Day."

Late that afternoon, the price control bill came to the floor of the House of Representatives. Congressman Adolph Sabath, the Chicago Democrat, opened the debate. "I hope this tremendous lobby that has been swamping us with hundreds of telegrams, air-mail special-delivery letters, and expensive booklets will not sway anyone. I hope you will stand by the people and not the interest of only a few."

The answer was a mocking clamor of voices: "OPA is holding back production . . . OPA is creating a black market . . . OPA is taking all the profits out of business."

But that was only a warm-up for Wednesday. For ten hours the House was burning with fever. Crowds of sight-seers roamed through the Capitol in the afternoon. They swarmed into the House gallery in relays, listened awhile to the belligerent voices, and then – puzzled – filed out.

Just outside the door behind the Speaker's stand, in the brightly lit hallway, a little group of men were arguing with Congressmen. These were the lobbyists. They sent page boys scurrying through the swinging doors. Representatives were drawn back into the dark corners and lectured on the OPA.

Some Congressmen shuffled their feet and turned their eyes away. Others marched back into the chamber with flushed cheeks and burning eyes.

Within the chamber, the members could not sit still. They paced up and down the aisles. They moved to the back of the House and smoked nervously.

The battle over price controls was being managed from two tables, one on each side of the aisle.

The Administration leaders sat on the right side. They were Brent Spence, the kindly and sincere old man who is chairman of the House Banking Committee; tall Mike Monroney of Oklahoma, and Wright Patman, the curly-haired Texan. A few days before they had been confident of success. The bill was voted out of the committee 22 to 1. Then the butcher, the baker, the manufacturer, the farmer had all written in from home – kill the OPA. The campaign was well organized, and it caught the gathering mood of discontent on the Hill. Scores of Congressmen from farm districts were deserting the Administration.

Across the aisle, at the opposition table, was Jesse Wolcott, a stout Republican from Michigan with thinning black hair. He knew, by the reports from his lieutenants and from the lobbyists, what his strength was and how far he could go. His strategy was well planned – cripple price controls with amendments and let the Administration take the blame for failure.

Spence pleaded with the House, "I know you have been subjected to pressure groups. The organized groups are always felt in the House and Senate. But there is another group, the unorganized majority, and believe me, from the letters I have received as chairman of the committee, 95 per cent of them do not want OPA destroyed.

"You are handling a force that is as dangerous as the misdirected force of atomic energy. You have lost sight of the effect that killing price controls would have on the economy of your nation. Do not be too sure, when you subject yourself to the influence of these pressure groups, that you are helping the American people."

Out in the hall, the lobbyists were busier than ever. They were trying to cinch the vote of every doubtful Representative.

Spence was still talking earnestly: "No people in the world are so willing to spend as the people of the United States. They have money now and there is no supply of the things they want. Turn them loose without restraint, let them go into the competitive market and compete for the few things available, and see what will happen. It will not only destroy them but it will destroy the dollar in your pockets and the savings of your lifetime. The disaster and tragedy of inflation will be as great as the disaster and tragedy of the war."

Congressman Rankin made his inevitable yowling speech and a motion to send the bill back to the committee. He cursed the OPA, the CIO, the PAC, and what he called "totalitarian regimentation."

Representative Brown of Georgia snapped up the challenge. He said, "That's fine. Let's settle the issue now – do we want inflation? I want a teller vote. Are you brave men going to undertake to say we will not stop inflation? The idea seems to be, 'To hell with inflation.' Let's meet this issue."

A thin trickle of Congressmen lined up to walk past the tellers for the Rankin motion. There, for one, was the ample figure of Jessie Sumner, the Congresswoman from Illinois.

Jesse Wolcott sat calmly at his table. The strategy was not to kill OPA outright. There might be a cry of "Murder" from the public.

The Noes filled the aisles and jostled past the tellers. The clerk read in his expressionless voice, "Thirty-four Ayes and 178 Nays. The amendment was rejected."

Wolcott had been waiting for this moment. He tossed in two amendments, one to end OPA after March first and another to compel OPA to grant cost of production plus profit on manufactured items.

Mike Monroney looked gravely across the table at Chairman Spence. Patman tried to stop the amendments, saying, "These amendments, if adopted, will successfully scuttle the bill. We are determining today whether or not the money of 52,000,000 people who are working today will buy a decent standard of living after the passage of this bill. If we have inflation in this country, Congress will be blamed. The rollcall votes of the House of Representatives will place the responsibility where it belongs."

The vote on the first Wolcott amendment came early in the afternoon. Members rose in their places to be counted. The clerk reported 126 for, 124 against. Spence asked for a teller count.

Almost all the Republicans moved into a thick, restless line in the well of the house. Les Arends, the GOP whip, and Abe Halleck, his energetic assistant, motioned Republicans out of the cloakrooms and beckoned to the few who sat stubbornly in their seats.

On the other side of the aisle, a number of Democrats were joining the parade. Monroney turned to look into their faces inquiringly. They pushed past him into the snake dance without an answer. The vote came out this time 171 for, 144 against.

For ten hours, into the cool night, the House was drenched with oratory. Angry men stalked to the microphone and shouted their maledictions on the OPA: "OPA is a sham and a fraud . . . OPA is holding down production . . . OPA . . . OPA." Through the shouts and the noisy undertone of conversation rose and fell the chant, "Vote, vote, vote," and the hammering of the gavel.

This was like some weird voodoo ceremony. Each speech stirred fresh fury. The Congressmen grew more restless, rising from their seats, walking a few paces, sitting down, getting up again. Only Jesse Wolcott sat calmly in the noisy chamber.

There were moments of diversion. Congressman Klein, a New York Democrat and the newest member of the House, got fed up with Rankin. He said, "I assume you have all heard the story about the boy who always cries 'Wolf.' Every time anybody gets up to make a speech which would help the common people and the underprivileged, the gentleman from Mississippi gets up and yells 'Communism.' "

Rankin was instantly on his feet shouting, "That's not true."

Klein paid no attention to him and calmly yielded the floor to a Pennsylvania Congressman.

Every time the House cooled down a little, Wolcott tossed in another amendment. The bill was being chopped to pieces. A worried Senator Barkley slipped over from the Senate debate on the British loan, which he was leading, to watch the stampede.

The farm bloc led the way, scuffling past the tellers on all the amendments. Congressman Barry of New York called to them scornfully, "I want to remind the members from agricultural districts that the shoe was on the other foot not so very long ago. As late as 1938 and 1939 the farmers received only 77 per cent of parity and members like myself who represent consuming city districts voted for millions and millions of dollars of parity payments. It strikes me as ridiculous for farm members to say they are now against all subsidies."

The House, still in its whooping uproar, voted 153 to 89 to abolish subsidies – the money paid to farmers to hold down the retail price. (The subsidy on milk, for example, amounted to two cents a quart.)

Amendments were thrown in from all sides. Congressman Spence shook his bald head and said gloomily, "Inflation is guaranteed. Price control is a corpse."

Representative Baldwin, the New York aristocrat, said politely, "I think there is a great deal of confusion here today. If we want inflation, go along the road we have followed today."

Monroney shouted mournfully, "This is a dark day for the American consumer."

In the middle of the babel, Congressman Kopplemann, Democrat, of Connecticut, introduced his ironic amendment – six words: "We sympathize with the American people." The House was so ready to vote on anything, a clamor of voices shouted, "Aye."

Late in the evening, the Congressmen stormed out of the warm, stale chamber into the dark night. The cool wind hit them with a sobering shock.

Some shivered on the steps. Others stared into the blackness and walked off into the night.

They were once again men – tired, troubled men – walking their separate ways.

Chapter XVIII

THEN came the deluge. Capitol Hill was snowed under with mail.

The already cluttered office of the Senate Banking and Currency Committee, which was considering the price controls, was jammed with letters, postcards, and telegrams. Paper boxes stacked full of unanswered messages sagged on top of a row of filing cabinets. In another room, clerks stared hopelessly at mailbags dumped on the floor.

A huge postcard leaned against the wall. In large English script the words said, "In order to keep living costs from rising, we petition you to remove all the crippling and damaging amendments from the bill extending OPA another year." The rest of the card was covered with hundreds of signatures. The return address was, "Employees, Outgoing Mail, General Post Office, New York 1, N.Y."

Both sides sent witnesses to plead with the committee. The housewives were represented by Miss Caroline Ware, a brisk, competent young woman in a gray jumper dress and black hat. She spoke for churchwomen, parents, teachers, women voters – all members of twenty-three national organizations.

She spoke clearly and distinctly to the old men around the committee table. She said, "We urge the Senate to pass a genuine price control act. We would like to bring our members here, to have you hear their hardship cases, but there is too great a need for speed. A peril faces the nation. The House bill fails completely and invites inflation. We urge you to reject each and every amendment."

The chairs on one side of the long room were filled with determined-looking women. They followed Miss Ware with intent eyes.

She said firmly, "It would be better to repeal price control outright than to approve the action of the House."

Senator Taft interrupted, "I don't see that."

Miss Ware explained patiently, "When the House took the major items on the cost of living out from under price control, there was virtually no protection left."

Senator Taft said coldly, "I object to this whole line of propaganda." Miss Ware flushed and the women in the audience stared angrily at the Senator.

With a side glance down the table at Taft, Senator Millikin began to work on the witness. He said, "Do you believe in control for control's sake?"

She said excitedly, "The primary job is to keep away from inflation, from boom and bust. We don't want to dive off the precipice."

Senator Millikin waved his hand carelessly and boomed, "Useless abstractions." He sneaked a grin at Taft.

Miss Ware said strongly, "They are not useless. I know when I go to the grocery."

"What is your remedy then?" the Senator inquired loftily.

She forced back her irritation and said, "Adequate enforcement."

Senator Millikin bent his head and lectured Miss Ware severely about what he called "Gestapo snoopers."

The witness smiled sweetly. She said, "I think one reason for the increase in the black market is the recent action of the House. Possibly you ought to put Congress in jail."

The Senator barked at her, "We have no such statistics about any increase in the black market."

She snapped back, "We have a good deal of common sense."

By this time every woman in the room was staring daggers at Senator Millikin. He did not indicate that he noticed this attention. A few minutes later he interrupted Miss Ware to grumble about "ill-considered and stupid controls on meat."

Miss Ware answered, "My butcher doesn't say that. He is an intelligent man. I wish you could talk to people who talk to the corner grocer."

Senator Capehart took on Miss Ware next. He began the old one-two-three technique to throw a witness off balance. He asked, "Who do you represent? Just how do you represent these people? How do you know they are for price control?"

Miss Ware replied stiffly, "Each organization has adopted a position in support of OPA." She looked around the table a little helplessly at each Senator and said, "You don't understand. This is of tremendous concern."

A foolish smile played around Senator Capehart's lips.

The CIO tried a new and unique method. A spokesman for the unions told the committee he would like to introduce, not experts, but workers from the factories.

A short, dark-haired young man sat down at the long committee table and stared belligerently at the Senators. He was Jack Saccocio, a welder from Schenectady. His wife, a pretty girl with big black eyes, sat shyly back on the sidelines watching her two children. Senator Wagner kindly invited her to sit by her husband. The CIO official explained apologetically, "If she sits by him, it will make him nervous."

Saccocio had no notes, just a rumpled sheet of paper with some figures scrawled on it. He began talking, uneasily at first, "We got some wage increases all right. But my take-home pay has gone down $15 a week."

He read the figures. They were his weekly budget – $10 a week, rent; $25, food; $8, clothing; $2.50, medical expenses; $3.29, insurance; $2, dentist; $6.30, income tax; 66 cents, social security; telephone, $1; and $1.50, utilities. This did not include a tonsil operation for one child. This totaled $60.25. His wage averaged $66 a week.

The little welder explained, "I'm a high wage earner. But we've got fellows whose wives have to go out and work to make both ends meet." He added bitterly, "God help us if OPA goes out of existence."

Jack Saccocio asked that all the black marketeers be put in jail.

Senator Buck asked him, "Where would we get the jails to put them in?"

Saccocio flung out, "Build more jails. Put them in concentration camps. Get the FBI after them." He paused a second to pull his thoughts together. "I'm pleading here. Don't hurt the OPA. Make it stronger. You are supposed to be representing the people – me and my wife. If this came up in the voting machines tomorrow, the people would vote for the OPA."

Saccocio told a story. Like many families of Italian extraction his used a good deal of cottonseed oil. He went to the neighborhood store but there was no oil on the shelves. The clerk tipped him off there was some in the back room.

The little welder told the solemn committee room full of people, "I went back and the oil was stacked in cases. I asked the manager why I couldn't get some. He set a gallon on the table and asked for six dollars. I put two dollars and a half on the counter, and he said, 'Where are you going?' I told him the OPA ceiling was two bucks and a half and either he could call a cop or I would."

Senator Tobey leaned forward. He said softly, "It's a very healthy thing for the committee to have you here. Nothing is finer than for the common people to bring these matters to Congress."

Saccocio blurted out angrily, "Lots of candidates make big speeches about democracy and then come down here and don't pay any attention to us."

Senator Tobey's voice rose to a roar. "The great danger to this country is that the common people are losing faith in government."

The little welder's fingers trembled and his dark eyes glared. He pointed a forefinger at the Senators and said in a high excited tone, "Most of you don't represent the people. We elect you . . . not the big boys. You fellows talk grand about democracy when you make campaign speeches, but what happens when you get elected? Our city councilmen up home made all kinds of promises. And then they get elected and they won't give any money for child care centers."

He stopped abruptly and said apologetically, "I guess that's all I've got to say."

Senator Wagner, the committee chairman, said gently, "Thank you very much. It was good to hear from you."

The other Senators sat motionless. Their eyes followed Jack Saccocio as he walked stiffly over to the corner.

There was a steady procession of sober, middle-aged businessmen telling their tales of individual hardship. They lined up their products in the committee room, from lawn mowers to electric heaters. Some flung long underwear on the committee table as exhibits. Another had dresses. Press agents busily passed out mimeographed denunciations of the OPA.

The heaviest blow was struck by Robert Wason, the husky, cold-eyed president of the National Association of Manufacturers. His appearance was preceded by a publicity build-up. The NAM sent out hundreds of copies of a leaflet, *The National Association of Manufacturers, for a Better Tomorrow for Everybody*.

Wason said deliberately: "NAM is convinced that all price controls on manufactured goods should be removed by June 30. . . . OPA drives goods off the shelves into the black market. OPA discourages the efficient production of established manufacturers. OPA has snarled production lines and crippled orderly distribution to the consumer. OPA discourages investment by attacking profit, which is the motive power of the economy. OPA by creating black markets is causing America to be a nation of law violators. . . . It is time to stop being bluffed by the phony figures and the misleading claims of the OPA. Savings will not be preserved if OPA's irresponsible scare campaign is continued. . . . Inexperienced men are telling American producers what they can produce, how much they can charge, what their profits should be, and how they should run their affairs. . . . There is no reason to fear a skyrocketing of prices if controls are taken off manufactured goods on June 30. . . . WE urge you to give the manufacturers of America a chance to turn out the goods with which to smother inflation."

Wason was given the respectful attention of the committee.

The farm lobbyists, big, confident men with bluff voices, came before the committee with their story.

Mark Pickell, the executive secretary of the Cornbelt Livestock Feeders' Association, pounded the table with a stubby finger, and shouted, "The situation is getting worse and worse."

The room was filled with cheerful farm leaders chewing on cigars.

Pickell said, "We feel the remedy is very simple. Encourage farmers to feed regardless of price and take price controls off meat. What the price would be is beside the point. Remove restrictions on grain and feed and take all the price controls off." His big fist lay doubled on the table.

Senator Barkley held up a yellow pamphlet and asked the witness, "Did you write this?"

He nodded his head. The Senator said soberly, "I'd like to read from it. 'Caesar became the ruler of the destinies as an absolute despot over his people. So did Mussolini. So did Hitler. They all died violent deaths. A few men, who have proved their inability to lead, but have brought chaos, confusion and shortages in food, have seized control of the destinies of America by seizing control of prices. They want to perpetuate their power. Their hold must be broken. OPA must go.'"

Barkley looked up and said quietly, "I would like you to name someone who wants to perpetuate himself in power for power's sake."

Pickell's face flushed. He said lamely, "The people in OPA want to stay in power as long as supply doesn't equal demand and it never will as long as they stay in power."

The Senator said sharply, "You didn't say that. I'd like to have these people who want power for power's sake identified. Name one person. Mr. Bowles?"

The witness replied, "Well, uh, Bowles seems to want to stay in."

This was one of those rare occasions when Alben Barkley was angry. He said heatedly, "Do you expect this committee to believe OPA is trying to stay in authority because of an individual's grasp for power?"

Pickell was not happy. He said sullenly, "I'm against the whole thing. It's wrong."

Barkley replied, "That's a matter of opinion. But to impugn the motives and honesty of men is not right. God knows, we all would rejoice if we could get rid of OPA tomorrow. I would thank God on bended knee if I never got another letter giving me hell about something."

Senator Butler, the white-haired Nebraska Republican, said sympathetically to the witness, "You based your conclusions on the OPA propaganda."

Barkley was not through. He said, "Of course, it's propaganda when you are against the OPA. And if you are against it, you feel free to attack the sincerity of men."

Pickell decided it was time to go. He stood up and said flatly, "We've got to get rid of this OPA."

The spokesman for the National Association of Real Estate Boards was a well-dressed, glib young man with beautiful charts. He asked for a "modest" rise in rentals of 10 per cent, explaining smoothly, "The property owners are more than entitled to more than 10 per cent."

The Administration sent its men up to plead for price controls. Tall Secretary of Agriculture Clinton Anderson had a firm prepared statement, "As long as the present inflationary pressures exist, strong price control measures are the first essential toward preventing disastrous farm depression."

The Senators began questioning Anderson about meat shortages. He said gloomily he hoped new quotas would channel cattle to legitimate slaughterers. But, he said, the packers were not very optimistic.

Senator Bankhead of Alabama became interested. He asked, "Suppose this new quota system won't work?"

Anderson blurted out, "We would have to try something else. One way would be to take price controls off meat." He caught himself and added hastily, "Of course, we wouldn't want to do that."

But the words were out. Senator Bankhead grimly kept after him. "How long should the controls be tried before they are given up?"

The Secretary squirmed. He guessed about ninety days.

Another Senator asked what would happen to the price of meat if controls went off.

"Well," Anderson calculated, "pork would go up to about seventy cents a pound."

"But," the Secretary added easily, "the people aren't worrying about food prices. Why, some people don't mind paying a dollar a pound for butter."

A Department of Agriculture aide sitting just behind the Secretary bit his lip.

Across the table, Senator Taft beamed. He said the Secretary's testimony was "very significant."

The Senate committee closed its doors and squatted on the price control egg for four weeks. A deathwatch of eight reporters patrolled the hall outside the committee rooms.

At the end of the fourth week, there was a crowd in the space at the end of a long, cool corridor of the Senate Office Building. Word had spread around that the committee was ready to report the bill. The story of what was happening behind those closed doors had leaked out. Amendment after amendment had been thrown in – taking away from OPA controls over food; lifting price ceilings on meat, dairy, and poultry; pulling out the maximum average price rule. There were amendments to benefit restaurants, manufacturers of cars and refrigerators, cotton growers and processors, and even work-glove makers.

All of the votes on amendments were close, with one or two votes tilting the scales. On one vote, a Northern Democrat voted with the Republican-Southern Democrat coalition. The amendment carried. Then the Senator changed his mind. The amendment failed. Finally, he decided not to vote at all. The vote stood eight to eight.

On this morning anxious lobbyists joined the deathwatch. They followed the little old lady committee clerk, asking her, "How long will the Senators be?"

The combination publicity man and legislative scout for the National Association of Manufacturers was talking easily with old friends among the reporters. The OPA liaison agent on the

Hill sucked on his pipe philosophically. Lobbyists for other groups – a slim man with a mustache, a big bluff old fellow who looked more like a Senator than did a real one, a well-dressed Tweedledee and Tweedledum – stood in the corridor.

Down the hall came a familiar figure trotting briskly. It was Senator Taft swinging a bulging briefcase. A reporter asked, "How soon will you be through?"

The Senator said confidently, "Very soon, now." The doors closed behind him.

One of the correspondents, a little man with a bald head and a wistful grin, offered some entertainment to the deathwatch. In a mournful, hillbilly twang, he sang a parody on Nellie Gray, "Darling OPA, they have taken you away and you won't be the same any more." Even the OPA man grinned.

Senator Mead of New York, on his way to the elevator, shouted cheerfully to the waiting throng, "Waiting for the verdict?"

Someone said, "We've already got a tip from the jury room. It's first-degree murder."

The NAM and OPA men were trading notes. The NAM agent said he thought the Republican steering committee would support all the amendments of GOP Senators. The OPA representative said he believed the President would veto the bill, if it passed the way it stood.

NAM generously offered some advice, saying, "You made the Senators mad with your propaganda."

The committee doors pushed open. The first man out was Senator Millikin. There was a grin on his large round face. A number of voices called, "Is the bill through the committee?" He nodded his head.

"Was it unanimous?"

The Senator replied merrily, "There was unanimous lack of enthusiasm."

Correspondents and lobbyists alike pushed into the room and circled around Alben Barkley. He stood patiently, chewing gum and answering questions.

He said, "I am making the report for the committee, but I

will make it plain to the Senate I neither endorse nor sponsor the bill."

The Senator was asked, "Is there anyone for the bill as it now stands?"

Barkley snorted, "I don't know of any."

Chapter XIX

SUMMER – hot and humid – came to Washington in mid-June. The flags on the Capitol hung limply in the warm sun.

Inside the Senate chamber, page boys placed a fat document on each desk. It was the price control bill bulging with amendments . . . amendments to remove price controls from meat, milk, butter, cheese and dairy products; amendments to push prices up on manufactured goods and products sold at retail and on clothing; an amendment slowing down OPA's enforcement program.

Alben Barkley began explaining the bill patiently and conscientiously but without enthusiasm. He spoke with all the weariness of a man crowded between intolerable pressures when he said, "All of us not only look forward to but yearn for the day when the government will no longer have to interpose its power or regulation to protect people against greed, rapacity, or unwise misadjustments of our economic system."

A few Senators were not just sure this bill was the remedy. Senator Vandenberg expressed the dilemma: "If we were to decontrol everything overnight, we would have chaos beyond description. But, on the other hand, if we don't get into full production under free competition, we are going to have economic chaos under OPA."

Senator Bob Wagner spoke sadly. "I cannot understand the wave of defeatism in the war against inflation. . . . These amendments would raise the prices of food, clothing, and household electrical appliances. More than half the cost of living would be affected."

Tall Senator Hawkes, a former president of the U. S. Chamber of Commerce, was more philosophic. He said, "We cannot reach the goal we seek without placing on the people some hardships which they must endure during the transition period."

The bill left the Senate on the beginning of its tortuous road. It stopped in a conference committee of Senators and Representatives to adjust differences between the two Houses.

While the conferees were still arguing, Chester Bowles was mapping his counterattack. It was as smooth a campaign of advertising and promotion as he ever planned for a corporation.

The object was to stir up a strong wave of pressure on Congress, but more specifically on the mild little man in the White House and his two economic-adviser cronies, John Snyder and John Steelman.

Bowles called in the leaders of organized labor for talks and pried out of those worried and anxious men an agreement to hold down strikes and encourage a high level of production, IF the cost of living line was not smashed.

He pounded a path around the government agencies, getting each one that had a stake in prices to make a statement. The State Department complained decorously that the international food program would be wrecked if grain prices shot up. The Department of Agriculture poured out statistics. Henry Wallace predicted a "rocky future" for American business if "we let down our guard against inflation." Secretary of Labor Lew Schwellenbach commented, "Labor is entitled to assurances that the value of its earnings will not be reduced by continuous rises in the cost of food, rents, and clothing." The chairman of the Wage Stabilization Board added that it would be necessary to change the government's four-month-old wage policy before the end of July, if price controls were lifted.

With all these labors completed, Bowles called a news conference. Reporters trudged through a dripping rain to his offices in that marble palace on Constitution Avenue, the Federal Reserve Building. Stacked up on a table were mimeographed copies of a six-page statement on the pending bill.

The heavily inked words referred to "booby trap amendments," and said, "It is unfair to expect OPA to hold back the flood of inflation with a sponge. . . . If such amendments as those appear in the bill which goes to the President, I feel strongly that a veto would be the only answer."

The mention of a possible veto was a gun pointed at the conference committee. The last thing Congress wanted was a veto, to have to go through the misery of writing a new bill or going home to the voters with no bill.

At the press conference, Bowles leaned over the back of a chair. His double-breasted coat was casually fastened by one button. He winked cheerfully at friends in the back row. He said easily, "Any questions about this handout?"

"Do you think the conference committee can come out with a good bill?"

He answered, "They have a hard task, because they've been shackled to some extent by the action of the House and Senate."

"What will happen to wage stabilization if the bill goes through as is?"

Bowles said mildly, "There won't be any. Labor demands will grow in intensity. There will be bickering and uncertain production."

He smoked continually, one cigarette lighted from another. He tossed back answers with no apparent effort in an easy slang. He talked about what he thought would happen if controls were lifted.

"There would be increases, a relatively short crack-up – not as long as in 1929, but the repercussions would be dangerous. There would be a big rift in the country – everyone searching for goats. It would set us back emotionally and politically." He ended with a shy smile and the tolerant comment, "If there isn't any good price control, I hope we'll keep our shirts on."

That afternoon, at his news conference, President Truman was asked if he would veto the bill. The President replied primly, "I never discuss pending legislation."

The bill rolled out of the conference committee much the same as it passed the Senate.

Alben Barkley – with an eye on White House reaction – told his colleagues, "We have produced the best bill possible in the atmosphere in which we were compelled to legislate."

Young Bill Fulbright said unhappily, "I am inclined to vote for the conference report, simply because it is a symbol. I am told there may be some beneficial effects in rents and a few other isolated instances. However, the greatest danger is that in adopting the report we shall lead the people to believe we have done something effective. . . . I am under no illusion that the report will maintain a reasonable level of prices."

More in sorrow (crocodile tears) than anger, the House and Senate passed the bill and sent it on to the White House. Senator Barkley and Congressman Spence told Mr. Truman, "This is the best we can do. Please sign it."

On a sticky, warm Saturday morning, about ten o'clock, President Truman's message on price controls came to the Hill for later reading. When Kenneth McKellar, the elderly presiding officer of the Senate, heard of the veto he swore a streak of emphatic and colorful profanity. Alben Barkley was stunned. All the lines in his face curved downward.

In the House, Representative Spence sat bolt upright folding and unfolding his fingers as a clerk droned off the message, "The Taft amendment promises peak profits. . . . It is a sorry jest which would wholly destroy wage stabilization. . . . This is a choice between inflation with a statute and inflation without. . . . The bill legalizes inflation . . . bonanza formula . . . enrich industry at the cost of the public."

At the conclusion of the reading, Spence plodded wearily to the front and in a low, almost inaudible voice said, "A great danger confronts the people. The conferees brought forth a bill. We did the best we could. I urged the President to sign the bill because I hoped it might work. But he has the responsibility of enforcing it. I will vote to sustain the veto."

The veto was sustained. But as the dark clouds rolled up in the sky and thunder muttered outside, the die-hards blocked a resolution to extend OPA three weeks. Wolcott in the House and "Pappy" O'Daniel in the Senate prevented the unanimous consent needed to consider the resolution.

The Senators and Representatives walked out into a torrential rainstorm that broke suddenly. These men who had hoped to find shelter from the hard pressures of price control were out in the storm again.

Week after week, a conference committee of Representatives and Senators met in Barkley's office just off a narrow dark corridor of the Capitol to write a new price control bill. They gathered in the morning, afternoon, and often at night. Reporters in the hall could look through an outside window and see men moving in the room.

The committee was stalled in stubborn deadlock. A majority of House conferees blocked the decontrol of food. They dreamed of angry consumers waving food bills at them when they asked for their votes. Most of the Senators were just as insistent that controls on meat and dairy products be thrown off.

Each noon, the reporters waited in the hall for Barkley. Any progress? None.

One day when the conferees were all talked out and sat looking glumly at each other, plodding Senator Radcliffe of Maryland had a brilliant idea. Why should Congress try to decide the dilemma of food controls? The idea was taken up enthusiastically. Sure, they could create a board to make the terrible decisions. Thus, the three-man Decontrol Board was born out of the weariness and disagreement in Congress. It could determine whether controls were needed on food and other products.

The House was worn-out and spent little time on the new bill. The Representatives were anxious to get it over. When the clerk read the vote, 210 for and 142 against the bill, there were no cheers or boos. Just a loud sigh of relief.

In the Senate, eleven members were at their desks when Barkley began a patient and detailed explanation of the compromise.

Senator Taft followed him, saying in that dry voice, "I intend to vote for the conference report, although I am not very well pleased with it." As other Senators asked questions, Taft defended the compromise. He gave assurances that production would not be bottlenecked, that manufacturers would get a fair profit.

The debate was subdued and orderly until midafternoon. Kenneth Wherry, the Republican whip, stormed to the floor. He faced Senator Taft, scowled at him, and said with heavy sarcasm, "I remember the words of the distinguished Senator from Ohio when he spoke recently on the radio. He stated this measure would give the Price Administrator more power than ever. Yet in all this confusion . . ."

Taft jumped to his feet. Wherry would not yield the floor. He roared on, "Senators speak against this report but they say they will vote for it." He looked hard at Taft and said deliberately, "We shall destroy maximum production."

Wherry was angry enough to provoke an open break in the Republican high command. Wherry – aggressive, emotional, a bitter enemy of almost any form of government control, a Midwestern isolationist – represented the predominant Old Guard wing.

Taft – the shrewd, one-man conservative brain trust, a candidate for President in 1948 – was willing to trim his sails for political expediency. He did not want to be charged with responsibility for high food costs.

Wherry pointed his finger at Taft. "Let me quote what the Senator from Ohio said during the debate, what he would do if he were made a conferee." He read the words, then rasped with sarcasm, "This is exactly the position I thought the distinguished Senator from Ohio would take. But the conference report comes back with meat not decontrolled, milk not decontrolled. Such leadership is weak-kneed, spineless, and does not meet the need of legislative authority."

Taft's face grew darker and his lips pressed tighter. At one particular pointed crack, he barked, "The Senator says so, but it is not true."

Wherry shouted at him, "I have just as much right to my opinion as the Senator has. I have the floor. I don't care whether the Senator from Ohio interprets it that way or not."

This went on for several hours. Senator Taft sat rigid in his chair. The attacks became so embarrassing, Senator Tobey of New Hampshire lectured Wherry as if he were an errant child.

The argument over price control ended as it began – in an atmosphere of confusion and anger.

A few days after the bill had been passed and Congress had

gone home, the Price Decontrol Board began its hearings. They were a refreshing experience to a Washington cynically accustomed to that mysterious power, "influence."

The three-man board showed the same friendly, objective attention to the big names of organized agriculture as to the fiery girl from Brooklyn who said, "You can't have democracy on an empty stomach." The board showed no special deference to the spokesman for the livestock growers just because he was introduced by a United States Senator, Tom Connally of Texas.

It was a curious setting for the final act of price control. The hearings were held in the Senate caucus room, which looks more like a Roman palace chamber than a battleground for so down-to-earth an issue as price control. Big marble columns line two walls. Dazzling cut-glass chandeliers hang halfway down from the decorated ceiling.

At the far end of the room, behind a long table, were the three board members. In the middle was the chairman, Roy Thompson, a big, rawboned man with a friendly, sincere face and a strong, stubborn chin. His white hair was cut short.

To his left sat Daniel Bell, the banker. He was a soberly dressed man with jet-black hair, skeptical eyebrows, and a dry voice. Bell has an orderly, logical mind and he kept after the witnesses with questions.

To the right of the chairman was George Mead, a Midwestern manufacturer, a small man with a wrinkled forehead and tired eyes.

The first witness was one of the most influential men in America, Ed O'Neal, president of the American Farm Bureau Federation. He and his organization have dictated farm policies and had a hand in the election of Congressmen for more years than Ed would like to admit.

He is a tall, suave old man with a delightful Southern drawl and a merry twinkle in his blue eyes. He began with disarming mildness, but his words grew tougher and tougher. In answering a question of Bell's about the effectiveness of rationing, he snorted, "No more practical than price controls. If you put price and rationing controls together, you'll be in a hell of a fix."

Another fabulous figure on the Hill brought his boys to the

hearing. He was "Judge" Joe Montague, a big, bald man smoking an enormous pipe. Tom Connally tagged along by his side. The Judge represented the livestock growers.

His spokesman was Colonel Jay L. Taylor, who said belligerently, "If you want production, you might as well face the facts. You won't get it if you put controls back on. Do you want production?"

The board was limited in what it could do. It could restore controls on meat, dairy products, grain, fats, and oils, only if it found that prices had risen unreasonably, the products were in short supply, controls were practical.

The decision of the board after four days of hearing and three days and nights of study was a distinct surprise, for it disregarded the heaviest pressures. Meat was put back under controls, despite the threat of the meat men that the country would not get meat. Dairy products were left alone, although the OPA and the Department of Agriculture in one of their rare moments of amity advocated price controls.

In a smudgy, barnlike building down by the railroad tracks the OPA began the discouraging task of pulling prices back down after the country had a wild vacation from controls.

The sprawling old building was once a warehouse, and it has none of the air-cooled elegance of the Social Security Building down the street. The big windows those summer days were thrown open to get any breath of air. In the windows came the grinding of freight trains and the cries of Negro children playing in the streets below.

The people who work there did not look like the cartoonist's dream of bureaucrats, well-fed people sitting back lazily before handsome desks. These were harassed men in shirt sleeves laboring in partitioned-off spaces.

In the early days of recontrol, the OPA called in the top leaders of business and industry to explain price controls, as Congress finally wrote them.

The businessmen were easy to pick out. They stepped briskly out of taxis, confident, well-dressed men with briefcases, and airplane tickets in their wallets.

The OPA-business meetings started out formally, but before long the businessmen, too, were in their shirt sleeves. The conference rooms became filled with a blue haze of tobacco smoke.

After an hour or so, the businessmen began to scratch their heads. What was this new law anyway?

An OPA "explainer," a cheerful young man with a pointed chin, said that under the new law goods would be priced not as a whole line of a manufacturer, but as separate objects.

At one conference, a puzzled businessman asked, "Does that mean I'll have to ask for price increases on each one of my products individually?"

"Sorry," the moderator replied, "that's the law. We didn't write it. We just administer it."

Another visitor held up his hand. "The law sets up the test of reasonable profit. What does that mean?"

The OPA official shook his head and answered, "We haven't figured that one out yet."

At the end of the long afternoon, the businessmen walked out of the old building. They had lost their springy step. They plodded along with the same worried look as the OPA workers.

Congress had succeeded in writing a law that pleased no one.

Chapter XX

THE issue of wages pressed the cheerful man in the White House. Soon after V–J Day, organized labor became restless. Requests for wage increases filled the dockets in the Department of Labor Building.

All across the country, thousands of workers were being laid off in war industries. They were slowly filtering back into their old jobs at less pay. The wartime bonus of overtime was becoming a pleasant memory. Prices were creeping up. Industry was protected against cutbacks in the contracts by guaranteed profits, but the workers had only the weapon of the strike.

The principals in this new struggle were:

That old rumbling warrior of labor, John L. Lewis. He had been carefully feeding an old grudge and was warily watching for the time and the place to break the Administration's economic policy wide open. His strategy was to let the more impulsive union leaders smash their heads while he snorted out threats. John Lewis was also building his fences in the American Federation of Labor to gradually take away the leadership from Bill Green. Lewis was looking way ahead to the 1948 elections.

Phil Murray, the cautious Scotsman who heads the CIO, had his hands full beating down the hotheads who wanted to strike and be damned with the consequences. They swore they weren't going to get shoved around. Murray had one eye on Congress, and he said privately that any wave of strikes would set back labor fifteen years. He had little faith in the Administration. The extreme left wing of the CIO was out to stir up trouble, and Phil Murray had to bat heads together and stretch his patience to the limit.

Lew Schwellenbach, the mournful Secretary of Labor, was unhappy. He hadn't wanted the job, and now he was plunked right down in the center of one of the worst storms to hit Washington. His long underlip drooped down. His deep-set eyes beneath thick, uncombed eyebrows were sad.

Strikes were coming up in automobile manufacturing, oil, coal, steel, and shipping. Congress was tired and angry. The desks on the Hill were full of bills clamping curbs on labor. Schwellenbach is a liberal but with a judicial, rather than an administrative, mind. All these problems left him with a helpless feeling. This was in the fall of 1945.

Harry Truman was gaily enjoying his first autumn as President. His days were filled with trips, little speeches to delegations in the White House, poker parties, and George Allen's jokes. He told Lew that labor was his problem. The White House was not going to get mixed up in it.

But Schwellenbach had no authority to settle the basic quarrel of labor – the cut in take-home pay. The Wage Stabilization Board was sitting on that lid. Wages were tied in with prices. All the Secretary could do was to plead earnestly with the angry labor men who hammered his desk, "Please, boys, let's talk this thing out before you do anything rash."

The weeks of autumn went by slowly the first year of the Truman Administration. The bright days disappeared.

It was during these dreary days that a streetcar and bus strike brought the labor issue home to Washington. This tangible evidence of the power of a strike inflamed Congressmen who had to compete for the busy taxicabs.

One rainy afternoon in mid-November, a news vendor stood before a barnlike hall in Northwest Washington. He shouted, "Truman takes over streetcars." The White House had jumped in with both feet.

In the hall was a scene familiar to many cities in America. A mist of blue-gray smoke floated around the bright center light. The big hall smelled of stale tobacco and sweat and that strange, strong odor of excitement. In the center below the light was a boxing ring. Men milled around in it aimlessly. A man with close-cropped curly hair stood in one corner with his fist clenched. The rest of the hall was dark and shadowy.

That afternoon President Truman had ordered the Office of Defense Transportation to take over and operate the transit system of Washington. These men in the hall were the strikers, now faced with the issue of striking against the government.

Harry Truman was mad. He called the strike a blot on the record of labor. He froze the union funds.

The dim figures of hundreds of men stood on the concrete floor or sat on the wooden bleachers. Men of all ages and types shared a fixed, tense look. A Negro stared with big, wide eyes. A fatherly gray-haired man took long, deep pulls on his cigarette. A younger fellow, still in his blue motorman's uniform, glared through half-closed eyes.

A union officer was speaking. The light struck his sweating face and emphasized the effort of his pleading.

"Boys," he shouted, "I'm with you. You've got to believe this. I'll go all the way with you. But when the President of the United States takes over, boys, I'm sorry. I can't go on with this."

There came a roar from the floor – "No. No."

The man with the clenched fist grabbed the microphone and yelled, "You know I'm with you. Let's walk out and not meet again until tomorrow."

Wild cheers filled the hall.

The union president, a solid-looking man in a blue suit, called back to the crowd, "I am ordering you back to work."

From the back of the hall a voice boomed, "Not until we get our thirty cents an hour increase."

The union president let the tumult die down and then said, "I want to do the right thing as much as you do. I want that thirty cents too. But these government people walked in, told us to go back to work, and then walked out."

A fellow on the stage yelled, "We'll stay here until they come back and lay their cards on the table."

Somewhere out of the confusion, a young man stepped to the center of the stage and waved for silence. The crowd, surprisingly, was quiet. The boy said, "I used to draw pictures, and I'm going to draw one for you. A lot of us have just come out of the Army. The right to strike was something we fought for. But the government says now, You are bad boys. The President of the United States has seized our assets. It's the biggest kick in the pants you ever had."

The speaker looked around the hall and went on, "Some of the men are slipping out. I don't blame them. They have kids to feed. The government knows that."

Then, in a rush of words, he said, "I'm as mad as you. I don't want to give up. But the government has taken over. What can we do?"

As he talked, a trickle, then a steady file of older men walked off the floor and out into the rainy night. There was no longer anger in their faces. Only the drained-out look of tired men. Three hours later, the streetcars of Washington were running again.

This had set a pattern for labor. The unions understood they could no longer expect any help from the White House. They had to fight their own battles as best they could. Industry understood this, too.

The same afternoon that the streetcar strike ended, there was a gentle air of melancholy in the Department of Labor. Workers were walking out all across the nation. The Labor Management Committee meeting in the long stone building on Constitution Avenue was split. The press relations man for the conference was apologetic.

He explained in his thin voice to the Labor Department press room, "The management group wants penalties for violation of contracts. The union boys want a clause on union security."

The uncertainty of tomorrow dragged on through the long months into January. Then, on a Wednesday afternoon, word whispered across Washington that a news conference by the Steel Fact Finding Board would start a new Administration drive to end the strikes.

Reporters jammed into the conference room. It had the sterile appearance of a hospital waiting room — clean white walls, green Venetian blinds. Outside there was a thin drizzle of rain.

The board's chairman, Nathan P. Feinsinger, a well-groomed young ex-brain-truster, was cheerful and confident. He read, "The board has been authorized to announce that collective bargaining negotiations will be resumed immediately in the steel industry."

A reporter asked gruffly, "Has a price increase in steel been offered by the government?"

Everyone in the room knew that was the key question. Feinsinger ducked it by saying, "This board has not taken a position on prices. That isn't our business."

But the story came out. Every day of this week, a group of men had slipped quietly through the east gate of the White House where they could not be spotted by curious newsmen. They were Lew Schwellenbach, Chester Bowles, and their assistants gathering for talks with John Snyder.

The Secretary of Labor wanted to stop strikes before Congress came roaring back from a vacation the next Monday. He had word that labor would snap up any reasonable offer. Chester Bowles was grimly and stubbornly determined to sit on prices. John Snyder, anxious and irritable, wanted industrial peace at almost any cost.

Snyder and Schwellenbach battered at Bowles. An increase in the price of steel would end the strike. Bowles stuck by his guns. He would agree to some rise, but the price suggested was too high. Prices would fly up all around him. Snyder listened nervously to all the talk. Then he broke in. He would decide the price of steel. Bowles could sit this one out.

When the meetings broke up optimistic whispers ran over Washington again. Snyder's assistants puffed their chests and talked to reporters. "We're going to settle these strikes. Steel is the key. Phil Murray wants to settle and he'll take less than two dollars a day increase. We'll give U. S. Steel a price increase, and they'll raise wages. Simple. Then we'll tackle General Motors, meat packing, and oil. You can look for a general 18 per cent wage increase."

John Snyder had found an easy formula for pushing away all this strike trouble . . . raise prices.

(A year later, John Snyder's successor as Reconversion Director, John Steelman, said in an official report: "Although many employees received increases of 18½ cents per hour set by the pattern in steel, the average wage rate increase for all industry is well below that figure. Between February 15 and June 30, 1946, the Wage Stabilization Board approved an average increase in basic wage rates of 14.7 cents an hour for more than 4 million employees. Thirty-seven per cent of these received less than a 15-cent increase.

("Despite the increase in wage rates and in straight-time hourly earnings, gross weekly earnings of all employees in manufacturing industries have decreased between April, 1945, and July, 1946, by approximately 8.5 per cent. This means that the average employee in manufacturing industry earning $47.12 in April, 1945, was taking home in July, 1946, $4.05 a week less, or approximately $43.07. . . . The money which the average working family has to spend per week has decreased further since V–E Day with a rise of 11 per cent in the prices of consumer's goods.")

Toward the end of the week, when the Snyder formula became the economic policy of the nation, two men walked out of the warm sunshine and into the White House lobby. They nodded pleasantly to a few reporters and strolled back to the President's office. They were members of the auto wage fact-finding board. One of them quietly told a correspondent, "Something is coming up pretty soon."

An hour later, a mimeographed press release, its ink still wet, was passed out by Charley Ross. Reporters bawled into their telephones, "Bulletin, fact-finding board recommends wage increases of 19½ cents an hour for General Motors strikers."

Friday was another cold and gloomy day. It was supposed to be the day when the strike jam would begin to break up. That afternoon correspondents waited in the quiet hall outside the Secretary of Labor's office to get the good news. It never came.

Regularly, as the hours wore away, Schwellenbach's assistants walked into the press room with a great show of casualness. They walked over to the news ticker, looked at it anxiously. No word from Detroit. It began to rain outside, a steady black downpour.

The Secretary's office lost its optimism. Each time the telephone rang, aides looked up expectantly. After the first call a stenographer asked, "Is the news good?"

The answer was, "No."

The girl remarked, "Dear, dear." She used that expression several times this night. General Motors refused to accept the recommendations of the fact-finding board. The steel conferences had broken up. The meat packing disputes were bogged down with disagreement.

At one o'clock on Saturday another long wait began, this time in the White House. A long black limousine drove up to the East Wing of 1600 Pennsylvania Avenue. Two well-dressed men stepped out and, without saying a word, strode briskly into the white building. The one with the black Homburg hat was Benjamin Fairless, the head of U. S. Steel.

Then a lone figure walked slowly up the curved driveway. It was Phil Murray. There was no expression on his tired, drawn face. He stopped and gravely waited for the photographers to take his picture. Schwellenbach arrived a few minutes later, and the meeting began with President Truman, Snyder, and Steelman, then newly appointed as a labor adviser.

The afternoon wore out. The sun set behind the buildings across the street. The stars appeared. The big light on the White House portico was turned on. People walking along Pennsylvania Avenue stepped briskly, for it had become cold with the night.

Shortly after six-thirty sleepy correspondents in the lobby painfully pulled themselves out of the red leather chairs. Phil Murray was coming out of the President's office. By his side was Benjamin Fairless. Both looked like men who had had a very tough day.

Murray's Scotch burr was rough with weariness as he said, "At the request of the President, I have agreed to postpone the strike."

Charley Ross read the reporters a statement from the President: "It is my belief that an agreement will be reached."

The solution was cut-and-dried. Steel prices would be increased so wages could be raised.

At seven o'clock the crowd of correspondents drained out of the big mansion on Pennsylvania Avenue. The lights were turned down in the West Wing. The White House retired to a fitful week-end rest.

Chapter XXI

A SQUARE brick building, looking like a six-story faded yellow mausoleum, squats on a busy Washington street corner. This is John L. Lewis's castle. The old mansion, a symbol of respectability, was deliberately selected by him. The mine workers could slouch through the rooms where Washington society had wined and dined, and pay their tribute to the big man who looks like an old Roman emperor.

In the spring of President Truman's second year, two cameramen lounged on the steps most of the day. They were keeping a vigil, waiting for Big John to come out.

On April Fools' Day, John Lewis had boldly demonstrated his power. With an oratorical flourish, he closed the mines. There was no thick, sooty smoke piling out over factory towns. Apartment dwellers and home owners were praying for an early warm spring. Curses and maledictions fell on Big John from Capitol Hill. Newspaper cartoons pictured a grotesque John Lewis with a big hand holding down reconversion. Headlines shouted, SCHOOLS, MOVIES TO CLOSE IF COAL STRIKE CONTINUES.

John L. Lewis sat calmly in his yellow mansion with his ducks all in a row. The miners were enthusiastically behind him. Besides the wage increase, he was asking for a welfare fund. During the war hundreds of miners had been killed, thousands injured in the pits. The fund was to take care of dependents and the crippled.

His United Mine Workers were not going to hog all the blame for shutting down industry. The eminently respectable railroad brotherhoods were taking a strike vote, too.

Big John had a couple of old scores to settle. He had made the mistake of assuming he was indispensable to Franklin D. Roosevelt and the New Deal. He had been coldly rebuffed. This time he would dictate his terms in the circular Presidential office.

There was the matter of Phil Murray, too. Murray had been Lewis's trusted lieutenant when they founded the CIO. But Murray had remained loyal to Mr. Roosevelt when Big John split with him. Lewis was going to show the country he could drive a harder bargain for his miners than Murray got for the steelworkers.

The negotiations, and they were only preliminaries, went on in the rear of the Labor Department's solemn auditorium. The gilt paint on the doors covered two lions' heads carved into the thick wood. The shaggy heads were cut into roaring grimaces.

John Lewis and Charley O'Neill, representing the mineowners, sat across the table like two stubborn lions. They were deadlocked on the welfare fund. Where would the money come from? Who would administer it? How much money should be set aside?

Harry Truman had innocently poked his nose into the argument. He told his news conference he thought the idea of building up the welfare fund from a royalty on mined coal was illegal.

During one of the negotiating sessions, Ed Burke, a mine operators' spokesman and former anti-New Deal Senator from Nebraska, was called out of the meeting by his press agent to comment on Mr. Truman's remarks.

Burke smiled slowly, listening to the account of the President's press conference. Then he told the correspondents, "I think the President is right. We can't run the risk of violating the law. Congress should make it a criminal offense for a union to ask for a royalty."

While Burke was talking, a miner – a big, broad-shouldered fellow with a toothpick in his mouth – came out to see what was up. His face was hard as he listened.

John Lewis was not talking. There would be plenty of time for that later on. He had planned his entrance at the most dramatic moment. His spokesman was Casey Adams, a hard-boiled little guy who edits the *Mine Workers' Journal* and looks like a Chicago reporter from the play *Front Page*. He wears a gray felt hat tilted over his forehead and calls all the girls "Betty."

Casey talked to the reporters, saying, "First, I have a little one-sentence statement. Here it is. The United Mine Workers have not received any proposals for settling the coal strike from anyone – and *that* takes care of that."

He was asked a question. Casey snorted, "I'm not falling for any gig-rigged questions. We are simply standing pat."

Someone said, "Say, Casey, have you got your winter's coal in yet?"

He grinned. "I think I can scare up two or three lumps."

Was it for burning or throwing?

Casey made a scat motion with his hand. "For throwing. The mine workers are not going to be trimmed this time. Now, be gone with you."

This was the atmosphere surrounding the coal negotiations. After fruitless sessions in the Labor Department, the conference room doors swung open reluctantly. A tired mediator announced, "The meetings are indefinitely postponed. No agreement."

They were not resumed until the scene was changed to one more to John Lewis's liking – the White House.

Meanwhile, on Capitol Hill, a storm had broken. It washed away all consideration of price control, atomic energy, and appropriations. Angry voices spluttered against labor.

The Senate Banking Committee was listlessly holding hearings on the OPA bill. John D. Small, the Civilian Production Administrator, was testifying halfheartedly until a Senator asked, "What effect will the coal strike have on production?"

Small sat up straight in his chair. His blue eyes sparked. His chin jutted forward. He said, "We are heading toward disaster if this continues." He paused, then bit off each word, "This country – cannot – run – if – small groups – are allowed – to stop – our economy." Then he subsided with a grim smile. That was off his chest.

But Big John still sat tight in his yellow mausoleum.

On the Senate floor, the British loan was forgotten. Handsome

Scott Lucas, the hand-picked boy of Mayor Ed Kelly of Chicago, rose in a wrathful mood. He thundered, "A catastrophe is coming to this country in every state in the Union unless something is done. I'm working on a bill to make it a criminal offense for a labor leader to conspire to break down and paralyze the industry of this country."

He was surrounded by Senators wanting to pump his hand. Pink-cheeked Harry Byrd, the Virginia county squire, had a bill to make royalty payments illegal. His high voice squeaked, "Why can't railroad workers ask for a per cent of every ton of freight they handle if Lewis gets away with this?"

Ed Burke wandered in and out of the cloakrooms adding fuel to the coalless fire.

The National Association of Manufacturers thundered in a press release, "The royalty tax demanded by John L. Lewis will pyramid into a multibillion sales tax on the American public."

Republican leaders were sitting back gleefully watching Democrats lead the wild cry against labor. Alben Barkley was playing for time, letting the Senate talk itself out.

John Lewis maintained an eloquent silence.

With antilabor sentiment running strong in the Senate, a group of twelve Senators who cautioned restraint took the floor and held it until tempers subsided. It was a filibuster.

Tall, stooped Jim Murray, one of the wealthiest men in the Senate, started it off. Speaking sorrowfully and gently, he said, "Labor disputes and strikes create grave public problems. But we have made great strides from the days when labor-management conflicts resulted in violence and bloodshed. Gradually a semblance of reason and law has been growing up in labor relations. We must not pass bills for the fleeting present, but for the long tomorrows."

He paused, looked over the floor trying to pick out from the facial expressions those who were leaning with him, and went on, "We should not overlook the danger of seeking a short-term victory through compulsory methods, and lose the long-term objectives of freedom and democracy."

Senator Lucas, who looks like a rotogravure section picture of the successful businessman at a country-club banquet, interrupted, "Can you guarantee to the American people that the coal strike will be settled?"

Murray answered, "I am not a prophet. But I can say with full assurance we won't settle it by restrictive bills."

Lucas remarked, "If I understand your position, there is nothing we can do. Is there no one in the Congress or the executive branch who can do anything? Are we a helpless, powerless group, unable to do anything?"

Murray plodded on, "If there is any fault, it lies with Congress in meeting reconversion problems. We should have provided for wage adjustments . . . a national health measure . . . many things."

Lucas, Joe Ball of Minnesota, and several Southerners stood on the floor. Each time Murray paused they heckled him.

George Aiken of Vermont was up next. He rose from the Republican side of the aisle, and said of the Lucas bill, "This is a plain statement that if a miner doesn't return, he loses practically everything of value outside his own family. He loses labor law protection. He loses seniority rights and his rights to collective bargaining."

Lucas replied stiffly, "I ask you whether the people are not entitled to some consideration?"

Aiken's usually mild eyes snapped as he said, "I am not in favor of casting overboard all concepts of liberty under which this country has been governed since 1776, in order to force one man against his will to work for another who will profit from his service."

Wayne Morse crisply added, "For the life of me, I don't know what bills we could pass that would settle the coal case on its merits. That, after all, is what we need to get coal mined."

Burt Wheeler, the old progressive warrior of the late twenties and early thirties, joined the debate. Like Achilles, Wheeler had shunned the wars during the latter part of the Roosevelt Administration. Now he was fighting again. He stood leaning over his desk, one foot on the chair, pointing with his finger, reeling off figures to support the miners' claims.

Claude Pepper held the floor hour after hour. Little Joe O'Mahoney, of Wyoming, the witty Irishman, added an hour or so to keep the antilabor bills from a vote.

At one time in the argument, Byrd said, "I am proud to be on the purge list of the CIO Political Action Committee, because that means they cannot control me in my votes in the Senate."

Pepper answered with studied, deliberate politeness, "There are others who get much satisfaction from being on the purge lists of reactionary business interests."

Byrd flung back sarcastically, "I'm glad there is at least something out of which we can get a mutuality of satisfaction."

Alben Barkley sat patiently. When reporters asked him what would happen in the Senate, he good-naturedly snapped his fingers. "Doggone," he replied, "I lost my Ouija board. Now I can't tell you what will happen here."

His strategy was to let all the voices wear themselves out. He had an ace in the hole – he could tack the poll-tax repealer as an amendment onto any antilabor bill. That would stop it.

At the White House, all was serene. Workmen were raking up leaves and planting grass seed on the broad lawn. The roses, planted in neat rows back of the President's office, were in full bloom.

Harry Truman was the cheerful host. A Baptist minister from a small town in Oregon stopped off at the White House with a gift of two dozen brown trout and a gavel made of myrtle. The minister mentioned that he was visiting Missouri in the summer. The President beamed. He sat down and scribbled off a note to his mother and told the visitor he must be sure to see her.

The coal strike apparently was not worrying the President. He told one Senator he was going to let the strikes "take their natural course." He was planning an airplane trip to Missouri to get another college degree.

At his news conference, Mr. Truman joked casually with reporters. While correspondents picked at him with questions, the President fiddled with a paper knife and straightened the edges of a pile of papers on his desk.

A voice inquired, "Do you think you can settle the railway dispute?"

Yes, he hoped to.

"What about the coal strike?" another voice called.

Mr. Truman smiled politely. Yes, he *hoped* to settle that one too.

Three blocks away John L. Lewis was having the time of his life. Photographers pleading, "Please, Mr. Lewis, one more shot." Senators and Congressmen denouncing him. Editorials in every newspaper. He strode majestically through the scenes of conflicts like a king. The massive head was held erect. A smile of victory hovered in his expressive eyes. He made up flourishing phrases for the delighted reporters.

He would walk out of the White House with a smile of triumph turning up his heavy lips. He had waited a long time to survey the world from the steps of the White House. This was it.

Harry Truman was fascinated and awed by this man. He had never seen anything like Big John.

The correspondents stopped Lewis in the White House lobby after one meeting. He surveyed them tolerantly like a monarch surveying his subjects. Someone asked him a question. Big John paused, then rumbled, "That gives one furiously to think."

There were chuckles of appreciation. Newsmen hastily scribbled down the phrase. Big John watched it all with a gleam of contempt and amusement.

On a Friday evening, Lewis decided it was time to act. The negotiating meeting had met in the morning. At noon, a brawny man pushed open the door and stepped into the cool hall. He was John O'Leary, Big John's first lieutenant.

"How did it go?" he was asked.

O'Leary answered, "We didn't make any progress. There is no use lying about it." He plodded on down the hall.

Big John opened the doors of his mausoleum and called the reporters in. In a voice like that of an old-fashioned country preacher he read a statement he had sent to the miners: "The nation's economy is being imperiled by the stupidity and selfish greed of the coal operators and associated financial interests, and demagogues."

But the story was – John Lewis had called a two weeks' truce in the strike.

Lew Schwellenbach brought to the White House soon afterwards a proposal to end the strike – an 18½-cent-an-hour increase and a welfare fund to be administered jointly by the government, union, and operators.

Twenty minutes after the Secretary of Labor entered the White House, a red-faced man puffed up the driveway. He was Charley O'Neill. Five minutes later, Big John strolled up the walk like a drum major.

An eager girl reporter stuttered something to him. One eyelid drooped. John Lewis rumbled, "How interesting," and strode on.

The meeting in Mr. Truman's office soon broke up. Lewis and O'Neill came out together. Big John was in great good humor. He was winning. The newsmen instinctively turned to him first. Lewis bowed ceremoniously in the direction of the mine operator and said, "After you, Mr. O'Neill."

O'Neill said they had discussed with the President his request to end the strike in five days. Lewis stood quietly, a flicker of a smile coming and going.

A reporter asked, "Did you talk to Mr. Truman about an increase in the price of coal?"

O'Neill said yes, he had mentioned it. Lewis boomed, "Not me."

Would the coal strike be settled in five days? Lewis again bowed to O'Neill and purred, "That depends on Mr. O'Neill and his associates."

But Charley O'Neill had the last word. He slipped in quietly, "And Mr. Lewis."

The two men smiled. They understood each other.

Chapter XXII

THE second big strike shut down the railroads. The engineers and trainmen left the locomotives and cars standing idly in the yards. This happened a few weeks after the coal mines shut down.

On a sunny May afternoon before the strike, two sturdy white-haired men with the determined faces of men long used to authority walked up to the White House. They were old personal friends of Harry Truman, and, in their own way, conservatives and aristocrats.

They were A. F. Whitney, president of the Brotherhood of Railway Trainmen, and Alvanley Johnston, president of the Brotherhood of Locomotive Engineers.

With John Lewis crowding the stage, the threatened railway strike had been shoved into the background. But this afternoon President Truman had called them in for a face-to-face talk.

They were not worried. They had been Harry's friends when he needed help . . . in Missouri politics, in the Senate. They had sold him to labor on a sweltering summer day in Chicago two years before. The man who was now President had always taken their advice with a grateful smile.

On this Thursday afternoon, Harry Truman was cold and hostile. His greeting was curt: "I brought you gentlemen here to discuss with you the emergency of a railway strike. I think you should call it off."

The men on the other side of the neat desk were startled. What had happened? Whitney answered gruffly, "Mr. President, this strike has been called for Saturday, May 18th, at 4 P.M., and unless we can get some rules, the strike will go on as scheduled."

(The rules were regulations which would raise the take-home pay of engineers and trainmen.)

Mr. Truman's underlip tightened, and he said, "My emergency board recommended 18½ cents an hour increase. I am going to support my board."

Whitney was angry too and flung back, "That would be tantamount to scuttling our program."

The more the bewildered men talked, the sterner their old friend became. The President told them coldly that unless they changed their minds, the government was going to run the railroads. He added curtly, "And you can put that in your pipe and smoke it."

These aristocrats of labor were not accustomed to such talk. Whitney blew up. He raged, "Do you mean the government will act as a strikebreaker?"

While Whitney sat back sullenly, Johnston tried another tactic. He said soothingly, "Mr. President, with all the many questions that come before you, I am convinced you do not understand this question."

That was hardly the diplomatic thing to say. Mr. Truman glowered and replied, "Yes, I do understand it. I know all about it."

Dr. Steelman, who had been quietly sitting by the President, found an excuse to break up the meeting. He led Whitney and Johnston into the cabinet room. There he tried to calm them. He apologized for the stormy scene in the President's office and explained, "The President did not have ample time to go into all the differences and there is some confusion."

John Steelman did not try to explain Mr. Truman's strange humor. Perhaps he himself did not understand it.

Harry Truman had been pushed into one of his stubborn moods. He had endured all the gibes he could take about nursing labor and letting strikes continue. He felt that now his old friends, Whitney and Johnston, were trying to hang him on the cross. That was too much. The President decided to be tough. There would be no more monkey business with these labor people who thought they were running the country. The President set his jaw firmly. No one could talk him out of his mood.

At Dr. Steelman's request, the railway negotiations were picked up again. The conferences soon bogged down. The railway owners had learned that the President was insisting the unions abide by the emergency board finding. As a result they would not budge. Neither would Whitney or Johnston. On Friday afternoon, the day before the scheduled strike, the two union leaders were called back to the White House. They reported stiffly to President Truman that the negotiations were deadlocked.

Mr. Truman pulled some papers on his desk before him. He said coldly, "All right, I will sign an order taking over the railroads."

The pen moved across the paper signing "Harry S. Truman." His old friends stood awkwardly before him. Was that all? Mr. Truman said curtly, "Yes."

Late that afternoon, Secretary of State Jimmy Byrnes and Dr. Steelman called Whitney and Johnston, and pleaded with them to hold off the strike a few more days. They agreed on a five-day moratorium.

Shortly after noon on the fifth day, Whitney and Johnston walked heavily into the White House lobby. They were tired, angry, and confused. Reporters surrounded them, firing questions. Without slowing down his stride, Johnston snapped, "We're here on invitation. That's all we know."

The hours wore on. One o'clock. Two o'clock. The strike deadline was in two hours. Within the Presidential office, Mr. Truman and his guests flared up at each other again. The President bit out his ultimatum. The unions would get what his emergency board had recommended and that was all. Period.

At four o'clock, the hour for the nationwide railway strike, President Truman strolled out on the broad back lawn behind his office for a garden party. He nudged Jimmy Byrnes and said with a grin, "They're still in session."

The worn-out conferees broke up in the evening. Deadlocked again. More conferences the next day. John Steelman raced back and forth between the two meeting places of the unions and the operators. No progress.

On Capitol Hill, the debate on labor legislation grew hotter.

The words "skunk" and "jackass" were thrown about the Senate.

By Saturday morning, Harry Truman had worked himself into a stubborn, angry mood. He announced he had broken off all further talks with the unions. Troops would guard the trains.

For the first time, Whitney and Johnston realized the President was going through with his threat. Frantically, they went to Jimmy Byrnes, whom they had known and trusted in the Senate. They offered to accept exactly what the President had thrust on them at the first meeting, plus assurances they could negotiate further and there would be no reprisals against union members. There was only silence from the White House.

Mr. Truman had been talking to Senator Harry Byrd. Senator Pepper, with proposals to end the strike, was refused an appointment. Byrd sold the President on addressing a joint session of Congress. He unselfishly turned over to Mr. Truman a copy of a Virginia law which permitted the drafting of strikers into the state militia. A power strike had been broken that way in Virginia.

At noon on Saturday, Whitney and Johnston gave in completely. They would call off the strike. Still no word from the White House.

All through the early afternoon, the House of Representatives swept through bills tying up labor. At one point the opposition sank to as low as fourteen votes. At four o'clock, Harry Truman, looking like an angry pallbearer, stomped up the aisle of the House. His lips were clamped grimly shut. The gray head bobbed stiff, mechanical greetings to the left and right. No smiles.

Cheers fell on him from the crowded galleries, from the floor jammed with Congressmen, Senators, and cabinet members. The President stepped purposefully to the Speaker's rostrum. The familiar voice with a Midwestern twang said firmly, "This disaster will spare no one." Mr. Truman rocked back and forth as he spoke, teetering on his brightly polished boots. Bursts of applause stopped and slowed the speaking.

But over the hall, there were those who sat quietly, their hands by their sides, not joining the applause . . . Jim Murray, Robert Wagner, Bob La Follette, Burt Wheeler. Mrs. Luce sat silently too, clutching a pair of red spectacles. Bob Taft wore a skeptical look on his face.

The President rushed on, speaking his words swiftly now. "A handful of men are striking against the nation." When he came to the section demanding that strikers be drafted into the Army, loud cheers and even a few rebel yells broke over the chamber. But less than half the lawmakers joined in.

A scrap of red paper was passed up to Mr. Truman. Jimmy Byrnes, sitting in the front row below the President, gave Secretary of Labor Schwellenbach a broad wink.

President Truman glanced at the paper, and announced proudly, "The rail strike has been settled on terms of the President."

All over the hall, Congressmen rose clapping and shouting their approval. Correspondents in the gallery scrambled to get their bulletins on the wire.

Mr. Truman plowed ahead, asking for injunctions against union leaders, the right to take seniority rights away from strikers, and criminal penalties. It was the stiffest labor legislation ever demanded in modern times by a Chief Executive. This small, grim man standing on the rostrum finished, "I urge immediate action on a comprehensive policy."

The response was the wildest ovation ever received by Harry Truman. He stood there stiffly listening to the thunder.

As soon as the floor was cleared and the House back in session, angry words tumbled all over each other.

Hugh De Lacy of Washington pleaded, "Ladies and gentlemen, I appeal to you, do not embark upon a course of action in which the Federal Government becomes an instrument of coercion against the working people." Boos rang over the chamber.

Charles Savage of Washington yelled over the uproar, "The railroad strike is over. I cannot vote for militarism in peacetime. The crisis is over. The time for hysteria is past."

Little Vito Marcantonio's dark face was almost crimson as he shouted, "God save the Congress of the United States from a repetition of what happened in the Italian parliament under Mussolini."

But the Democratic leadership, egged on by the Republican

high command, pushed through the bills. Joe Martin, the Republican floor leader, said righteously, "I do not like to give the President all this power, but I find no alternative."

The House was a tumult of noise and confusion. In less than an hour, the House passed a bill embodying the Truman provisions. The vote was 306 to 13.

In the Senate, Alben Barkley dutifully rose to ask unanimous consent to consider the Truman labor bill. Taft snapped, "I object." The bill was stopped until Monday morning.

Monday morning, rain dripped outside the Capitol and dark clouds threw gloomy shadows over the skylight.

Bob Taft was moving about amiably, a smile on his face. He had never seemed quite so tall.

Alben Barkley rose heavily from his desk. The familiar smile was not there. He was a soldier performing a distasteful task. He held a printed copy of the Truman bill in his right hand.

The galleries were crowded. Several Senators' wives leaned over the railing. A delegation of CIO workers from New York sat in silence. Soldiers and sailors and their girl friends whispered back and forth. Every space at the long press and radio benches was taken.

Senator Taft asked Barkley, "What is the ultimate sanction against strikers who refuse to go back to work? Suppose they are drafted and refuse?"

Alben Barkley stared unhappily at the green carpet. Well, he replied, if the workers would not obey the orders of the President of the United States, they could be treated as traitors.

Taft smiled triumphantly. "Then," he proceeded, "the ultimate sanction is not drafting. The President could make everyone work for ten cents a day, and – if they refuse – they could be court-martialed."

Stung, Barkley snapped, "This is one way to secure operation of the coal mines, not wait until there is a complete collapse."

Senator Revercomb, a Republican from the coal-mining state of West Virginia, batted next. He asked, "Would not the inducted striker be subjected to the same punishment as a soldier – court-martial, death or penitentiary?"

Barkley answered glumly, "He is inducted into the armed services."

Revercomb pressed on, "I do not see any sense in giving the President the power to execute a man because he doesn't obey an order of the President."

Bob Taft stood in the aisle watching with sharp eyes. He was the field general planning and timing the attack.

Barkley retreated a step, saying, "Frankly, I don't like the section either. It would be used only as a last resort in an extreme situation."

A few men spoke for the bill. Scott Lucas, scowling like a movie villain, grumbled, "What good is it to protect civil rights if you have an emergency crisis, and there are no civil rights anyway?"

Senator Overton of Louisiana added, "Wouldn't you rather have a dictatorship by the President than a dictatorship by John L. Lewis?"

Other men dug at Barkley – Saltonstall, Wherry, Aiken. Sheridan Downey, the California Democrat, walked across the front of the Senate. He stopped at Barkley's desk, leaning over to whisper to him. Barkley reached out, clutched Downey's arm, and pumped it. There was a wistful smile on the majority leader's face. Then Barkley plodded out.

Downey began speaking. "I have had many amazing experiences. But I must admit I am now like a person in a dream. Here we are debating the most harsh and dictatorial law of which the human mind can conceive."

Mrs. Downey, a small woman in a brown dress, sat in the gallery following every word of her husband. He was a solid man with curly gray hair. His voice was husky with emotion as he said, "I doubt if anyone can point to a single act by Mussolini or Hitler before the war began as extreme as this proposal. Are we willing to say, 'You serfs, you will work or go into the Army. You shall labor or you shall die by a firing squad'?"

Senator Morse interrupted, "Do you know that the White House knew at noon Saturday the railroad workers were ready to go back?"

Downey answered politely, "I believe the President announced it during his speech at four-ten that afternoon."

Morse's neat black mustache quivered as he said, "I think that was one of the cheapest exhibitions of ham acting I ever saw."

Unexpectedly applause clattered across the gallery. The presiding officer pounded his gavel.

Little Carl Hatch, the self-appointed defender of Harry Truman in the Senate, popped up like a jumping jack. He spoke in outraged tones. "I do not think any Senator has the right to stand here and refer to the President as a ham actor. I think every Senator ought to resent that statement. I ask consent for the words to be stricken from the record."

Morse flung back angrily, "I will repeat those words, if necessary, to put the facts in the record." He and Hatch glared at one another.

That afternoon Millikin held the floor for nearly an hour while a circle of Senators gathered around him. He took the Truman bill section by section, pounding it with cold and legalistic arguments. He said, "In my opinion, this violates the due-process clause of the Constitution. . . . This is nothing less than peonage, a violation of the Thirteenth Amendment to the Constitution."

The next day worried Democrats tried to get word to the White House. Harley Kilgore, facing re-election in the coal-mining state of West Virginia, pleaded with Mr. Truman to withdraw the bill.

This was the morning of remorse for Harry Truman. He was worried, surprised at how far his anger had taken him, and sorry. He told Senator Kilgore sadly he would like to help his friends in the Senate. He would like to withdraw the bill, but he was afraid John Lewis would not sign a contract if the bill were not hanging over his head.

Senator Burt Wheeler was blunt. He lectured the President as though he were an errant schoolboy. Wheeler said the bill was political suicide, and added, "Even if you don't care about your own political future, don't sacrifice every Democrat in Congress. Call back the bill."

After this stiff talking-to by the older man, Mr. Truman was meeker than ever. He indicated to Senator Wheeler that he would recall the bill. But that night, the President changed his mind. He called Wheeler on the telephone and told him so.

Two days later, on May 29, John Lewis triumphantly strode into the White House and signed a coal contract. Harry Truman watched with a happy smile.

On the Hill, Les Biffle brought word of the end of the coal strike to Senator Barkley. He walked quietly into the chamber and whispered to the Senator.

This had been Bob Taft's day in the Senate. Men from both sides of the aisle . . . Wagner, Pepper, La Follette . . . had consulted with him. Even as Biffle was talking to Senator Barkley, Taft was saying, "The idea of drafting men to work is the most extreme form of slavery."

Soon after Barkley announced that a coal contract had been signed, Democratic Senator Tydings moved to adjourn. In an instant, Taft was on the floor protesting. The Democrats watched anxiously. Would they be forced to vote on the Truman bill? Les Biffle had hopped up on the rostrum and was advising the current presiding officer, Brien McMahon.

Barkley settled the argument. It was more important to keep the rules straight in the Senate than to gain a point. The voting began. Old John Crockett called off the names. The first one was Briggs, a Democrat from Truman's own state. He voted a clear "Yes," to throw out the White House draft-labor provision.

Every Republican voted against the Truman proposal. Taft looked over his men with a smile of victory. Thirty-four Democrats voted the same way. Even old Kenneth McKellar, the president pro tem of the Senate, and Lister Hill, the Democratic whip, both Southern Democrats, broke with the President. The President was left with ten Southern Democrats, plus Barkley, Hatch, and Lucas.

At his news conference a few days later, Mr. Truman spoke back. He stood behind his desk, a small, well-dressed man in a blue suit and polka-dot tie. There was a trace of coolness in his voice. It was a warm morning and the doors were opened on the garden.

The questions were blunt. "Do you agree with Whitney that you have signed your political death warrant?"

Mr. Truman replied dryly that he had no comment. The questions piled up, pricking at him. Finally, his reserve broke. He stormed that the draft provision of his bill had been grossly misrepresented. In an emergency, a sheriff could deputize anyone. He needed to deputize people to run the railroads.

A voice from the center of the tightly pressed crowd asked, "Do you still support your legislation?"

The President pressed his lips tight, then replied stiffly that he would not have recommended it if he had been going to change his mind later. The House of Representatives – he emphasized the words – felt the same way. He appreciated it.

A few minutes later, the President took another swipe at the Senate. Why hadn't he appointed a council for full employment? He said it was hard getting people to serve. They saw what treatment *some people* got before the Senate.

That afternoon, the lines were re-forming in the Senate. Alben Barkley was more like his usual calm, self-assured self. This time he was doing it the way he wanted to. He had a fistful of amendments taking the teeth out of the bill in his desk.

This, too, was the end of President Truman's honeymoon with the Senate. There were no more regular parties in Les Biffle's office with Harry Truman as the guest of honor that summer. Those days were over.

Chapter XXIII

A YEAR before the strikes, another great crisis was growing behind a wall of secrecy.

The sad days of that lovely spring of 1945 checked off the calendar. The shock and sense of crisis following the death of Franklin Roosevelt gradually wore away in the hot summer months. There were moments of wild, delirious joy . . . when Pennsylvania Avenue in front of the White House was filled with shouting singing masses. War in Europe was over!

The story of this crisis began on October 11, 1939, when a bustling bushy-haired little man, Alexander Sachs, saw President Roosevelt in the White House. He came bearing a message from a group of scientists.

Sachs, a kind of itinerant economist, philosopher and scientific interpreter who wandered in and out of the New Deal, read the President a carefully prepared memorandum:

"I trust that you may now be able to accord me the opportunity to present a communication from Dr. Albert Einstein to you, and other relevant material bearing on experimental work by physicists with far-reaching significance for national defense. . . . The experimentation that has been going on for half a dozen years on atomic disintegration has culminated this year in the discovery . . . that the element uranium could be split by neutrons. . . . This new development holds out the following prospects . . . the construction of bombs of hitherto unenvisaged potency and scope. As Dr. Einstein observes, a single bomb of this type carried by boat and exploded in a port might well destroy the whole port together with some of the surrounding territory."

When the excitable voice with the heavy accent finished reading, Franklin Roosevelt said thoughtfully, "Alex, what you are after is to see that the Nazis don't blow us up. This requires action."

Almost six years later, on July 16, 1945, a still summer night on the lonely desert of New Mexico was lighted with a flash so blinding that men shivered. The first atomic bomb was exploded. The world moved into a new and more precarious era.

But the impact of the atomic bomb did not sink into Washington until that fall. It was about two months after Hiroshima fell apart.

Early in September, young Senator Brien McMahon introduced the first atomic energy bill. The Kilgore committee interrupted its hearing on the science bill to listen to reports of the fantastic new world. These hearings struck Washington with a stunning shock.

The atomic energy testimony was given in a small, borrowed room on the top floor of the Senate Office Building. The room was crowded and smoky. At the head of a long table with green cloth, like a pool table, sat Senator Harley Kilgore of West Virginia. He had a large round face, a pleasant deep voice, and a light, sometimes cynical, smile.

On either side of him were Senator Warren Magnuson of Washington and Bill Fulbright of Arkansas.

Jammed into the room were scientists – Dr. Vannevar Bush calmly smoking a pipe – generals, admirals, and reporters.

One of the first witnesses was Rear Admiral William R. Purnell, the Navy's expert on atomic bombs. He is a sandy-haired man with bushy eyebrows.

Senator Fulbright poked around in his pocket, brought out a frayed clipping, and drawled, "The Associated Press here says the Naval Affairs Committee knows of an effective countermeasure against atomic bombs . . . some way to detonate the bombs a distance from our shores."

The Senator paused, smiled eagerly at Admiral Purnell, and asked, "Do you feel there is a defense?"

The Admiral shook his head soberly, and answered in a low tone, "I do not know of any defense. The people who made the bomb have thought about any possible countermeasure, and of ways to evade them."

Bill Fulbright twisted around in his seat to face the Admiral. His high forehead was creased in anxious wrinkles. He asked the Admiral, "Do you suppose there will be any warning of the attack starting the next war?"

"No," Admiral Purnell replied quietly, "and we will have no time to develop countermeasures. The war might last only thirty minutes."

The low, background murmur in the room was hushed. The only sound in the pause was the scratch of the reporters' pencils moving hastily over the yellow copy paper.

Senator Fulbright asked, "Is it possible we might attack first?"

The Admiral answered crisply, "No sir, that is impossible under our Constitution."

Bill Fulbright, almost talking to himself, said, "Then, in event of a paralyzing attack, we are at a disadvantage. We are the most vulnerable. If we have any defense, it must be in the political field. We must have a strong world organization."

Admiral Purnell spoke in a whisper, "That is not in my field, sir."

The small room had become cloudy with smoke. Senator Fulbright stared at the ceiling, and commented, "This seems so much more powerful than ordinary weapons, our conventional ideas do not apply. We've always thought defenses could be developed for anything, so we wouldn't have to worry."

Admiral Purnell smiled dryly and remarked, "There must be an exception to every rule."

The questions dropped over the table. . . . Could we defend ourselves by digging underground like moles? No, not even that. Atomic bombs could be made to penetrate the deepest underground shelters. Could the bomb be kept a secret? The theory was wide open, but only the United States now had the industrial resources.

Admiral Purnell suddenly opened the door to more strange possibilities. He said earnestly, "There is only one thing we lost sight of. We started out to develop this bomb with nothing but figures on paper. As soon as we conquered one problem, we went on to the next. We didn't stop to find out if there were a cheaper or a faster way. We do not know if the scientists left short cuts behind them. Any nation may find these short cuts."

Senator Magnuson asked the Admiral if he felt the atomic bomb would change the role of the Navy.

Admiral Purnell reflected a few seconds, then replied slowly, "Frankly, I get lost just thinking about it. I don't think the best scientists know where we will be fifteen years from now. It might wipe out the Navy, or Army, or air forces. Atomic bombs might be launched from submarines, or planes, or by rockets. *The atomic bomb is the most powerful weapon ever found.*"

The air in the small room was suddenly very close. This was Washington's introduction to the atomic age.

There were a series of greater shocks at the hearing the next day . . . a beautiful fall morning in Washington. Indian summer. The trees near the Capitol were splashed with bright reds and yellows. A warm sun shone and a smoky haze rolled across Congressional Hill.

The committee room – this time in the basement of the Senate Office Building – was jammed. A pretty Wave sat in the front row. A gray-haired Admiral was near the back. There were: An intense man in a war correspondent's uniform. Visiting scientists. A small old lady who took copious notes. A neat handsome man with black hair turning gray at the sides squeezed in at the press table. He was Boris Krylov, the shy Russian news agency correspondent. Senator Kilgore presided, cheerfully chewing gum.

The crowd had come to see the principal witness, Dr. J. R. Oppenheimer, research director at Los Alamos, where the atomic bombs are made. Dr. Oppenheimer has a fascinating aliveness about him. When he smiles, he has a merry, pixy quality. He is a slim, long-legged man with penetrating blue eyes. He has long, slender fingers that are never still, a high forehead on a long face, big ears that stand out from his narrow head, and close-cropped black hair.

Dr. Oppenheimer began by telling of the giant machines at Los Alamos – how they could be used for biology and medicine, as well as for death. They are the huge piles, or chain reactors. He called them "a big sledge hammer to hit the mosquitoes of science."

These machines are too expensive to be duplicated by private industry. They belong to the People of the United States and Congress must decide what we shall do with them.

Dr. Oppenheimer spoke in a low, meticulous voice. His pronunciation was a little academic. But there was a gathering, hypnotic quality in both his words and their sound.

The military aspects of atomic energy, the scientist said gently, "are really rather terrifying."

He damned the wartime practice of surrounding scientists and their research with secrecy. This policy, if carried into peacetime, would stifle progress and discourage scientists, he said. Back of the atom bomb were years of free exchange of scientific knowledge.

"All we did," Dr. Oppenheimer said, "was to take a tree ripe with fruit and shake it hard. Secrecy is not possible. The nature of the world is not secret. Only policy is secret. You cannot keep the atom secret."

Senator Fulbright asked thoughtfully, "Can we keep the techniques of atom bombs secret?"

"That," Dr. Oppenheimer replied, with a slight smile turning up at the corners of his long mouth, "is like why don't you stop beating your wife. The immediate problem, it seems to me, is to get confidence among the nations, not force them apart by trying to build up a great secret. Other countries will say – keep your secret. We'll do it another way."

Dr. Oppenheimer looked around the room, catching the fixed, fascinated expressions. Krylov had his chin in his hand.

The scientist went on, "The intolerable state is very close. It is only necessary for other nations to decide to pursue an independent course in atomic research. How little it would take to close the door! If I were a Russian scientist, and had this pulled on me, I'd say, 'Boys, let's get to it.' I think they will."

Helen Gahagan Douglas quietly slipped into the room, and took a chair in the corner.

"Are there any defenses against the atomic bomb?" Dr. Oppenheimer was asked.

The answer was given in a clear, convincing tone. "There are no specific countermeasures for atomic bombs. There never will be. Our bomb cannot be exploded before it hits the target."

Dr. Oppenheimer looked around the room. "I will offer to wager half my savings, small as they are, to anyone who can explode a bomb made at our place before it reaches its destination. The atomic bomb is the two-billion-dollar straw that may break the camel's back."

The room was painfully still. Through a basement window was a tiny scene . . . legs briskly walking by . . . a patch of sunlight . . . one corner of the big fountain in the park. But it was a different world.

Senator Fulbright, his face concentrated in thought, asked if there were *any* defense.

Dr. Oppenheimer replied, "No country is ever thoroughly alerted. Atomic bombs will be a cheap way to make war. They can do so much with so little. . . .

"I suppose," he said reflectively, "it is a natural human reaction to wish so hard for a defense against this thing that people already begin to believe there is a defense. But this comes to a world already at the breaking point, so far as weapons are concerned."

Mrs. Douglas sucked in her breath. A low, shocked murmur ran through the crowded room.

Bill Fulbright thought aloud, "We in government have a real job – to make sure the people understand the importance of this new power."

Dr. Oppenheimer said quietly, "We scientists are willing to be circus performers, to move into the glare of publicity, if we can somehow make the people understand."

The room was quiet for a moment, lost in thought. Then Senator Fulbright inquired, "Could our one hundred and forty million people be wiped out in one attack?"

Every eye was fixed on Dr. Oppenheimer. He answered slowly, "I am afraid that is true."

The gray-haired woman bit her lip. Krylov had forgotten to

write a word. There was a long ash on Senator Kilgore's cigarette.

The scientist continued, "The atomic bomb has weakened the military power of the United States. Ten or twenty years from now atomic bombs will be very cheap."

Bill Fulbright answered him. He said, "That is a compelling reason why we must undertake some other means of defense. I feel the only way is through government opposition to nationalism. Governments must agree to some world system of control."

"Yes," Dr. Oppenheimer said, looking at the Senator, "there are no technical problems. Only political ones. And even in solving the political problems, the world traditions of science will help." Dr. Oppenheimer smiled, "I am not envious of the tasks of the foreign ministers."

Senator Magnuson remarked, "You know it might help if we put the scientists in the political field."

"Perhaps," Dr. Oppenheimer replied, "that might work. Scientists have always belonged to a world fraternity. Many times on the development of the atom bomb, we thought the war might end before we had a bomb. But some of us did not stop, because we wanted the world to see the atomic bomb. It was to us the greatest argument for world peace."

Senator Fulbright said slowly, "Yes, it took the shock of Hiroshima to wake us up."

Then he turned, facing the scientist directly. He said earnestly, "Dr. Oppenheimer, if all the people could hear you, I think it would give us the motive to really build the peace."

The dilemma of the atomic bomb swept over Capitol Hill like a fever. A few weeks later, there was so much fascinated curiosity that the atomic scientists held a forum especially for the Congressmen. It was held in the big House caucus room, which looks like an eighteenth-century ballroom. The chamber was full of men and women of all beliefs and parties from Arthur Capper, the stooped, deaf old Republican from Kansas, to Jerry Voorhis, the square-jawed New Deal idealist from California.

The first speaker was Dr. Leo Szilard, an anti-Nazi German whom Dr. Einstein had brought to see President Roosevelt. Szilard is a round-faced man with a streak of gray running through his curly black hair. He spoke so intently – the fervor of his words, the effort to speak clearly in English – that his face shone with sweat.

He warned we have reached the valley of decisions. Bombs may be manufactured to destroy hundreds of square miles. We can either organize for peace or wage a preventive war.

Dr. Urey, the Nobel Prize winner, spoke with quiet force. The world has not reached its peak of destruction, he cautioned. There are other processes many times more powerful than a split atom . . . a mesatron releases billions of volts of energy.

At that moment, a plane roared overhead. The man sitting in front of me shuddered.

The last speaker was a prophetic figure . . . lean, dressed in black, a long serious face and black hair. He was young Dr. Borst (perhaps not yet thirty), one of the atomic scientists.

He spoke slowly and in a soft voice: "We are the young people. We wish to live our future lives in freedom. We wish to be creative, not destructive. We wish to live at peace with the world and our consciences. It is our duty to enlighten the people of our democracy."

The Congressmen sat silent, and perplexed.

A few days later, Secretary of State Byrnes held an uneasy news conference. The Soviet Foreign Commissar, Mr. Molotov, had said defiantly that Russia, too, would have atomic power.

At this news conference, Secretary Byrnes had deep lines in his forehead. His lips were tired, drooped downward. He looked thin and fragile.

One reporter brought up the Molotov speech and asked, "Would you say, Mr. Secretary, that the atomic race is on?"

Mr. Byrnes pursed his lips, took off his glasses, and replied simply, "I hope not."

It was more than an answer. It was a prayer!

Chapter XXIV

THROUGH the glorious, bold days of that autumn and into the sleepy winter, the specter of the atomic bomb grew and spread its wings over Washington.

A frightened and bewildered Senate passed the resolution by freshman Senator McMahon of Connecticut for an investigation of the problems of the atomic age. For five mornings a week the McMahon committee sat like children fascinated by the dreadful tale of the ogre, while generals, admirals, and scientists poured out the story of the bomb.

At noon, on one of these days, Big Ed Johnson, a bluff, towering man, walked out of Room 312 in the Senate Office Building and down the bustling corridor. A thin reporter tagged along, asking questions in a pleasant Southern drawl.

Big Ed's voice boomed, "We've got a bear by the tail. We can't hang on, and we can't let go."

The reporter grinned, bobbed his head, and replied, "Thank you, Senator, that's just the line I needed."

The two had come from the McMahon committee, known more informally as THE BOMB committee.

This room, 312, is small and genteel. It really belongs to the sober, deliberate Finance Committee. A large mirror in a heavy gilt frame glitters at one end. Red curtains hang at the long windows. The committee sat around a curved wooden bench. A big policeman with a grin on his face stood at the door like a traffic cop. People flowed in and out as in a movie theater.

In one corner of the room sat the atomic scientists. They wore baggy dark suits, slouched in their chairs, and blinked sheepishly when the photographers snapped their pictures. The other spectators craned their necks at this picture-taking and looked at the scientists with an expression that said, "Who in the heck are these guys?"

The Senators around the bench were a jury sitting on the fate of mankind. They sat with solemn faces and attentive eyes.

Only a few feet separated the Senators from the scientists . . . a few feet of red carpet. But there was another great gulf . . . the one between the dreamers and hard practical politicians. At one point in the hearings, Senator Johnson blurted out angrily, "You scientists have made the world insecure with the atomic bomb. Now, you come to us politicians and ask us to patch up everything."

One of the first witnesses was Major General Leslie Groves, director of the Manhattan (atomic) District of the War Department. He is a stocky, genial man with a bushy mustache and a paunch that bulges his uniform at the waist.

In the professionally cool voice of the military man, he testified, "I would like for a minute to discuss what happened when the bomb dropped over Japan." He read some figures into the quiet, gray room. Seventy to one hundred and twenty thousand dead and missing at Hiroshima. Seventy-five to two hundred thousand injured. All buildings in a radius of two miles wiped out . . . gaunt, twisted frames, and piles of rubble.

The General gave the story of an eyewitness, Father Seming, a priest. "He was standing in front of a window in the Hiroshima suburbs. He was seeing what a beautiful day it was. Then, there was a terrific flash of light. He was scratched some. Father Seming didn't know what had happened until the refugees streamed past."

(It was raining outside Room 312 in the courtyard. But those of us in the room could almost see through the drizzle this miserable little band of people trudging past the monastery.)

General Groves went on, "There probably were some people killed by radioactivity. But they would have been killed anyway . . . from the blast, or the terrible heat."

A nervous little laugh ran around the room.

He was asked, "What is the heat?"

General Groves answered quietly, "I would rather not say in an open hearing."

Senator McMahon leaned across the bench. "I think I can tell you," he said, "it is like a piece of the sun . . . several million degrees."

A general went on, "A Japanese officer told us you could do something about other bombs. You could stand up against it. But this was unendurable."

One of the scientists clenched his fists and bent his head forward on his chest.

General Groves described the light from the bomb. Another scene – a nightmarish scene – stood out from the streaks of rain on the windows. It was a dark night at the New Mexico testing ground. Men lay flat on the earth wearing dark glasses. Out of nowhere came a light so blinding, so brilliant, no man can describe it. There was only a numbing ache in the eyes.

General Groves went on in the even voice of a professional guide, "I looked at it a second after the bomb went off. It was so beyond human experience we were overpowered. I was not interested in the blast or the noise. The light was so dumbfounding we lost our keenness of observation."

Senator Hickenlooper, a small-town Iowa lawyer, had forgotten his doodling. The pencil lay still. Senator Tydings mused, more to himself than to the committee, "Sooner or later, we've got to protect ourselves and the world."

Hickenlooper asked, "Is there *any* encouragement for a defense?"

The General said, "No-o-o. You might stop some. But enough would get through to kill forty million people."

Senator Vandenberg leaned forward with his elbows on the desk, letting cigar smoke drift slowly from his lips. He said grimly, "The answer is no encouragement . . . Period!"

(Thunder rumbled across the sky outdoors. Several people in the room started nervously.)

Dr. Urey was called next. He read a paper like a professor talking to his class. Senator Tydings teetered in his chair. Senator

Hart, the former admiral, a straight little man wearing a high, starched collar, made notes with a gold pencil in a neat hand.

Dr. Urey outlined three stages. . . . The present, when we alone have the bombs. Next, we have a stock pile of the best bombs. The world fears us. Third, all nations have enough bombs to destroy each other. The tension develops beyond anything we ever had before. Every ripple on the world scene causes man to wonder if a bomb will ever come in the cool morning.

"This building," Dr. Urey said, "is an important target." Senator Connally looked down at him over his glasses. The scientist put his paper to one side. He lost his schoolroom manner and pleaded, "This next war will be disastrous for victor and vanquished. When can we interrupt this chain of events?"

Senator Tydings, like a man talking in his sleep, asked, "Could an enemy agent smuggle bombs into Washington, set them off with a clock, and destroy the President, Cabinet, Congress, and Joint Chiefs of Staff?"

Dr. Urey nodded his head. The Senator whispered, "We would have demoralization far beyond anything we could imagine. . . . Do you think the horror of the bomb would prevent nations from using it?"

The scientist studied a second. Every eye in the room was fixed on him. He answered deliberately, "No. I don't trust it."

"Have we anything better?"

He replied very earnestly, "We must try to induce other nations to outlaw the bomb, and bring violators to justice."

Another Senator asked, "If any large power refuses to agree, should we go on making bombs?"

Dr. Urey spread out his hands helplessly. "Yes, what else is there to do?"

Another witness was Dr. Langmuir, associate director of the General Electric Laboratory, and a Nobel Prize winner. A lock of gray hair fell over his forehead. He spoke in a small, precise voice. His testimony might have come from the Book of Revelations. "The time will come when bombs can be made a thousand times more powerful. We may not reach this stage first. There will be enough bombs to treat all the United States the way of Hiroshima."

He stuttered in earnestness, "Men must learn to live together. We must have world agreement. . . . If the fact that we have bombs and large atomic factories creates fear and suspicion, we ought to destroy all our bombs, the material and the factories. Drop it all in the sink." Dr. Langmuir clasped his hands tightly under his chin.

"This is not too big a price to pay. The alternative is simply appalling. This is a million times more dangerous than anything we ever had."

The great political dilemma rested before the committee. Senator Connally said gruffly, "We are all interested in getting a world plan. But there is still a risk."

Dr. Langmuir replied flatly, "The alternative is a war of atomic energy."

Connally grumbled, "Unless we get more bombs."

The scientist said quietly, "That won't help you any."

Senator Austin, a judicial-like man with pince-nez, spoke. "It narrows down to a simple, a spiritual matter – a question of world discipline."

Senator Byrd shook his head glumly. "Human nature doesn't change."

Ed Johnson had the last word. "You scientists have gotten a long way ahead of human conduct. I favor we speed up."

The Senators grew more and more restless as the dilemma settled down more firmly. At one session, a scientist recommended earnestly, "We must use the next twenty-five years to establish human relations to prevent war."

Senator Johnson said wearily, "Why don't you scientists go back to your laboratories and work on a defense, instead of giving us political advice?"

The scientist answered gravely, "I am afraid, Senator, the only answer is in the political field. I don't believe there ever will be a way to stop the atomic bomb. The buck is passed to the politicians. It's the toughest problem ever handed a statesman."

The restless questions were asked every place where members

of Congress gathered. General Eisenhower held a seminar on Capitol Hill to discuss the draft. A Congressman asked him the question gnawing at so many minds, "Do you believe if we share the secret of the atom bomb with the world, we open the door to attack?"

The General replied easily, "If we could establish a complete interchange of knowledge, you could give away the secret."

The audience of Representatives and Senators applauded, first timidly, then with more vigor.

The General continued in that flat, earnest, Midwestern twang of his: "Let's be realistic. The scientists say other nations will get the secret anyway. There is some point in making a virtue out of necessity."

Another old question came up, "Is there any defense against atomic missiles?"

The General of the Armies replied, "No sir. A strong air force could keep enemy planes from reaching our shores. International agreements could prevent the establishment of rocket bases close enough to bombard us. Those are our defenses."

On the Senate floor, too, the disquieting problem was debated. It was tossed back and forth during the discussion of the United Nations.

One afternoon "Ole Tawm" Connally roughly chided Senator Taylor for advocating world government.

Senator Ball pulled his long figure out of his chair. He said, "I would like to ask the Senator from Texas, who is so firmly opposed to any step toward world government, how many more world wars he thinks this earth can stand, now that the atomic bomb has been discovered."

The Senator's silence covered the earth.

Chapter XXV

BEFORE the first soft snow of winter fell on Washington, a storm over control of atomic energy swept across the city. It involved the President and split his Cabinet. The storm raged for days in Congress.

The issue was – who would control this terrible force, the military men or civilians?

The Senate Atomic Investigation Committee teetered back and forth unwilling to make up its mind. Chairman McMahon favored civilian control. Ed Johnson and former Admiral Hart wanted the generals and admirals to be in charge.

The military spokesman before the committee was a man almost as fantastic as the atom bomb. He was Major General Leslie R. Groves, an obscure army officer in the Corps of Engineers. After working on the construction of the Army's mazelike office building, the Pentagon, the General was suddenly ordered to take charge of the new Manhattan District.

For fifteen years Groves toiled obscurely as a first lieutenant before he got his promotion in 1934. Ten years later he was the boss of a two-billion-dollar project employing the best scientific minds of America and turning out the greatest destructive force the world has ever known.

Early in the project, General Groves went to the University of Chicago laboratory, where much of the basic work was being done. The conference room had been used an hour earlier by a freshman physics class. The blackboard had not been erased and the symbols were still on in chalk.

General Groves glanced at the board. His eyes brightened. He turned to one of the learned scientists and said heartily, "It's been twenty years since I took physics, but I can understand these things you men are talking about."

There was nothing subtle about the General. In his appearance before the McMahon committee, he proposed a program as militaristic as anything the old *Junker* could have conceived.

He wanted the Army to continue its control of the Manhattan Project until Congress had established a commission and, in his words, "It really has a chance to understand what problems it is going to be faced with."

Senator Vandenberg asked him, "Suppose there is an international decision to outlaw the atomic bomb. Could the world be successfully policed?"

The General's big brown eyes clouded over with skepticism. He shook his head. "I don't think so unless the United States is ready to start war against somebody who has taken the first step to prevent an inspection."

He went on. Inspection was too big a job. "We've got to have inspectors who can go everywhere, who can go into every man's house, and nose into everyone's business throughout the world."

Later, General Groves said lustily, "It's awfully hard to think of the kind of inspectors you'd need – the shrewdest and the sharpest people – who could never forget their national loyalty. I certainly wouldn't recommend any man that I thought was capable to be one of these world inspectors who would ever forget for one minute he was a United States citizen."

The General added virtuously, "I was, of course, brought up on the U. S. first principle."

Senator McMahon had been sizing up the witness like a lawyer at a trial. He said, "Wait just a minute, General. That suggests that if your inspector found some secret works going on in one of our big corporations, he ought not to report it."

The General replied brusquely he would not want any part of it. He said, "You cannot just say that everyone in this country now ought to owe allegiance to some international organization."

He had his own plan to keep the United States as the world's dominant power. He advocated that this country have ten thousand atomic bombs scattered about the country ready to be launched at any aggressor.

McMahon kept after him. Suppose the enemy planted forty bombs in the U. S. and set them off mechanically. What good would our ten thousand bombs be?

General Groves replied stoutly, "The survivors could still win the war."

Senator McMahon pursued him, "How would they know where to launch our ten thousand? Let's assume that country A takes over nation B, a smaller country. From all we can find out, the forty bombs come from this little country. On that suspicion, are you going to launch the ten thousand bombs at country B?"

General Groves plunged on, like some heavy animal trampling the underbrush. He said, "If I were running the government, I certainly would not hesitate very long on that."

McMahon protested, "But they might be innocent."

The General began, "Well, if they are innocent . . ."

Senator Dick Russell of Georgia filled out blithely, "They are out of luck." General Groves glanced at him gratefully.

There was a fascinated, strained look on McMahon's broad face. He said slowly, "In other words, it is too bad for us or too bad for them, the innocent country." The Senator shook his head. "I don't know of any system of morality that would work in that kind of a world."

None of the other Senators on the committee said a word. The two elder statesmen, Connally and Vandenberg, merely chewed their cigars.

Some wanted to know what nations could compete with us.

General Groves replied sarcastically, "I understand that most of these nations say they can't even subsist without money from the United States. So, it's a little difficult for me to see how they can embark on something of this scale so easily. . . . They are going to have to consider how much they will have to reduce the rations of their people, and how much money they are going to have to borrow from the United States to build these plants with which to attack us."

The General stumbled amiably on through the hearings. He

offered six words in defense of military control of atomic energy – "World peace is not guaranteed now."

He advocated a nine-man board of part-time commissioners to control atomic power. The board would be independent of the President or Congress, but its decisions would be subject to a vote of the Joint Chiefs of Staff.

General Groves cheerfully ruled out his most vigorous opponents, the atomic scientists, as commissioners. He said bluffly, "You can't find nuclear scientists who are disinterested. I feel very strongly that no one belongs on such a commission who is interested in any way in anything that will really cross swords with his duty as a member of the commission."

Senator McMahon lifted his eyebrows and asked, "Would your nine-man commission be all civilians?"

"Oh no," the General said hastily, "the military should be on. The bomb is *the* most important of all military weapons."

He warmed up to his subject. The military members should have special qualifications. He said blandly, "They ought to be officers on inactive duty. I don't want a man who has to go to the Secretary of War or Chief of Staff to be told how to vote."

The General plowed on. The decisions of the commission should be reviewed by the Joint Chiefs of Staff.

Senator McMahon attacked from the flank. "Do you think the bomb will lose its military dominance in a year or two?"

Groves replied stubbornly, "No sir."

"Well," the young Senator asked, "do you see any sign that we can think more about the peaceful uses of atomic energy than of the bomb?"

The General answered bluntly, "I don't think we can ever shift to peacetime uses until we are certain there will be no more wars. You cannot have a weapon of this power subject to a civilian majority on a board."

Mr. Vandenberg puffed slowly on his cigar, weighed the balances – war and peace.

Senator Hickenlooper asked, "Who ought to appoint the administrator – the President or the commission?"

The General did not hesitate. "The commission. If he was

named by the President, he would be under his direction."

Senator McMahon injected with a catlike smile on his handsome face, "General, it would seem that the bill of particulars you draw up for the administrator could fit you pretty well."

General Groves smirked, "They would have to argue with me to take it."

The Army, using General Groves (who could be quickly repudiated) as a feeler, had outlined an ambitious program – control of the world's most powerful force by militarists subject to no supervision.

The Navy was more cautious. Its views were presented by the straight-backed, terse Secretary of the Navy, James V. Forrestal. He said briskly, "The military use of atomic weapons must be decided by the Joint Chiefs of Staff. We can re-examine this later . . ." his voice trailed off . . . "perhaps in 1950 if the atomic bomb is abolished by the United Nations."

A light, cheerful room on the fourth floor of the Senate Office Building was a curious setting the day Forrestal testified for an exploration into a dim future with its terrifying scenes. A weapon of two centuries ago, an Indian tomahawk, lay on a bookshelf. The Indian's protection against the supernatural, a small, orange totem pole, leered down on the committee.

It was a young audience sitting in the stiff folding chairs . . . a sprinkling of soldiers, a youthful Catholic priest, a Wave lieutenant, young women taking notes.

Ed Johnson brooded, "I hope war can be stopped, because of the atomic bomb."

Secretary Forrestal said stiffly, "I am aware that wishful thinking might mislead us."

His recommendation was for an atomic commission, composed of the Vice-President, the Secretaries of War, Navy, and State, four full-time members named by the President, and an executive director appointed by the White House. He said smoothly that of course the Army and Navy would have to retain controls over military applications of atomic power. The Secretary warned, "I do not want it to come to pass that someone will be able to say to the military – this is as far as you can go."

Ed Johnson thought out loud again. He boomed gloomily, "Nothing is done to separate military and civilian aspects of this thing, except a vague hope that it is safe to close our eyes to the military use."

Tamping tobacco into his pipe with a thumb, the Secretary strung out his advantage. He added, "You have laws against murder, but people still use revolvers."

He sat puffing his pipe with satisfaction while around the table Senators with frowns on their faces spoke up dourly against entrusting atomic energy to civilians.

Senator McMahon tried to break the mood. He asked Forrestal with almost timid courtesy, "I want your views on putting the responsibility on the President whether to use atomic weapons."

The Secretary commented, "That is too big a responsibility to dump on him."

During this discussion, Secretary of the Interior Harold Ickes slipped quietly into the room. He plopped down at the table and squinted his lively curious eyes at the Senators.

Forrestal left with a parting shot, "We must not limit the military until the world has reached the pattern we all hope for." It was delivered piously. Around the table, the Senators nodded their heads solemnly. McMahon, outnumbered ten to one, let his lips droop disconsolately.

Ickes took the witness chair. He hunched up his shoulders and looked pugnaciously around the table. He spat out the words, "A democracy cannot afford to keep secrets from itself. . . . I object to making a scientist get permission from an army officer to analyze an atom. I hope the day will never come when scientific thinking can be hedged about with petty restrictions." Secretary Ickes sneered over the phrase "petty restrictions."

He went on with a rush, "If a push of a button can destroy a city, no nation can allow this button to be in private hands. . . . We have only a little time to negotiate for world security, and we can't get it with a monopoly of knowledge. The military is suspicious. If you look through military eyes, all you can see is wreckage. And the answer, more wreckage."

An Army corporal stood by the door. His two small children, a boy and a girl, were restless by his side, innocent of all this big talk.

Ickes went on, "We need to have civilian control. I hope our victory will not lead to military control of science and industry. Then we would have co-ordinators of co-ordinators."

The Secretary rumbled happily over the rest of his statement: "I don't think it ought to be a crime to own fissionable material, because I wouldn't know it if I stumbled on it. I might have some on my farm, and I don't want to be put in jail."

The Senators were grateful for the introduction of some humor. Some laughed openly. Others smiled. Ickes catered to the mood, saying, "I don't say anyone who steps up to the counter should get a pound of plutonium."

Senator Hart fussed with his papers, coughed, and asked in his pinched, dry voice, "Do you believe we should disclose to *all* the atomic bomb secret?"

Ickes looked up in surprise. "If that means the nations that fought with us to win the war, YES."

Hart looked primly disapproving. He asked severely, "Who has proposed that the military take over and run atomic energy?"

The Secretary answered, "If no one has, I'd like to put in a negative. Perhaps I cried before I was hurt, but I don't want to be hurt."

At that moment, the supporters of civilian control were losing the hard struggle. The black headlines cutting across the newspapers with stories of division among the Allies, the nameless fears of this unknown creature of science, were clubs in the hands of the Army and Navy.

Senator McMahon was almost ready to admit defeat. The atomic scientists, desperate and with uneasy consciences, would not give up. In their dingy, crowded, fourth-floor walk-up office, they plotted the counterattack.

It was placed with Senator McMahon by the two scientist attachés of the Senate committee, serious Dr. Edward V. Condon, and Jim Newman, the mathematician with a sense of humor.

Chapter XXVI

It was now a fight to the finish. No holds barred. The counter-attack for civilian control moved off boldly.

A gentle man with graying hair and deep-set eyes threw down the challenge to the military. He was Henry A. Wallace, the Secretary of Commerce. Wallace was carefully picked to hit the first blow. He has a dreamy, mystical quality that identifies him with the future.

Wallace came to testify before the Atomic Energy Committee. He looked across the table at the Senators and said slowly, "There is no more important problem before Congress than the control of atomic energy."

Senator McMahon allowed a faint glow of satisfaction to flicker in his eyes. These words were music to him.

The Secretary went on, "The answer may determine whether our civilization and whether the human race itself shall continue to exist."

There were perhaps fifteen young people in the room – all devoted followers of Henry Wallace . . . a pretty, red-lipped college girl, a cadet in blue uniform, two boys with open shirts. They bent their heads forward to hear their prophet.

Wallace moved in to the issue – who shall control atomic development? – by saying, "At no time in the history of the United States has it been more important to follow the constitutional pattern of subordinating the armed services to civilian representatives of the people."

A severe-looking Army captain, the War Department's observer, wrote busily in his notebook.

The Secretary turned on the War Department's pet atomic bill, the May-Johnson bill. "The peculiar wording of the bill would set up the most undemocratic, dictatorial arrangements that have ever, to my knowledge, been proposed to Congress in a major legislative measure." Wallace's voice was soft and reserved.

He swung again, not bothering to look up from his paper. He did not change the easy pace of his reading. The Secretary said, "One of the government contractors at Oak Ridge has stated – with the approval of the War Department – that some five thousand new devices capable of ordinary industrial applications were developed by it. Although the Commerce Department is interested in making these developments available to American business, we can't get any information. . . . Apparently even this matter is still shrouded in military secrecy."

The Army captain was having a hard time keeping up with Wallace's remarks. He gripped his pencil tightly and wrote on hurriedly.

One of the Senators leaned over and asked, "Did you try to get this information from the War Department?"

Wallace was ready with another blow. He looked up from his paper and answered, almost casually, "Yes. General Groves, the Army administrator of the atomic project, turned down our request for information."

Senator Millikin boomed, "I suggest we get to the heart of this, and get General Groves up here. We ought to clear this matter up."

Secretary Wallace read on his warning, "We must insist that atomic energy be used to better the human race and avoid the pitfalls which would lead to the destruction of our civilization and world suicide."

The Senators and Wallace turned back to the terrible, puzzling question of peace (Can it be hoped for? Can dreams be trusted?) and atomic energy. The Secretary teetered back in his chair. A question would be fired at him. He would study for a few seconds, then thoughtfully speak his answer. His followers never took their eyes off this gentle, yet quietly passionate man. Senator Millikin asked, "Doesn't the whole decision rest on whether the biggest nations are sincere in saying they want peace . . . ?"

Wallace looked intently at this solemn man with the large head, almost as though he were following the thoughts still forming in the Senator's mind.

"The question," Senator Millikin insisted stubbornly, "is whether there is a peace on which we can rely."

Wallace's voice took on a new quality. He was a prophet crying out. "This atomic power is so terrible – there has been nothing like it before. It can make a durable peace, or create fear and hatred."

Several days later, the reporters were called into Senator McMahon's office. The Senator looked like the cat who had just swallowed the canary. There was a pleased smile on his face as he said, "I have a letter from the President."

When McMahon read the letter, his good humor was explained. President Truman was completely supporting the civilian control. The letter said:

The atomic control commission should be composed "exclusively of civilians.". . ."The government must be the exclusive owner and producer of fissionable material. . . . It is essential that devices utilizing atomic energy be made fully available for private development through compulsory, nonexclusive licensing of private patents, and regulation of royalty fees to insure their reasonableness. . . . Legislation must assure genuine freedom to conduct independent research and guarantee that controls over the dissemination of information will not stifle scientific research. . . . The commission should be in a position to carry out at once any international agreements relating to inspection, control of production, dissemination of information, and similar areas of international action."

The last line of the letter read, "To your committee – pioneers in legislation of vast promise for all people – there beckons a place in history."

The Senator looked out of his office window over the terrace of the Capitol and down the long green Mall to the shaft of the Washington Monument. It was a bright sunlit day. History beckoned. Atomic power was on its way out of the Army's lockbox.

McMahon had stolen a march on the military by having the letter prepared along lines favorable to the most influential members of his committee. He presented it to Mr. Truman, who took the good-natured view that whatever the boys on the Hill wanted was good enough for him. He signed.

The Army was furious. The Truman letter prevented the generals from lobbying openly against the McMahon bill and civilian control. Their propaganda campaign to revive the May-Johnson bill, which even Ed Johnson referred to sheepishly as the "so-called May-Johnson bill," was stopped in its tracks.

The first big test came the week spring moved in on Washington. It was April. The windows in the big granite government buildings were pried open. Girls in bright new dresses strolled along the Tidal Basin looking dreamily at the cherry blossoms and the boys in uniform. Workmen pruned the dead limbs from the spreading trees on the White House lawn. The air was filled with the fresh new scent of growing things.

Sight-seers were everywhere. They tramped enthusiastically through the gray halls of the Capitol. On Tuesday morning, a little before noon, a crowd of visitors – soldiers in town for the day, mothers with restless children, newlyweds holding hands – stood in the North Wing of the Capitol around a guide.

He pointed to the paintings worked in the colored walls of the alcove and said in his flat, professional voice, "The portraits are of the signers of the Declaration of Independence." The sight-seers craned their necks around to stare.

Out of the corners of their eyes they could see down the hall a nondescript group of perhaps fifteen men and women standing before a white painted door. A sign identified it as the room of the Senate Foreign Relations Committee.

Behind that door, the Atomic Energy Committee was making a final decision. It might be considered one day as important as the decisions made by the signers of the Declaration of Independence. The people lounging awkwardly around the door were the deathwatch . . . reporters assigned to the story.

Noon came and went. The correspondents grew restless. Had something gone wrong? The committee was still in session.

The Senators at their last meeting had passed the Vandenberg amendment by a vote of ten to one. Only Senator McMahon voted against it. He called it military domination of the atom. Then came the mail. Thousands and thousands of letters. The writers were passionately afraid of the power of the atom, and of military control.

The newly organized Committee on Atomic Information had gone to work. Religious and civic groups were contacted. In one day alone church members sent fifteen thousand letters to the McMahon committee . . . against military control of the atom. This was one of the greatest avalanches of mail ever to fall on Washington.

A woman wrote from Los Angeles: "I wish to applaud your valiant efforts to keep the control of atomic energy out of the inefficient, greedy power of the military. We Gold Star mothers demand that Congress, not the military, run the country. Our world doesn't stand a chance for survival unless atomic energy is controlled by the Federal government in the public interest."

A man from Peoria, Illinois, typed: "Ever since the inception of atomic energy, I, like millions of Americans, have watched the action of those people in strategic positions in our government. Most certainly the control of atomic energy belongs to the greatest champions of peace, the people."

A young woman from California told the committee: "Get busy in the name of youth and all that you hold sacred. We, the youth of today, are not ready to die yet and I doubt if you are either."

Some of the other letter writers said:

An Army sergeant: "This is purely a personal expression and I in no way tend to express the feelings of any of my superior officers. It is my sincere hope that the future of science and civilization will not be retarded by shortsighted measures."

From Westfield, N. J.: "If international good will is to be maintained, atomic weapons must not be kept as a private plaything of the army."

From Uvalde, Texas: "The last frontier for killing has been found. Now we should learn to protect."

From New York City: "The atom bomb is being used as another militaristic bugaboo to frighten money out of the taxpayer for the aggrandizement of an undemocratic military clique."

Six clerks had to be brought in to handle the Senate committee's mail. Organization mail came from such oddly assorted groups as the Kiwanis Club of New Britain, the Texas Association of University Students, the Brotherhood of Railway Trainmen, the League of Catholic Women of Boston, the Flatbush Women's Committee. . . .

The volume of communications went up to near one hundred thousand. Only five letters were recorded in favor of the May-Johnson bill.

This day of the deathwatch, the Senate committee was meeting to reconsider its vote on the Vandenberg amendment. The mail had been a persuader. Senator Vandenberg himself does not like to be criticized by respectable people.

At nearly half-past twelve, Senator Vandenberg pulled open the committee door and stepped outside. He smiled jovially at the reporters and held up his hands playfully as they crowded around him. He seemed almost human.

In his deep voice the Senator said cheerfully, "We've passed a new amendment. It's being typed inside."

"Was it your amendment?" he was asked.

Vandenberg bit off the end of his cigar and replied pleasantly, "Yes."

"Was it unanimous?"

The Senator nodded his head and said with a smile, "I hope the reaction is as unanimous in the Senate as in the committee."

"What does the change do, Senator?" the reporters persisted.

Vandenberg said bluffly, "Oh, there is no change in the objective. We found in exploring the situation we had common ideas. I found there was no disagreement on complete, fundamental civilian control and the right of the military to be consulted *only* in matters affecting national security."

The Senator paused. "Security is a matter of language. We've worked that out. You'll get the text inside."

He genially waved good-by and strode confidently down the hall.

(At the Senate committee hearings on confirmation of David Lilienthal as chairman of the atomic energy commission, Senator Vandenberg displayed a dignity and fairness that increased his stature.)

A few minutes later, the big door opened wide and the deathwatch filed in impatiently. The room was one of the old rooms of the Capitol with a gold-framed long mirror on the wall and a dazzling cut-glass chandelier hanging from the ceiling.

There was a triumphant smirk on Senator McMahon's face. He spoke very deliberately to the reporters. "You have the rewritten provision for military liaison. As you will see, the entire emphasis is on civilian control. The atomic energy commission is required to consult the military only on military applications. . . . This is an invitation to the military to restrict itself to its own business. If the generals are not satisfied, they can appeal to the Secretaries of War and Navy."

McMahon added firmly, "I consider this new amendment tends to put the military relation into its proper focus."

At the other end of the table, a committee clerk was whispering enthusiastically, "The other Senators found they were out on a limb and McMahon was holding the trunk. They had come to him. Brother, this was one of the biggest mail campaigns of all time."

On June first, the atomic energy bill came quietly before the Senate. It had been formally approved by the President and the Secretaries of War, Navy, and State. The committee unanimously endorsed its bill.

On this afternoon, only a few correspondents were in the press radio benches. A group of restless schoolchildren and a row of attentive Nisei WACs were in the gallery. On the Senate floor, Arthur Vandenberg was sprawled out comfortably before his desk. Big Ed Johnson was talking about uranium and mining to an audience of one Senator, who was the only one paying any attention. Other committee members who had statements to make rose and gave them calmly. There was no excitement, there were no raised voices.

Finally, Brien McMahon, a solid, heavy, middle-aged man, stood by his desk. "Mr. President, I move the passage of S1717."

The Presiding Officer, stirred out of his drowsiness, said, "All in favor say aye." There was a rumbling murmur of ayes. "All opposed . . ." The Senate was silent.

A startled reporter, suddenly realizing that the atomic energy control bill had passed the Senate, raced out of the gallery. By the time he came back, the Senate had turned to other business.

Thus ended the first act of the struggle for control of the atom.

Chapter XXVII

THE McMahon bill left its safe and friendly home in the Senate and began a stormy journey across the long central corridor of the Capitol.

Congressman Andrew Jackson May reached out a big, flat hand and grabbed the bill. He did not let go of it until he was subpoenaed by the Senate War Investigating Committee and suffered a heart attack.

Andy May's interest in atomic energy had none of the fear and awe of the scientists. He was more practical. This atomic energy looked pretty important, and if anyone was going to have his finger in it, why not Congressman May?

May gave the Senate bill a shrewd look. The only way he could keep his fingers on atomic energy was to keep it under the Army. As chairman of the House Military Affairs Committee, Andy had his ways of "persuading" the Army to do his bidding. The answer to this equation was easy – this business of civilians controlling atomic energy would have to be squelched.

A back-room conspiracy was planned. Representative May did his part ruthlessly and thoroughly. For weeks S1717 gathered dust in his committee. A few desultory hearings were held with Andy serving as Judge and prosecuting attorney. The witnesses favoring civilian control were skillfully hushed. Those on the other side were led on with gracious smiles.

At a time when a chunk of committee members were off on junkets or politicking, May swiftly called up the bill for a vote. He tacked on his amendments and voted the curious creature out by using the proxies of absentees.

The May amendments were cold-blooded amputations. Two military men could be placed on the five-man atomic commission. The Army was authorized to continue its atomic work independently. This meant the Army would continue to control the big atomic plants. The new commission would be left with a formula. The Army was also authorized to keep on making atomic bombs.

The generals were in this plot, too. They acted like little boys behind a barn. Major General Leslie Groves whispered with May, advising him on the amendments.

Rumors, sly hints, dark innuendoes were manufactured and whispered over Washington. "Shh, these scientists are a bunch of damn Communists and they're trying to seize control of the government with this atomic bill. . . . Look, it's all off the record, but we've uncovered a plot. These atomic scientists are nothing but a bunch of dirty Reds."

To give these whispers a breath of realism, the War Department blandly announced it had dismissed several civilian employees from an ordnance laboratory. The Army admitted stiffly they were members of a – well, a union!

This was all John Rankin needed. He sent Ernie Adamson, the counsel for the House Un-American Committee, to Oak Ridge, Tennessee. He'd expose this conspiracy. Rankin licked his lips in anticipation.

This was the strange, unreal setting for the House debate on atomic energy.

One last effort was made to break this mood of suspicion and misgiving.

The National Committee on Atomic Information scheduled an institute on world control of atomic energy one day before the House opened its debate.

Outside, it was a sultry Monday morning in mid-July. But in the Department of Interior, where the institute opened, the halls were cool and hushed and remote.

The auditorium was half full. Most of the audience were women. There was not a Congressman in the room. Registration slips, tossed into a paper box, showed visitors representing the Association of University Women, the League of Women Voters, the Coal Institute, and even the Republican Party. One writer had scrawled, after ORGANIZATION REPRESENTED, "Personal interest."

Henry Wallace, grayer than ever, opened the meeting. He had the secretly gloomy look of a man who knows the world will fall apart on a certain day, but is willing to try to prevent it. The Secretary spoke slowly and deliberately. "This is one of the truly significant gatherings in Washington. Perhaps the newspapers will not think so, but history will." He looked down at the scattering of reporters in the two front rows with a gentle smile.

"Some say the atom bomb came sixty years too soon. The atomic age may bring peace or race suicide. There is no escape from the past. Our decision is how to survive and prosper. We still do not have the legislation for civilian control. Only recently the United Nations commission got to work. This is like a time bomb ticking away."

Wallace stared grimly out into the auditorium. "We cannot afford to wait a whole generation. The people cry for new and revolutionary measures to control new and revolutionary dangers, and they are right. . . . I bid you Godspeed and success."

The next speaker was a crippled young man with burning eyes, Dr. Philip Morrison, the brilliant scientist who had followed the atomic bomb from the laboratories in Chicago to the New Mexico desert, to the Pacific, and then to Hiroshima.

The intense young scientist hobbled up to the speaking stand. Down below, the Russian reporter who had been sitting quietly, even listlessly, during Wallace's talk picked up his fountain pen and notebook. Dr. Morrison was a scientist.

The clear, distinct words took the audience thousands of miles away and back in time. "It was just one year ago that we lay on the desert in the cold hour before dawn to see the sun rise twice." A little shiver passed over the people before him. "Everyone who saw that first test was changed. We were all struck dumb with surprise and awe. The green glaze left on the desert is the footprint of the atomic bomb."

The high, emotional voice told of the take-off of the bomb-laden plane from a tiny island in the Pacific. "The field was quiet. Just a few people out in the middle of the night. One plane . . . a city destroyed in a minute."

He told of his discussion with Dr. Nishina, the leading Japanese physicist. This little old man with twenty-five dollars' worth of equipment had already learned many basic facts of atomic fission.

Dr. Morrison spoke very quietly now. "The secrets of the bomb can be learned by scientific inquiry. The only safety is not in manufacturing more bombs, but in some form of international control. Atomic energy is already tamed. We need political and social controls."

The speaker's mood changed again, to fierce intensity. "It is our commitment as scientists to see we do not appear in history cursed and damned, but as symbols of good."

The debate opened in the House the next afternoon. The chamber was almost half full. Senator McMahon and some of his assistants sat anxiously in a dark corner of the gallery. The reporters had yellow copy paper strewn before them. They hardly knew what kind of story they would file that night.

The debate opened in a curious mood. There was none of the remoteness of the Interior Building auditorium. None of the evangelism of the scientists. Not even the sober earnestness of the Senate discussion.

It was a wild and angry atmosphere, like one of those sudden storms that whip up on a hot and calm day, lashing the trees and brush with furious winds and beating rains.

Rankin and J. Parnell Thomas had tried to stop the atomic bill from coming on the floor. Thomas blustered into the Rules Committee with a report from Ernie Adamson of the Committee on Un-American Activities, raising the old scare.

Chairman Sabath of the Rules Committee was mad. He rose in the House, pointed his finger across the aisle at Thomas, and spluttered, "The gentleman from New Jersey stated the Army should control this astounding and world-shaking new knowledge which may change the fate of all mankind, apparently because some of the civilians named to the Commission might believe in world government, although he did not mention that some military men might believe in military government right here."

Sabath was so angry his voice thickened with his Czech accent. His face grew red as he cried, "To support his fears, the gentleman read to us what he called a report from Adamson. I understand Adamson is a lawyer and not an expert on atomic fission. As a result of this brief investigation, Adamson concludes that the Army should keep permanent control over atomic energy."

The indignant voice went on, "It's difficult to believe this so-called report should be taken seriously by anyone. . . . It will be recalled this man Adamson has denied that the United States has or should have a democratic form of government. He is trying to suggest that these brilliant scientists are not wholly loyal to this country. It is character assassination by innuendo, by insinuation, by association of ideas."

Sabath stared defiantly around him. His little white mustache bristled. Thomas stared back sullenly. Sabath said of the Senate committee: "They passed on every clause and phrase. They discussed and debated it. They agreed on it. That should suffice for any man who has the interest of the country at heart, who is not trying to leave the insinuation. . . ."

Thomas was rising swiftly to a boil. He jumped out of his seat. He yelled, "Just a minute. Are you insinuating that I have not the interest of the country at heart?"

The Speaker kept pounding his gavel for order. Only a few members were paying any attention to the Sabath-Thomas feud. Congressmen were roaming aimlessly up and down the aisles. The cloakroom doors were swinging back and forth. The galleries were almost empty.

Andy May sat at the majority table with a broad smile on his face. As chairman of the Military Affairs Committee, he could control the debate, recognizing whom he chose and for as many minutes as he liked. Across the aisle, Dewey Short, as acting minority head of the committee, could parcel out speaking time to the Republicans.

Sabath spluttered, "This so-called Adamson report is the machination of his warped mind."

Les Arends, the blond, sleepy-eyed Republican whip, stormed against the Senate bill, "This bill sets up the most totalitarian authority in history." (He wanted military representatives on the atomic commission.)

Representative Elston, a little man with a fringe of white hair, burst into oratory. "This bill takes away from the American people their liberties. It is the most dangerous bill ever presented to Congress. They are trying to frighten us into adopting this bill." He was building up to a climax like a Fourth of July fireworks display. "All the secrets will be turned over to . . ." he paused for dramatic effect . . . "civilians. It will place shackles on private industry by making the patents available to . . . the government."

A group of young sight-seers had quietly filed into the gallery. They stared at the scene below with the bewildered look of people who had bought tickets for the theater and had gotten into the burlesque house next door by mistake.

J. Parnell Thomas bellowed, "I see no reason why we should take up this bill in the closing days of the session. There is one man who is more interested in this bill than any other human being. It is Gromyko, the Russian delegate to the United Nations Atomic Commission. He is sitting there in New York laughing up his sleeve. This bill will do the very thing he is trying to do – make it possible for other nations to get all the atomic secrets."

Out of all the noise and confusion there arose a few voices of sanity and reason.

Congressman Johnson, Republican, of California, spoke solemnly. "This bill is a bill for survival. I can't believe we can solve the dilemma by looking at it merely as a military matter. To listen to the discussion here, you'd think that no one of the Military Committee was in favor of the Senate bill. As a matter of fact, a majority of the members are for the bill or a reasonable modification of it.

"If you assume that atomic energy can only be used for military purposes, you might say that civilization itself is ready to crack up and die. . . . If the bomb is controlled or dominated by the Army, you will generate suspicion through the world that we are preparing for the atomic war."

A voice from the floor boomed, "Would the gentleman give it to Russia?"

Johnson answered calmly, "I would not give it to anybody, and the bill does not provide for giving it to anybody."

Congressman Andresen said darkly, "You give it to the scientists."

The House manager for the McMahon bill was a ruddy, gray-haired Texan, Robert Thomason. He is a hard-working, earnest

Representative. His voting record, seen against the background of the other Texans, is surprisingly liberal. When he got the floor he was thoroughly disturbed and angry.

Thomason stormed, "To say the House will not consider the bill at this critical time is indefensible. We'll just see if all the people behind this bill are Communists." The Congressman read off the names of scientists, educators, businessmen, and the members of the Senate committee. He wound up sarcastically, ". . . and Admiral Hart. And there are Secretary of War Patterson and General Eisenhower, two more distinguished Communists, I suppose."

The week of the debate was a confused nightmare. Up in the gallery, Senator McMahon's usually cheerful face sagged into gloom. A number of the scientists sat with long, shocked faces. Every isolationist in the House yowled against the McMahon bill.

Dewey Short became enraged all over again at the British loan and shouted, "What suckers we are. We have given away everything but the dome of the Capitol. It's all give and no take."

Like the end man in a minstrel show, Congressman Harness yelled, "And we're doing all the giving."

Short bowed to him in appreciation.

Rankin and May indulged in a boasting contest. Each claimed he had been the subject of the most criticism, as if it were some badge of honor. Rankin had the last word – "The gentleman from Kentucky has merely had the first dose."

Rankin almost succeeded in killing the bill by offering a motion to send it back to the committee. The House was restless and even while Rankin was going through all the familiar paces of waving his arms and shouting, the impatient roar rumbled, "Vote. Vote."

This was not a record vote. The members merely moved down the aisles to be counted. Most of the Republicans filed past the tellers in favor of the Rankin motion. The final count was 131 to 102 against the motion.

Clare Boothe Luce made a speech. She was the actress in a great role – a trim figure in a black dress with a white blouse. She wore a red rose and her wavy, golden hair brushed her shoulders. All that was lacking was the spotlights.

She said dramatically, "If a man in order to get home safely must walk along the brink of an abyss, he does well to take that trip with his eyes open and in clear weather. We want, if we can, to skirt the abyss of atomic warfare. It seems that the only road home does skirt that abyss; and unhappily it is the totalitarian road of the legislation before us. Let us take it if we must. But, in the name of all our liberties, let us take it with our eyes wide open."

The male members of the House showed their gallantry by reducing the usual loud background murmur a few decibels.

Mrs. Luce was gracious. She praised Senator McMahon. She was severe, calling attention to the several books of printed testimony before the Senate committee, which she had read and her audience had not.

The Congresswoman in a clear, ringing voice asked for passage of S1717 and criticized each House amendment. But after each demand, she added such words as, "Some sections of this bill might have been written by the most ardent Soviet commissar . . . socialistic implications. . . . This bill was forged in the fires of totalitarian action . . . the inherent threats in this necessary bill. . . . If America is eventually sovietized as a result of the wartime discoveries of atomic energy it will be because Congress, in fear and funk, allowed itself to be duped."

The already bewildered Congressmen were all the more confused after her talk. There was quite an argument among the reporters as to whether she was for or against the bill.

As the debate jerked on by spurts, it was obvious the House was held together by one common bond – ignorance. Even the most ardent Administration supporters, when their oratorical phrases wore out, had nothing left to fall back on.

One Southern Representative, who is usually quite positive, said plaintively, "I spent much time listening to the debate. I find myself in the same position as 90 per cent of the House, in a state of general confusion."

Another spoke up sadly, "I am inflicted with indecision. I wish atomic energy could be placed back in the secrets of the universe."

In a final dreary action, the House passed the bill to get it out of the way. It was littered with amendments.

That night, the National Committee for Civilian Control of

Atomic Energy worked over an outraged statement. It was signed by such an assorted group as bankers, newspaper and magazine publishers, religious leaders, and college presidents.

The statement condemned these House Amendments:

Placing military men on the commission and permitting the Army to manufacture atomic bombs independently.

Removing the authority of the commission to allocate funds for private research.

Striking out safeguards to protect scientists from "arbitrary charges."

Senator McMahon and his assistants were already planning their strategy. It was based on the scenes they saw in the House gallery. The plan was for the Senate members of the conference committee on S1717 to hold a forum for the House members.

The conference committee met in Andy May's office behind closed doors, in deference to the House. Senator Vandenberg went over the arguments for civilian control point by point. Little by little, the Senators won over one, then another of the House members. The Senators generously made concessions to the Representatives on every minor point, and held the big issues until the last.

There was an unexpected break for Senator McMahon. The Senate War Investigating Committee announced it was summoning Andy May to answer questions on his connection with the Garsson munitions empire. That evening, May's physician announced he had had a heart attack and would be confined to his bed for several days. Andy did not return to the conference committee or the floor of the House.

When the bill went back to the House from the conference committee, the Senators had won on every major point. The only bow to the military was an amendment placing a general in charge of the Division of Military Control, an administrative section of the atomic commission.

The debate in the House this time was short. The same loud voices said the same things over again. But the House was tired. The Representatives were sick of argument. They wanted to go home. The revised McMahon bill passed.

Atomic energy had come of legal age!

Chapter XXVIII

(On the day President Roosevelt died, American foreign policy was a magic formula. It envisioned a brave new world of peace. It was a religion and a hope.

Mr. Roosevelt died during the brief honeymoon of the victors. Harry Truman and Jimmy Byrnes inherited the stresses and strains of the postwar world and its terrible need for leadership. Under them, foreign policy jolted along like a mule-drawn wagon. Often it faltered and changed its course.

The story was not contained in the State Department alone. It took reporters to the White House, the Senate, Henry Wallace's office, and the War and Navy Departments. Each had its part to play in the dawn of the atomic age.)

THE State Department is an ancient and dingy gray building on Pennsylvania Avenue just west of the White House. The checkerboard tiled halls are worn with the tread of years. The wooden slat doors lining the corridors reach only part way down to the floor and give the building the absurd appearance of a public toilet.

The Department has an atmosphere all its own. It is nothing like the air-cooled elegance of the Social Security Building or the remoteness of the long and quiet halls of the Interior Department. The State Department has a mood of aged dignity and decorum. It is a fussy old maiden lady who strongly disapproves of these giddy times.

The Department's press room has pale green walls and little booths for the regular correspondents. There is none of the normal hubbub found in the cramped White House press room across the alley. The reporters speak quietly and talk learnedly about such little known corners of the world as Albania and Mongolia. Foreign languages are spoken as familiarly as jitterbug lingo at the corner drugstore.

Across the way in the White House, the reporters play a raucous game of poker, take a nip of whiskey to warm them on a cold morning, and listen to the World Series. In the State Department, the correspondents, for that is what they are called, play more intellectual games – chess and fan-tan. The desk drawers are jammed with diplomatic reports. None of them hides a half-full whiskey jug. During the World Series broadcasts, the men and women were arguing over Yugoslavia.

The dean of the correspondents is Larry Todd, a thin man with a pinched face and red complexion. He is an encyclopedia of diplomatic information and his questions at press conferences are carefully thought out. Todd writes for an audience he never sees. He is the correspondent for Tass, the Russian news agency.

The chief British correspondent is Paul Scott Rankine, an irritating little man with a talent for double-edged questions. The French reporter is Jean Davidson, the keen and vivacious son of sculptor Jo Davidson. The press room includes three very affable Chinese, a solemn black-haired young lady who was secretary to Maxim Litvinov when he was the Russian Ambassador to Washington, a sophisticated girl who sends stories to a Greek-American newspaper, and a pipe-smoking Phi Beta Kappa who reports for the Communist *Daily Worker*. The most important correspondent is probably Bob Hightower, the soft-spoken, studious young man who is diplomatic correspondent for the Associated Press. His stories set the tone for State Department reporting.

The press conferences twice a week are a chance for the reporters to get a somewhat blurred peek at American foreign policy and to question the State Department spokesmen. These sessions are conducted in the carefully obscure language of diplomacy. The tenser the conflicts become, the vaguer the words used by State Department officials. They give a reporter the odd sensation of having intruded into a world of fantasy.

At a time when the United States and Yugoslavia were glaring at each other, the correspondents were trying to find out just how far Washington would go. Would the case be taken to the United Nations?

Undersecretary of State Dean Acheson said politely that our demands were being complied with. We would apply to the United Nations only if there was a threat to peace. If our demands were complied with, we would presume that was not the case.

When the Navy sent an aircraft carrier steaming down the Mediterranean near the time Greece was voting on return of the monarchy and Turkey and Russia were squabbling over the Dardanelles, a correspondent asked, "Is there any significance to this trip?" Acheson replied with deliberate casualness that the carrier's tour was nothing more than a "good will and courtesy tour."

This is the language of diplomacy. To interpret it, the correspondent must watch the inflection of the voice, the droop of an eyelid, and the length of a pause. The reporter must look beyond the words to find the objective of a casual conference remark.

State Department announcements are sometimes as flamboyant and inconclusive as political campaign oratory. The Department's note of October 18, 1946, to Yugoslavia might have been turned out jointly by Senator Bilbo and the Department's expert on long words.

In sensational, headline-catching words, the Department accused Yugoslavia of holding American citizens without trial and as forced laborers. Real, blood-boiling charges. The Yugoslav Embassy denied that the persons they were holding were American citizens. They were either naturalized or Americans of foreign descent who had left this country during the depression. The ties binding them with American citizenship were stretched very thin. The Embassy charged the individuals held had been Nazi agents. There was nothing in the State Department note to indicate the status of these "Americans." The inference was that they were visitors, or officials or relief workers.

Correspondents have other opportunities to pick up the State Department's policy — at off-the-record conferences, and by reading so-called "confidential" cables.

The two men who handle the day-by-day press relations look amazingly unlike diplomats. Mike McDermott, Secretary Byrnes's press agent, looks like a retired wrestler who has mellowed and grown moderately prosperous running a tavern. Lincoln White, head of the Department's press division, is a tall, beamish young man with the exuberant manner of a shoe salesman. Both are masters of the "planted story," an old State Department technique. If they want to stir up headlines for a pet project of a higher-up, they drop the right words in the right correspondents' ears. They can execute a crisis with remarkable ease. Just a few words and the world will quiver with anxiety. Mike and Linc are often the "diplomatic authorities" and "sources close to the State Department" quoted in dispatches.

The Secretary of State during the first two years of the Truman administration, James F. Byrnes, of Charleston, South Carolina, is a small and nervous man with a pinched, florid face, a long nose, tight lips, and little blue eyes. Wisps of white hair lie indifferently across his head.

Secretary Byrnes was always bustling from one anxious situation to another and never appeared completely relaxed. He would pop through the door into his press conferences as though he had been hurled out of a cannon. While questions were being asked, he wrinkled his forehead, pursed his lips, and stared intently at the ceiling. As he talked, he fingered his watch chain or tapped on the table. As soon as the conference was over – whisk – and Secretary Byrnes had hurried back through the door.

At his press conferences, the Secretary was transparent. If he felt sure of himself, he was cheerful and expansive. Upon his return from the Moscow meeting, Byrnes gave so much information, including secret agreements made at Yalta, that a startled correspondent asked if it were off the record. The Secretary beamed and said not at all. He congratulated the reporters on their questions.

But when Byrnes was uncertain of himself or under attack, he was irritable and snapped back in monosyllables. He did not enjoy these meetings with reporters and showed it.

Jimmy Byrnes has a quick wit and temper, a not excessive

amount of Southern charm, and a sharp mind. He seems to enjoy hard work and takes himself and his ambitions quite seriously. Byrnes has many of the characteristics of a professional politician. He is agile in changing sides of an argument to be on the winning team. He has all the intolerance of a campaign orator for his opponents. In addition, he has a brusque temper and rarely forgives an enemy.

Jimmy Byrnes is essentially a politician, an expert craftsman at the business. But he lacks the imagination and boldness that made Franklin Roosevelt an artist in this field.

Somewhere there is a line dividing politics and statesmanship. Whether Byrnes crossed this line is a decision history must make. A politician knows how to gauge the pressures and how to bow gracefully to the strongest. A statesman knows how to arrange the pressures to fit his own program, and he has the courage to defy them all.

As Senator Byrnes of South Carolina, Jimmy scurried around Capitol Hill lining up support for Roosevelt's program. He was never considered a full-blooded New Dealer, but rather a willing and able field commander for the Democratic administration. With cheerful and flattering words, he talked sullen Senators into going along. He found the happy compromises – an amendment, a clause reworded in a bill, a patronage appointment. He knew almost by intuition the weak points of the opposition.

There was never any necessity for Senator Byrnes to show outstanding leadership. Franklin Roosevelt did not like to have strong leaders around Washington. He was the leader. Byrnes was the handy man. If Jimmy had decisions to make, he consulted either Mr. Roosevelt or Bernard Baruch, the towering, white-haired financier. Baruch discovered Byrnes as a young court reporter in South Carolina and has been his guardian angel.

President Roosevelt rewarded Jimmy for his Senate chores and placed him on the Supreme Court. During the war emergency, Mr. Roosevelt needed him again. Jimmy obediently took off his black robe and gave up the title "Mr. Justice" for "Assistant President." As Director of the Office of War Mobilization, he dived into the center of the hubbub. When there was trouble on the Hill, Byrnes rushed into a White House limousine and used

Senate Secretary Les Biffle's office for hurried conferences. If a war agency was breaking down with internal conflicts, Jimmy interviewed all concerned and made a report to the President. If there were unpopular decisions to make, Jimmy announced them. The brain trusters did the planning. Mr. Roosevelt made the decisions. Byrnes saw that they were executed. He was a combination buffer, errand boy, and hatchet man for the White House.

His introduction to foreign affairs was due to his early talent, shorthand reporting. When the President was packing for the Crimea Conference, he remembered Jimmy had been a court reporter and brought him along. FDR dictated secret memoranda to him.

Byrnes, like many other men who had worked long and selflessly for FDR, thought he should be Mr. Roosevelt's running mate in 1944. He imagined, along with several other prospective nominees, that he was the White House "favorite." Byrnes sulked at the selection of Harry Truman. His off-the-record comments on Truman were scornful. A few weeks before the President's death, Byrnes packed up and went back to South Carolina. He saw no future in being a whipping boy for the White House.

When the new President moved in, Jimmy scurried back to Washington and hung around the White House like an expectant father. He obviously hoped to be the power behind the throne. All this was embarrassing to President Truman, who did not like Byrnes well enough for that and resented the inference that he needed a "guardian."

George Allen made one of his adroit suggestions. Reshuffle the deck. Put Byrnes in as Secretary of State. That would remove Edward Stettinius, whom the President instinctively disliked because he was a big businessman from New York. This shuffle would please the Senate and keep Jimmy busy.

Secretary Byrnes seemed to enjoy his job more when he was away from Washington at the conferences. When he was in his office he was wedged in between conflicts and indecisions. The career diplomats never accepted him. He never knew when the White House was going to jerk the props out from under him. The Army and Navy kept prodding him.

Jimmy Byrnes's shadow was Ben Cohen, the shy, intellectual

member of the old New Deal team of Corcoran and Cohen. Ben was the idea man and Corcoran the aggressive salesman. In every photograph of Byrnes at Paris or Lake Success, Cohen was at his side staring apprehensively at the Secretary. Cohen looks like an anxious mouse. He dresses plainly in dark blue or gray suits. His eyes are soft and gentle.

He is a congenital pessimist, and certainly his job at the State Department was no inspiration for blitheness. He seemed to resign himself to defeat and frustration, even seeming to enjoy his helplessness. To his old friends, Cohen unburdened himself and complained that he had been "tied down" by career diplomats and military brass hats.

He gained his greatest fame when he had the aggressive Irishman Tommy "the Cork" Corcoran carrying the ball for him. Ben needed his punch, and Tommy needed Ben's brains. After the team broke up, Ben worked quietly and inconspicuously for Byrnes in the Office of War Mobilization. He did a good job. At the State Department he was in a strange and fanciful world, where he needed some of Tommy's charm and his stubborn chin.

Dean Acheson, the Undersecretary of State or second-in-command, is one of the most popular men in the Department. From a distance he looks like a villain in an English play. He is a tall, carelessly groomed man with one of the most villainous mustaches in captivity. It is sandy, almost red, and bushy, with the ends tapering down to points. His friendly, intelligent blue eyes belie the villain.

The Undersecretary enjoys the confidence of correspondents because his conferences are witty, friendly, and, quite often, frank. He never takes offense at tough questions or loses his good humor. His conferences have much of the same intellectual give-and-take as Mr. Roosevelt's and none of their grimness.

One morning Acheson neatly prevented what might have been a diplomatic crisis. His press conference, scheduled for eleven o'clock, was unexpectedly postponed. The correspondents were buzzing with a report that Soviet Ambassador Nikolai Novikov had been held incommunicado at LaGuardia Airport because he would not sign a customs declaration. As a diplomat, he did not have to. The Soviet Embassy was furious and sent a stiff note to the Department.

Sitting in the press conference room waiting for Acheson, the reporters concocted rumors . . . Acheson had been called to the White House in this crisis . . . he was talking to Secretary Byrnes by transatlantic telephone.

Twenty minutes later, Acheson strolled casually into the room, smiled at the crowd, and said, "I was delayed reading a most inspirational comment in *Punch*, the British humor magazine." He spread the publication on the table and read with a straight face, "It is reliably reported from Washington that a state document to be released by a newspaper columnist has come into the hands of the State Department."

His blue eyes twinkled. The room broke into chuckles.

Acheson readily admitted the Department had received a protest from the Soviet Embassy. He was asked, "What do you know about the incident, and what do you intend to do?"

He replied, "I will have to give you the celebrated answer of Dr. Johnson – 'Ignorance, madam, pure ignorance.' "

The atmosphere of crisis was broken. One of the reporters going down the winding stairs commented sadly, "I haven't got anything to write about now."

Acheson is a well-bred Easterner, Yale, class of 1915, Delta Kappa Epsilon, and Episcopalian. He chose law instead of diplomacy, and was for two years private secretary to that great liberal, Supreme Court Justice Brandeis. From the Justice he acquired strong convictions about civil liberties.

At one of the many cocktail parties he attends, Acheson was approached by a Midwestern Congressman who grumbled, "When are you going to get rid of the Communists in the State Department?"

The Undersecretary replied politely, "I am not aware of any Communists being in the Department. If by Communists you mean liberals, I shall certainly do all I can to keep them."

The career diplomats, backbone of the Department, are difficult creatures to trap, identify, and describe. They will duck into the men's room to avoid a reporter walking down the hall. They rarely say anything for the record. They run in their own small circles like some shy and nearly extinct breed of animals.

The career men are preponderantly wealthy and aristocratic. Their economic and social outlook has not changed much since 1900. They entered diplomacy when it was regarded as a "career for gentlemen." Independent wealth is almost a necessity for a diplomat, because he must do a great deal of the extravagant kind of entertaining.

The careerists have a stranglehold on the Department. Even their bitterest critics admit sadly the State Department would fall apart if all the career boys were thrown out. The reason is that the careerists have control of the key jobs, the so-called political desks, such as the French desk, the Russian desk, and so on. The career men have the records, secret cables, and memoranda on their particular area. Everyone else in the Department must come to them for information. Many of the career diplomats have been squatting on their own private corner of the world for years.

No little gadget like the atomic bomb is going to make them change their minds about the prejudices they have carefully tended over the years.

One of the career employees is a czaress in her own right. She is Mrs. Ruth Shipley, Director of the Passport Division. Her word is law and even Jimmy Byrnes was afraid of her. She approves or turns down applications for passports on the basis of voluminous confidential files relating to the loyalty or lack of it of government personnel and public figures.

Many high officials have sputtered and fumed because Mrs. Shipley refused a passport for one of their key men to travel abroad. Her name has been mentioned heatedly at cabinet meetings. Mr. Roosevelt would laugh and remark how odd it was that a mere woman could bluff his cabinet members. But he did not try to budge her either.

One White House assistant who has clashed with Mrs. Shipley many times says, "The trouble with her, damn it, is that she is right sometimes."

Franklin Roosevelt, who had much the same social and economic background as the career men, did not trust them. Harry

Truman, the small-town judge from the Midwest, resents them and instructed Jimmy Byrnes to "clean house." The Secretary never quite got around to it. In fact, at the Paris Conference, smiling meticulously by his side, was one of the deans of the career clique, James Clement Dunn.

Three of the Assistant Secretaries of State, independently wealthy men themselves, have bucked the career men. One is Bill Benton, the former advertising man and partner of Chester Bowles. His job is selling American foreign policy. His greatest difficulty is that no one ever tells him what it is.

Assistant Secretary Will Clayton, who is in charge of economic affairs, is a practical businessman. He was the Texas cotton king and a conservative who occasionally supported Republicans. Clayton is an intelligent and shrewd operator who lives in the twentieth century and has some of the ablest young men in Washington working for him. Clayton hit it off well with President Truman and Congress.

Spruille Braden, Assistant Secretary for Latin American Affairs, is a huge, bluff man who is a chain smoker. He punched back blow for blow against an alliance of career man George S. Messersmith, Ambassador to Argentina, and the military services. Braden insisted that Argentina must become a democratic "good neighbor" while the Army and Navy, with Messersmith's help, were demanding that the United States form a military alliance with dictator Perón.

This is the State Department, where even the elevator operators wear starched handkerchiefs in their breast pockets.

Chapter XXIX

(After every armed struggle, the victorious warriors are strong and confident. They are public heroes. But where are the new worlds, the new fields to conquer? In the early history of man, war was so eternal that conquering generals ran society. As civilization developed and became more complex, the warriors became the servants of politicians and statesmen and dictators in the more highly organized nations. They were robbed of their ancient power. But after the Second World War, the leaders of the mightiest Army and Navy lost none of their authority.)

JAMES F. BYRNES walked into his new job with a springy step, a happy smile, and blissful ignorance.

His head was full of wonderful dreams. The position of Secretary of State would give him the character of statesmanship he had always missed. The country was united on foreign policy. Even the Republicans were going along. The world was looking to the United States for guidance. The grateful citizens of the forty-eight states might look on the man who led them confidently to a new era of international friendship as a candidate for President in 1948.

Secretary Byrnes was given a rude, awakening jolt upon his return from the Moscow Conference.

He was happily unaware of the future when he held his first news conference after coming back to Washington. Jimmy was in high good humor. He expected to be praised on all sides for doing a good job. The reporters had never seen him so friendly before.

When the Secretary trotted across the street to the White

House, Admiral Leahy growled at him, "Jimmy, what in the hell did you get from those Russian so-and-sos in return for what you gave them?"

In the Senate, Arthur Vandenberg, Jimmy's friend, criticized American foreign policy and urged a tough line with Russia.

President Truman was stiff and cold toward his Secretary of State. At a White House press conference a few days after Byrnes's return, a reporter started to ask the President a routine question. He began, "Do you support the State Department policy of . . ."

Mr. Truman's lips tightened. He snapped at the reporter before he could finish the sentence, saying there was no foreign policy unless it was approved by him. The State Department, the President said firmly, could have no policy of its own.

Jimmy Byrnes discovered a scheme well under way, engineered by Admiral Leahy, to toss him out and bring in a general as Secretary of State.

A sadder and wiser Secretary Byrnes found out that a lot of people were interested in foreign affairs and were just waiting for Mr. Roosevelt to get out of the way before they jumped in. While Jimmy Byrnes was across the seas, they had cut the ground out from under him.

Secretary Byrnes did not need any divining rod to locate the strongest pressures. His coattails were scorched from the hot breath of the Army and Navy.

The services had poked their heads into foreign affairs and had no intention of getting out. Their instrument was Harry S. Truman, the World War I captain of Battery D.

His views on the world when he became President were pretty much those of the man on the street in Independence, Missouri. He was curious about the Russians. The British annoyed him. He was bored and bewildered by the details of foreign policy. During the Palestine controversy, delegations of all kinds descended on him. On the fourth day, he told a visitor, "I wish someone would come to talk to me about the United States." It was a wholly natural reaction to him.

President Truman turned to Admiral Leahy, who had been with Mr. Roosevelt at the conferences with Churchill and Stalin.

The venerable Admiral taught his willing pupil the ancient doctrine of all professional military men – the only sure way a nation can be secure is to have the biggest damn army and navy; the professional officers are practical men with wide experience around the world and thus better able to handle relations between nations than striped-pants diplomats.

All armies and navies must have some potential enemy in mind as an excuse for their existing. Admiral Leahy among friends casually referred to Russia as "our enemy," and said gruffly that that kind of people just thought our "appeasement" was a sign of weakness. You had to treat them rough and make them like it.

Jimmy Byrnes did what was natural for him with his experience in politics. He could not lick the Army and Navy, so he would join them. They would become allies. Secretary Byrnes bowed, and opened the door to the services.

He could not have expected the results.

By early October of 1946, the cautious Foreign Policy Association warned: "The United States now relies on military and naval strength in achieving its aims of foreign policy to a greater degree than ever before in its peacetime history, and the War and Navy Departments have an important part in shaping America's foreign relations. . . . So long as the President encourages the military to share in the formulation and execution of foreign policy, Congress will have the serious responsibility of laying the foundations for a consistent and sound military policy. . . . The President, in turn, bears the responsibility of making sure that military agencies do not gain domination over our foreign policy."

The *Washington Post* said tartly, "Some of our military men seem to think their department is the State Department. They behave and itch like frustrated diplomats."

The brass hats were showing off their muscles. Admiral "Bull" Halsey put the military philosophy very simply. He said, "It's nobody's damn business where we go. We can go anywhere we please."

Not to be outdone by the Navy, General "Hap" Arnold shouted, "The first line of defense for the United States is no longer the Atlantic and Pacific Oceans but the Arctic. Attack, if it comes, will come over the North Pole." (No one had to be clairvoyant to figure out his fist was shaking at Russia. It was the only nation with access to the North American continent by way of the North Pole.)

Vice-Admiral Denfeld, who was being prepared for the Navy's top job, Chief of Naval Operations, chorused, "We must be ready to defend ourselves at the drop of a hat. Until world-wide peace is an established reality, we must maintain an Army and Navy sufficient to lend firm conviction to the voice of our statesmen at the international tables."

In the period of a few months, the military gained a firm foothold in the Department. Policy in the occupied areas of Germany and Japan was dominated by generals. General MacArthur in Japan coldly ignored policy directives from Washington. The services began seriously advocating that Japan be developed into America's Far Eastern base with the explanation that "after all, the Japs are good soldiers."

The diplomatic rolls revealed military titles – Lieutenant General Walter Bedell Smith, the Ambassador to Moscow; Admiral Kirk, Ambassador to Belgium and Minister to Luxembourg; General Holcomb, Minister to the Union of South Africa, and General Hines, Ambassador to Panama.

While Jimmy Byrnes was busy snapping at the Russians over the conference table in Paris, the Army and Navy in Washington were gnawing away at the foundations of the State Department.

There were countless arguments with the services over military proposals to establish bases all over the world, and to send fleets and air squadrons on muscle-flexing "missions." The Army and Navy competed with each other. The Navy wanted to send a whole bristling fleet unit down the Mediterranean to impress the Greeks at the time of their elections and to buck up Turkish resistance to Soviet pressure. This was pared down to one ship, ironically the carrier *Franklin Roosevelt*. Secretary of the Navy Forrestal proudly announced that the Navy was "an instrument of foreign policy." Not to be outdone, the Army wanted to send a squadron of B–29's built to accommodate atomic bombs soaring around the world.

Each time the State Department said "No" to War or Navy Department proposals, Admiral Leahy slipped out of the White

House and across the street. He cautioned against interfering with "military preparedness plans." The President would not like it.

Oddly enough, the business press kept the closest tabulation on the growing influence of the Army and Navy.

Business Week reported in September of 1946: "Quietly, behind the scenes, Washington's ideas are beginning to cluster around the theme of industrial mobilization for war. Top policy men are beginning to think in terms of gearing industry for a quick shift back to a war basis. When President Truman goes before Congress in the spring, he will ask money and authority for continued stock-piling of critical materials, for a program of stand-by munition plants, for educational munitions contracts to industry. He may ask permanent authorization for a civilian mobilizing-planning agency. . . . It's not impossible to envisage the day when a spokesman for military needs sits in on every major business decision."

At the same time, the *American Machinist* announced: "Legislation setting up a five-year industrial preparedness program will be proposed in January to the 80th Congress. Army-Navy Munitions Board is working out a preliminary outline."

A month later, *Aviation News* wrote: "The Pentagon is worrying about relations with Russia far more than the civilians. As a result, Washington news men are running into a curtain of secrecy that is reminiscent of wartime."

The top military planners were the four members of that mysterious and powerful body known as the Joint Chiefs of Staff. It was created under the wartime emergency powers given President Roosevelt by Congress. The chairman is Admiral Leahy.

A brief, disturbing look at the Joint Chiefs was given Congress by the testimony of a former member, Admiral Ernest J. King. He told the Senate War Investigating Committee that the Joint Chiefs considered themselves an agency of the President and were not responsible to the civilian Secretaries of War and Navy. It was a "common practice" of the Joint Chiefs to mark the files "top secret" whenever other government agencies of Congressional committees tried to poke civilian noses into their business. In the case of the $135,000,000 Canol project to bring oil and aviation gasoline to Alaska, the Joint Chiefs accepted the report of a subordinate military group without studying it, and completely disregarded the protests of the War Production Board and Petroleum Administration for War.

Military penetration into foreign policy broke out into the open where correspondents could report it in October of 1946. The story began when War Department press agents called reporters and advised them not to miss the press conference of Assistant Secretary for Air Stuart Symington. He would have "some real news."

In the Pentagon conference room, Symington, a tall, handsome, self-confident Missourian, read a statement: "The flight of the B–29 *Dreamboat* over the Arctic wastes is but another proof that General Spaatz is right when he stresses the danger of an attack over the Polar regions, this because of the far shorter distances that way to the United States from all industrial countries."

Boris Krylov, the small, neat Russian correspondent, was sitting in the fourth row. His face was expressionless during the reading. Symington read on briskly, "In the future, if America is attacked, our retaliatory attacks will be immediate. It will be necessary to either drop or land troops."

Then Symington dropped his own bomb, saying, "The air forces will send a group of B–29's on a flight around the world in two or three weeks, *if* the State Department approves." This flight would cross Egypt and India and move up the Pacific to the Arctic.

The Assistant Secretary read further, "The specific reason for this flight is to work out technical problems of moving large groups of large planes long distances. The purpose is to train and maintain an air force capable of carrying out an assignment as may be required under the United Nations."

The first question shot out. "You say this flight will take place, if the State Department approves. Isn't that putting pressure on the Department?"

Symington smirked, "Oh, we wouldn't do that."

A correspondent said sarcastically, "Would the flight involve courtesy calls?"

The Assistant Secretary knew he was being heckled and he did not like it. He tried the bland approach used by masters of ceremonies to quiet annoying voices from the crowd. He said coldly, "If the State Department requests them."

Had the White House been consulted? he was asked. Symington was frigid by this time, answering that he saw no reason to consult the White House.

Every correspondent in the room resented the patronizing manner of the man up front and went to work on him. This can be a pretty rough deal for even the most polished and experienced official. Symington was neither.

Another question was, "Could this flight be compared to the trip of the carrier *U.S.S. Roosevelt* through the Mediterranean? Does the Army expect the same criticism of waving the big stick?" The question was asked with a disarming pleasantness.

The Assistant Secretary was sulky. He replied stiffly the flight would not be made unless it was approved.

A reporter inquired, "The Secretary of the Navy said fleet operations in the Mediterranean could be considered a part of foreign policy. Are the air forces thinking of the potential use of B–29's in the same manner?"

Symington rose enthusiastically to the bait. He dropped his defensive attitude and said proudly, "We like to think of the air forces as an instrument of national policy."

One of the older correspondents asked, "Will the flight of the B–29's allay or increase the fears of the world?"

The Assistant Secretary froze again. He replied, "What we want to do is to further military training. Other matters are outside of the War Department." He wore one of those irritating, distant smiles that are usually saved for poor relatives or idiots.

He was asked, "How do you consider this flight will help the United Nations as you suggested in your statement?"

Symington replied, "We have a responsibility to the United Nations."

The correspondent kept after him. "I'm sorry, I don't understand how this is a responsibility to the United Nations."

The Assistant Secretary snapped, "Perhaps you had better see me later, and I will explain the details. Under the United Nations we have a responsibility to further the development of our military knowledge."

A little blond girl reporter in the front row spoke up. "Is this flight in the interests of peace?"

Symington was mad. He had taken about as much as he could. He said to the girl with elaborate politeness, "Do you think so?"

She murmured that she was not being interviewed. He said coldly, "This is not a matter for the War Department."

By that time, the whole room was in a mood of rising irritation. Some thoughtful aide closed the conference.

At his news conference several days later, Undersecretary of State Dean Acheson went as far as he thought he could go. He said mildly he had only heard of the flight vaguely, and did not know where it was going, when, or how. He still did not know. The air forces had never made any official request to the Department. The correspondents thought they were on the trail of a real controversy. Symington had spoken out of turn on foreign policy. Would he be given the boot like Henry Wallace?

President Truman was asked for comment. He said casually that no decision had been made on the flight yet. Then he went on gaily to announce that he was sending Admiral Leahy and a squadron to Chile to represent him at the inauguration of a new president.

If the President was not concerned, much of Washington was. This was an open attempt by the Army to get its oar in foreign policy. The well-bred *Washington Post* in an editorial labeled "Muscle Flexing" said, "Inevitably the tour would bring distrust and suspicion of our motives. This would not be a logical extension of our firm policy toward Russia. It would be a form of braggadocio which, instead of calming war jitters, would do the opposite."

The Navy chose a different method, more discreet and more dramatic, to express itself.

One dim and cloudy afternoon of early autumn, a sleek naval transport lay beside a pier in the Washington Navy Yard. The blue-gray ship had been scrubbed until it gleamed in the mist. This was the *U.S.S. Burleson*, back from the Pacific after atomic bomb tests at Bikini with a hold full of atomic-sick animals.

A string of reporters shuffled along behind an officer and climbed up a ladder. The procession squeezed through narrow, white-painted corridors reeking with the familiar antiseptic smell. This was a small group – the tall stooping Swede who writes for scientific magazines, the regular gang from the Navy press room, two intent Englishmen, and a small, red-haired girl.

Once inside the wardroom, the correspondents were handed a crisp, five-page statement, which said, "Deaths may be expected even months after the animals are exposed to atomic radiation sickness. Animals affected become apathetic, lose appetite, appear weak and are prone to develop secondary infection causing death. . . . Radiation sickness is painless in its effects on animals. Since the animal has no knowledge of the disease, there is none of the mental anguish that assails a human being. The animal merely languishes and either recovers or dies a painless death. Suffering among the animals was negligible."

Vice-Admiral Blandy, deputy chief of naval operations, strode into the room as a captain barked, "Attention." He nodded with an impersonal cheerfulness to the group, and began speaking. His words rose clearly above the throbbing of the engines: "The best way to avert war is to be prepared for it. Our slipshod methods in the past have resulted in great loss of life and dislocation of our economy. We have a chance to prevent the next war – I do not refer to any specific war – by preparing for it."

A junior officer by his side nodded gravely. He looked like a younger brother – the same stiff and efficient bearing.

Admiral Blandy turned over the conference to the medical officers. These were men from another world. There were no hard creases in their uniforms or rows of ribbons on their jackets. Their coats were wrinkled. Their eyes were alive and their words tumbled out enthusiastically.

A reporter said, "A scientist died at Oak Ridge the other day from atomic radiation. Have you had any successful results in curing atomic sickness in human beings?"

One of the medical officers replied, "At Hiroshima and Nagasaki, individuals by the thousands were exposed, but the treatment was primitive and disorganized. Until the Bikini tests, no attempt was made to treat experimentally early in the disease. We hope we will learn methods to save those exposed to moderate amounts of radiation."

The medic stressed the word "moderate," and added thoughtfully, "I do not believe it will ever be possible to cure those with heavy doses of radiation."

The correspondents were leaning forward. Some were so absorbed they neglected their notes. The doctor was asked, "Is there any cure for radiation?"

He answered, "No, only against the effects such as anemia. I hope our discoveries will prove useful in the case of some Japanese victims. Some are hanging between life and death."

The officer answering most of the questions was Captain Shields Warren, a reserve officer who was returning soon to his university laboratory. His bright eyes looked through an individual, as though staring at some distant, faraway point. He spoke with a boyish enthusiasm.

A reporter inquired, "What do you call a heavy and a moderate dose of radiation?"

Captain Warren commented, "That depends upon the animals. Insects can stand up to 100,000 R units. If man gets from 300 to 500 R units, that is sufficient to kill. The rat is more resistant."

The Swede asked for Captain Warren's views on sterility. He answered, "Anyone ill from radiation would be harmed. The sex cells of the body are more sensitive to radiation. It is possible for animals or man not to be killed, but to have the sex cells destroyed. In some animals, there is evidence of atrophy of the testes. The mice were not harmed."

Another officer said cheerfully, "We are very happy to report very few animals died of accidental causes. Almost all died from atomic radiation."

Captain Warren explained that all of the pigs, which are slightly more susceptible than man, were killed in the second atomic bomb explosion.

A reporter mused, "I assume if men had been on the ship, they would all have been killed then."

The captain said he supposed so unless they were all evacuated immediately. He referred to what he called "the unique effect of the atomic bomb."

Admiral Blandy was asked, "Are the results of the test being made internationally known?"

He stated firmly, "No, they remain secret U. S. property."

A British correspondent who had been taking few notes scribbled this down.

The conference moved on – was there anything to the idea that electronics might be used as protection against atomic warfare? The Admiral replied, "This has not been pursued. It is just conjecture. I do not believe it is feasible."

What structural changes on shipboard were contemplated in the atomic age? The Admiral dropped his cool, official manner and remarked dryly, "Principally, removal of the patient before exposure. The best protection is not to be there when the bomb goes off."

Ending the session, Admiral Blandy said, "I cannot tell you the positions of the animals. I have a security directive from the Joint Chiefs of Staff. This is top secret. . . . We are bringing some of the ships back to the naval yard to acquaint personnel with the hazards in a possible war."

Captain Warren led correspondents up and down ladders to see the atomic animals. They were lying listlessly in the straw. Down in the laboratories, the throbbing of the engines was louder than ever. The air was stuffy. Naval technicians bent over microscopes testing the blood count of animals. On another bench the Geiger counters, large metal tubes, were attached to a metal box. There were many dials and little lights flickered off and on.

The little crowd of reporters walked across a gangplank and out into the rain. A few unconsciously took a deep breath. They walked in silence across the Navy Yard, passed the busy ship repair shops and gun factories, and went out into the familiar din of a Washington street.

Three of us bundled into a taxi with a Navy officer who said cheerfully, "The best thing to do in the next war is to scatter. These cities will be bad. Too crowded."

One of the reporters grumbled, "The thing to do is not to have another war."

The red-haired girl said sadly, "That is too intelligent."

The conversation languished.

Chapter XXX

(Veto power over a foreign policy is nothing new to the United States. A few old men in the Senate have exercised this authority for generations. Less than thirty years ago, a few embittered Senators vetoed Woodrow Wilson's hope for peace, the League of Nations. The United States Senate still holds the veto power over the President and Secretary of State.)

SENATOR ARTHUR VANDENBERG has one obvious advantage over Jimmy Byrnes. He looks like a statesman. When the two were photographed together, Secretary Byrnes always managed to look like a harassed male secretary.

The impressive, white-haired Senator has other advantages. He is not the Secretary of State. His party is solidly behind him. He has a helpful sense of humor. At the San Francisco Conference Vandenberg kept the American delegation in good spirits with his quips. Whenever the Senator is kidded about being a Presidential candidate, he replies with a smile, "I'm not a candidate because by 1952 I would be too old to run for a second term."

Arthur Vandenberg is influenced greatly by John Foster Dulles, the Republican Party's foreign-policy expert. Dulles was quoted in the *Congressional Record* as having said on May 24, 1946, that "the United Nations was relatively impotent and negotiations at Paris failed because Soviet leaders consider American ideas of freedom to be obsolete."

Vandenberg is also directed by his reactions to public sentiment and his hearty dislike for all things New Deal. Vandenberg's pet New Deal peeve is Henry Wallace.

After Mr. Roosevelt's death Vandenberg dominated all foreign-policy decisions in the Senate, where American views toward the world are traditionally made. An incident in the 1946 political campaign illustrates the Michigan Senator's influence. Blustering Clarence Brown, Republican Congressman from Ohio, was debating with Democratic Representative Wright Patman of Texas on a radio forum. The moderator asked if foreign policy was an issue. Brown snorted, "Why should it be? Arthur Vandenberg is running our nation's foreign policy." Unhappy Congressman Patman said nothing.

The spirit of internationalism was highest in the Senate during the winter of 1945–1946. The magic of Franklin Roosevelt's salesmanship hung over the Senate on a raw winter afternoon. The members were about to decide the powers of the American delegate to the United Nations Security Council.

A few isolationists were stubbornly protesting turning over a limited number of American troops to the Council. Reporters sat in the crowded gallery with long tally sheets before them. The teletype lines were open to New York, London, Paris, and Moscow. This vote was a part of the brave new world.

Senator Bill Fulbright lounged in his chair, absent-mindedly fingering his gold watch chain. Burton K. Wheeler, last of the great orators among the dwindling number of isolationists, spoke in a low and tense voice. "The time will come when not my voice, but the voice of the common man will be heard in Congress – the woman knitting by her friends, the soldier back from the war, the worker."

Sheets of crumpled white paper lay scattered on the floor around his desk. The Senate listened indifferently. Old Tom Connally lumbered down the aisle. He did not even glance at Wheeler or indicate he knew the Senator was speaking.

Fulbright argued back in his easy Arkansas drawl, "The old policy so obviously failed, something new ought to be tried. We ought to try the United Nations."

In the gallery, a young lieutenant with a row of ribbons on his chest leaned over with his chin on his fist. A grandmotherly lady who had been there all afternoon slumped in her seat.

Senator White nervously paced the chamber while Senator Willis of Indiana spoke slowly and laboriously. Bob Taft jingled a key ring. Senator Revercomb of West Virginia shouted, "We never before gave such powers as in this bill."

Then Barkley walked through the swinging doors into the dark chambers. Les Biffle trotted by his side. The buzzers in the cloakrooms started to ring. A quorum call before the final vote. Senate clerk John Crockett called out, "Mr. Aiken, Mr. Andrew, Mr. Austin . . ."

At six-ten the vote was counted – 65 to 7 for the United Nations bill.

Little by little the hope of that afternoon died away. The commanding figure at every stage was Arthur Vandenberg. He made the reports to the Senate. It was Arthur Vandenberg who turned a new pressure on Secretary Byrnes in the spring of 1946.

The Senator had returned from the Moscow meeting. He was irritated by the Soviet stubbornness and by what he considered Jimmy Byrnes's too moderate approach. Arthur Vandenberg and John Foster Dulles talked things over. They decided the time to challenge the U.S.S.R. was at hand.

One afternoon soon after, Senator Vandenberg addressed an unusually well-attended session of the Senate. Clerks and Congressmen sat in the benches around the rear. The galleries were crowded. Vandenberg had received special permission from Tom Connally to speak first.

Arthur Vandenberg was the superb actor in this scene. His deep, husky voice said slowly and deliberately, "I return here with no illusions that automatic peace awaits the world." A long breath whispered out through the gallery. A shabby old man in a black suit bent his head and closed his eyes to hear better. A young soldier tightly clutched the hand of his pretty girl friend.

Vandenberg stood like a preacher at a pulpit. His manuscript lay before him on a wooden stand. He continued, "But I also have an overriding conviction more emphatic than before, that the world's only hope of organized peace is linked with the destiny of the world. I cannot, and I do not, share the melancholy pessimism heard in some quarters that the United Nations will be unable to cope with world realities."

The Senator raised his right arm and his face grew stern. "The United Nations must be made to succeed if we are to avoid unspeakable catastrophe in this atomic age when the first casualty list may be the last."

With his dramatic shift from gloom to hope to gloom, Senator Vandenberg had the audience with him. A slight shudder shook the shoulders of the old man in black.

Vandenberg was now ready for his punch line. His voice thundered mightily, "This is an individual challenge to the Soviet Union and to the United States. . . . These two rival ideologies are face to face with the desperate need for mutual understanding. The future of the United Nations is wrapped up in this equation."

His eyes flashed. "I assert my own belief that we can live together in harmony if the United States speaks as plainly on all occasions as Russia does; if the United States just as vigorously sustains its own purposes and ideals as Russia does."

The Senator's voice filled with scorn. "If we abandon the miserable fiction that we somehow jeopardize the peace, if our candor is as firm as Russia's always is, and if we assume a moral leadership we have too frequently allowed to elapse. We must have positive foreign policies."

With each pause, a long silence held the Senate chamber. When the flow of words stopped with a pious prayer for peace, applause fell on Senator Vandenberg from the floor and gallery. He stood tall and triumphant. If any man was the master at this hour of American foreign policy, it was Arthur Vandenberg. Not a dissident voice was raised that afternoon. With one speech, Arthur Vandenberg had switched the line. The new "get tough with Russia" policy was born. The line was echoed again and again that spring by Dulles, Taft, and other Republicans. Tom Connally's more moderate tone never caught on.

Days later, after Secretary Byrnes turned around to catch the Vandenberg policy, there was a lone protest in the Senate. The

United States had lined up with the British against Soviet expansion in Iran, and Claude Pepper objected.

He held the floor for half an hour. His voice rose and fell with sarcasm and bitterness. His face was flushed. His hands were constantly in motion. The Senate sat in stolid, disapproving silence.

Pepper asked, "What has the American delegation to the United Nations done to get all foreign troops out of foreign territories? I have not seen the Secretary of State as a white knight on a gallant charger moving in to the liberation of Indonesia. All that I am asking is for an American foreign policy that will say to everyone, 'Get out of everybody else's business.' "

Senator Connally stared coldly at Pepper and brushed some lint off his sleeve, as though to dispose of him. Senator Hatch stood by his seat waiting to shout down Pepper.

The Florida Senator moved into the aisle. He cried, "There was a time when struggling peoples seeking independence could feel sure that here in the great heart of America there would be a dynamic echo to all their hopes and aspirations. I hope American foreign policy will not get hardening of the arteries. Now when over the earth there are these anguished cries for independence and a new life, I want to see the strong hand of America stretched forth."

His voice fell to almost a whisper. "The way to avoid an imperial scramble is for all of us to get on our knees before the graves of the dead, and say, 'It is a new earth the dead have given us. Now let us remake it.' "

He raised his arms above his head. "If the United Nations really wants to carry out its destiny to mankind, let the nations go back to the council table, and ask each one what she is willing to give up. We cannot have peace and keep this *status quo* of power politics. When America becomes the shining light for a new order of nations, then the dead can sleep in peace."

The Senate adjourned during an August heat wave in a cynical mood. The last act of business was to mutilate a resolution accepting the authority of the World Court. The chief slashers were not Henrik Shipstead, the glum isolationist from Minnesota, or Burt Wheeler. Instead, they were the two Senate "architects" of American foreign policy, Tom Connally and Arthur Vandenberg.

Senator Morse, author of the resolution, had been trying for weeks to pry it loose from the Senate Foreign Relations Committee and out on the floor. Two days before the Senate adjourned, Morse buttonholed Elbert Thomas, the gentle and tolerant Utah Senator, who headed a subcommittee studying the resolution. Morse asked bluntly if Thomas intended to report out the resolution.

Senator Thomas, one of the kindest and most philosophic men in the Senate, was embarrassed. He personally was for the resolution and would support it, but he did not intend to bring it up. Senator Connally did not want action on it.

That afternoon, Senator Morse defiantly told the Senate he was introducing the resolution. Connally lumbered to his feet and raised a point of order. Senator Austin, Republican, of Vermont, chosen to be the American representative on the United Nations Security Council, spoke about "*ipso facto* jurisdiction" and asked whether the resolution was the correct method.

Morse, tense with impatience, said, "I only wish to say that every intuitive cell in my body convinces me that it is of the utmost importance that the Senate vote on this resolution before it adjourns. I know of no responsibility more grave upon our shoulders than to demonstrate that we believe that international disputes should be settled by way of the World Court."

The Senator from Oregon pleaded, "I do not see how we can possibly go home with the world upset and torn as it is without adopting this resolution. There is no valid reason for not adopting it at this time."

Senator Millikin – a lawyer so able that he can make his statements sound respectable and judicial – said, "I think we may be a little profligate in rushing this through in the closing hours of the session."

Connally allowed a grim smile to flicker in his eyes. Senator George, the veteran Southern conservative, went to work next.

He said harshly, "A large number of Americans think that by adopting resolutions and hastily entering into international agreements, we can make certain and steadfast the peace of the earth. We are not going to put an end to war with laws or resolutions, or by adhering to every kind of international agreement which anyone can think of."

By the next afternoon Senator Thomas had decided to lead the fight for the resolution. This Senator, a former Mormon missionary with a religious faith in peace and justice, sat patiently at his desk. A young Foreign Relations Committee clerk was beside him.

One Senator was eating a lunch of milk and crackers at his desk. Tom Connally shuffled across the floor, stopping to lecture Wayne Morse. The Oregon Senator listened without any expression on his thin face.

As Senator Thomas rose to read his speech, Senators streamed out through the swinging doors. Only seventeen remained. Thomas, no orator, spoke with plain and honest sincerity. He said, "Why should any nation with a clear conscience be afraid to accept the impartial judgment of a World Court? If the United Nations is to succeed, the system of power politics must be displaced by justice." The calm voice read on, "So long as nations can place themselves above international law, there can be no hope for peace."

At this point, nine Senators were listening. Senator Capper tottered out and then there were eight.

Thomas glanced up from the typed pages and looked appealingly around him. He said, "I cannot help but say the peace of the world depends upon our action. I know of no better way for the United States to set an example for the world."

Connally slouched across the floor. He held in his hand a copy of the bill. There were pencil marks through it – an amendment he had just constructed. Connally bent over and showed it to Millikin. Millikin nodded his approval. Connally smiled in satisfaction.

Arthur Vandenberg began the attack on the resolution. He opened up with sharp questions. There was a touch of irritation in his deep voice. He used many important long words . . . "multilateral case, reciprocity of international justice." He asked pompously whether the resolution was in conformity with the recommendations of the State Department and the Republican foreign-policy expert, John Foster Dulles.

Thomas answered mildly, "I think there is no inconsistency as I read the English language."

Vandenberg continued his questioning and after a very involved legalistic statement said, "The Senator from Utah then agrees that the situation defined in this suggested *reservation* is the situation which would exist . . ."

Senator Thomas was upset. His tolerant eyes snapped and he said firmly, "Since the Senator has used the word *reservation*, I think that word is one that can well be avoided and dispensed with. It would be disastrous to the whole United Nations structure, after we have gone through the process of accepting obligations of the United Nations, for the Senate to pass any measure which would in any way affect the structure of the United Nations. That is my stand. I would guard against any such action."

In the manner of a gentle teacher lecturing an errant pupil Thomas added, "I do not want anything which we do here labeled as a reservation."

Senator Austin followed with a learned dissertation which said, in effect, that the World Court did not have any business deciding questions of a domestic nature.

Tom Connally, chairman of the Foreign Relations Committee, threw in his amendment – twenty-two damaging words – which would prevent the World Court from considering "disputes with regard to matters which are essentially within the domestic jurisdiction of the United States, *as determined by the United States*."

Senator Donnell asked Connally if he agreed with a Foreign Relations Committee statement, "The committee therefore decided that a reservation of the right of decision as to what matters are essentially within domestic jurisdiction would tend to defeat the purposes which it is hoped to achieve . . ."

Ole Tawm snorted, "I do not agree with it. I think we have the right to adhere 100 per cent, if we choose, and we have the right not to adhere at all."

He said scornfully that the Court might decide that immigration, tariffs, and navigation of the Panama Canal were international questions. He did not want that.

Senator Thomas was asked whether he thought the Connally amendment was "consistent with the provisions of the United Nations charter."

Thomas answered mildly, "The amendment will have to be changed. For us to adopt an amendment which would be inconsistent with the charter would cause us to go back on our pledged word – and that would be a very bad thing to do, of course."

Senator Morse rose in his seat and his cold precise voice was edged with emotion. He said, "I think that on this issue as on so many that arise in the field of international relations, we have only fear to fear, as the late President Roosevelt was wont to put it. Why should we fear the Court's jurisdiction? There is no realism in the argument that it might attempt to encroach upon our domestic problems. . . . Obviously we would lose our world standing at once if we welshed on our agreement to be bound by the World Court under the pretense that in a given case domestic issues were involved. I fear the amendment may cause some nations to form a false opinion that we are not ready to go all the way in supporting the World Court."

The next afternoon Tom Connally's amendment was voted through, 51 to 12. All the old men who shape foreign policy in the Senate – Connally, Vandenberg, George, Austin – together with the isolationists – Langer, Shipstead, Millikin, O'Daniel, Revercomb – voted for it.

Only twelve, ten Democrats and two Republicans, opposed the Connally amendment.

The Senate moved ahead to a final vote on the scarred resolution, 60 to 2.

In its last day, the United States Senate had shown its colors.

Chapter XXXI

(A great dream was forming in Franklin Roosevelt's mind the last year of his life. This dream kept a tired, sick man alive. The outlines were clear to him – a world where war was banished forever, a world in which all nations were secure and prosperous.

The plan was so daring, Mr. Roosevelt talked of it only to a few intimate associates. The world must share its resources and services, so that never again would there be weak nations controlled by a few wealthy and powerful countries. This was the final philanthropy of Franklin Roosevelt.

The plan was born of a conviction that the basic evil of the world was economic pressure building up into political movements and exploding into war, and a fear that organized civilization could not endure a war in the atomic age.

Mr. Roosevelt was searching for a way to relieve crowded population pressures in sore points of the world. He asked Dr. Ales Hrdlicka, the anthropologist, to study population pressures and to suggest how they might be relieved by mass transfers of people. The President had engineers, biologists, and horticulturists surveying the possibility of transforming wastelands into fertile areas, and economists and educators thinking of ways to raise the standards of literacy and living. He was thinking of public works far beyond the boldest projects in America.

But basically, Roosevelt planned to pool and reallocate all the basic wealth of the world. He wanted nations to share their ports and lines of communication and transportation. One program was for pooling the world's shipping and reallocating it by percentages. No one nation, then, would be dependent on another to carry its goods.

When the President heard a briefing of this shipping plan, he smiled and commented, "Our British friends won't like this, but who the hell cares?"

Mr. Roosevelt was irritated by the British leaders, as one is annoyed by an old friend whose habits and idiosyncrasies are too well known. He trusted the British statesmen as far as he did Governor Dewey, and for the same reason. Governor Dewey was his political opposition in the United States. The President considered the British his political opposition in the world.

Soviet Russia was a challenge to Franklin Roosevelt, a man who enjoyed challenges, Mr. Roosevelt was willing to gamble that he could soften the harshness of Soviet Communism and its imperialism. Part of the formula was to quiet Russian fears for its own security. The price was expansion to the west.

There is a legendary story of a Roosevelt-Stalin meeting. Stalin is supposed to have told the President, "We have much to learn from you in political democracy. You have much to learn from us in economic democracy. One day, perhaps, our two systems will meet.")

IN his innocent, well-meaning way, Harry Truman started alarms ringing all over the world in the early spring of 1946. A trip that was to change the mood of many nations began in a gay, holiday atmosphere. It was one of those lovely glowing days after the frost of winter. Some forty reporters and photographers trotted briskly through Washington's Union Station to board a special train. In this group were two Englishmen, a cheerful French correspondent, a Chinese, and a serious Swiss.

The usual crowds in the station patiently waiting for trains looked up curiously. Little by little, a throng began to drift over to the iron gate leading to track fifteen. The whisper moved through the crowd, "Churchill and Truman are coming."

By the time Secret Service men had cleared a path, hundreds were grouped around the gate. Soldiers craned their necks. Pretty girls stood on their tiptoes. President Truman waved his hand and smiled happily. Winston Churchill, looking like an aged cherub, ponderously raised his hand in the famous V-salute. The crowd roared with delight.

Through the sunny afternoon, the train rumbled and shook past smoky blue hills and rolling farm lands, green with the first fuzz of spring. Farmers leaned against their wooden fences staring into the windows flashing by. Children stopped their play to watch. Fat cows idly munched the grass. The earth had been broken by plows and lay turned over, rich and brown.

President Harry Truman was taking his distinguished guest to little Westminster College in Missouri to make a speech. Mr. Truman was as pleased as Punch. It was a great day for Missouri. He wandered happily through the train. He kidded with the conductor – "What are you going to do with me? I haven't got a ticket." He climbed into the cab of the big Diesel locomotive, looked at the gadgets and – like a boy – eagerly put his hand on the throttle. Being President was fun sometimes.

Winston Churchill lay behind windows with the curtains drawn. The sick and tired old man was asleep, storing up his precious strength like a miser with a treasure. When the wartime Prime Minister awoke, he and the President chatted about the scenery. Churchill, the scholar, drew from his storehouse of knowledge. He talked like a guide crammed full of historical facts. Harpers Ferry? Oh yes, that was where Stonewall Jackson seized McClellan's stores.

As the sun sank below the hills and the shadows of night spread over the sky, the correspondents gathered in their compartments for the usual diversions, talking and playing cards.

A little gray-haired English reporter looked out of the window. He was fascinated by the figures gathered at the small, red brick stations that flashed by in the twilight. He turned to his friends and said enthusiastically in his Scotch burr, "These *are* the Americans, you know. This is the way to see your country."

The talk leisurely wandered over to the atomic bomb. The Englishman said seriously, "If this thing isn't settled in a year or two, I'm going to refuse any assignment in New York or Washington. I'll go out on a farm. I don't want to die that way."

The train raced on through the now black night. The mournful hoots echoed over the hills.

The other British correspondent – a solemn man – mused, "This may be Churchill's swan song. . . . The old boy may not have too much time left."

The easy, relaxed mood of the Presidential special train dropped like a fallen mask at ten-thirty that Monday night. The mimeographed text of Mr. Churchill's speech was passed out. The official British spokesman, Charley Campbell, a friendly young man with a drooping walrus mustache, was asked, "What do you think the lead is, Charley?"

He answered briskly, "If I were writing it, I'd say – Churchill proposes Anglo-American alliance as Russian shadow darkens over world."

The reporters hustled back through the swaying train to their compartments and then read the forty-five hundred words through. Some whistled in surprise. Others muttered to themselves. This was dynamite!

The words on the long, coarse mimeograph paper were hard and blunt. They described the hopes of Europe after the last war. Then, the black, heavily inked text said, "I do not see or feel the same confidence or even the same hopes at this time." This line was hurriedly underlined. So was the proposal for an Anglo-American alliance, and a bitter attack on Russia.

After the stories were handed over to the telegraph man, the reporters crowded into each other's rooms. They wanted to check with each other, get rid of that horrible sensation of being alone with a loaded weapon. Do we all feel the same?

In one compartment, a slim correspondent shook his head. "Things aren't going right," he said. "I'm getting scared."

Another commented gloomily, "This might wreck the United Nations."

A usually stolid fellow spluttered, "If this had to be said, why couldn't *we* say it? Why can't the United States speak out for itself?"

Up and down the cars, the restless reporters wandered deep into the night. The two British writers said stoutly, "It is a good speech. This had to be said." The jolly Frenchman was mournful. "It is dangerous." The Chinese was indignant. "What does he mean talking about Christian civilization and the English-speaking powers?"

Throughout the lengthy night the men debated. How official was this? Was there any significance to President Truman's sitting on the stage with Churchill? Let's see – what about those conferences between Churchill and Senator Vandenberg, John Foster Dulles, and Secretary of State Byrnes? What would the world think? How would the story hit Moscow?

In the club car three card games were going on. Correspondents who seemed unable to sit still came in and began talking about the speech. The games broke up.

On and on through the night the train rushed on its way. At crossroads towns faces blurred past. This was an eerie, uncomfortable feeling to race past these American faces knowing that tomorrow Winston Churchill's speech would explode in the world.

The next morning – when the dawn lifted – there was the city of St. Louis gleaming in the sunlight. Then the fertile fields, green and brown with overturned earth. Shocks of corn from last year stood in the fields. And again, those haunting faces at the stations. Some were the faces of children . . . bright, eager, and happy. What kind of world would they inherit?

The caravan of cars wound into Fulton, Missouri, at noon. The little town had a carnival atmosphere. Balloons for sale. Hawkers shouted, "Get your C–T Day banners here." The streets were lined with curious folks . . . farmers who took the day off to get a long-remembered glimpse of an historic face . . . bobby soxers . . . little children. As the limousines drove slowly by, one little girl said tearfully, "Daddy, I didn't get to see Churchill."

Then to the small campus of Westminster College with its cool green lawns and old brick buildings. This college, so remote from war and conflict and politics, is tucked away in a valley between the hills of Missouri. It is the kind of small college that middle-aged graduates remember with nostalgia. The audience crowded into the little gymnasium. A pretty organist in a black robe began to play softly, "Come, all ye faithful."

A long file of men in black academic robes, with vari-colored capes, moved slowly down the main aisle. Mr. Churchill shuffled in the rear, a dramatic figure in a scarlet robe. President Truman was almost inconspicuous behind him.

A tall and earnest young man moved to the front of the stage to read the prayer. His clear voice said, "There can be no peace save in the hearts of men."

Harry Truman, unfamiliar in the black robe and mortarboard hat, said, "This is one of my greatest pleasures and privileges since I became President of the United States. Mr. Churchill is one of the great men of our age. I know he will have something constructive to say."

The clatter of applause fell off into a deep silence.

Winston Churchill walked slowly down the center of the stage. Before him the scene was like that of a high school commencement in a drowsy small town. A gymnasium decked with bunting. Solemn professors in their black robes. The clean-cut young faces of the students. The audience dressed in Sunday best seated uncomfortably on wooden bleachers. Baskets of roses on the stage. Big windows tilted open to let in the warm, fragrant breath of spring.

That flaming, scarlet robe gave Winston Churchill the appearance of a fallen angel. A warm smile began in his eyes and moved over his smooth, round face. He stood back about two feet from the speaking stand. His shoulders were characteristically humped over.

In this pause, as every eye focused on him, Mr. Churchill slowly put on his heavy shell-rim glasses and fingered his gold watch chain. The old warrior was gathering strength from the warmth of his audience. He pressed his hands against his black vest and began to speak. The familiar voice began faintly – long pauses, stumbling over words and phrases. As he fell into the mood of the words and felt the intent interest of his audience, vigor poured into his voice. It rose and fell with humor, with sarcasm, with gloom.

For forty-five minutes, this man sick and weary from the old fevers of war and world politics spoke his mind. There was the pessimism of a man who in a crowded life has seen too much evil, the imagination of a dreamer, the bitterness of an unheeded prophet.

The audience sat quietly under the power of oratory. It was a warm afternoon and people fanned themselves with the paper programs.

Mr. Churchill paused, looked over his spectacles, and said slowly, "Our supreme task and duty is to guard the homes of the common people from the horrors and miseries of another war."

From the side a pair of eager hands began the applause. It spread like fever across the small hall. Then, quiet again as the somber voice read on.

Once again, several minutes later, applause moved over the gymnasium. Mr. Churchill said, "It would be criminal madness to cast the atomic bomb secret adrift in this still agitated and disunited world."

Down he went through his speech, calling for a United Nations air force, free elections throughout the world, and an Anglo-American alliance. Over the auditorium there was the deep silence of a warm afternoon.

Twice the audience roused into applause – for mutual use of British and American naval and air bases, and exchange of military cadets.

Halfway through the speech, Mr. Churchill's voice dropped to almost a whisper. Softly, slowly, and dramatically, he said, "A shadow has fallen over the scenes so lately lighted by the Allies' victory. Nobody knows what Soviet Russia and its Communist international organization intends to do in the immediate future, or what are the limits, if any, to their expansive tendencies. . . . It is my present duty to place before you certain facts about the present position in Europe."

President Truman, sitting behind Mr. Churchill, played idly with the golden tassel on his mortarboard hat. Admiral William Leahy, the grim old Chief of Staff to the President, sat stiffly attentive.

The voice picked up strength again. Mr. Churchill coldly and deliberately bit into the words, accusing Russia of wrongdoing in Europe, Asia, and the Near East.

The audience sat in complete, bewildered silence.

Winston Churchill grumbled gloomily, "Last time, I saw it all coming and cried aloud to my fellow countrymen and to the world. No one paid any attention. This last war might have been prevented without the firing of a single shot, but no one would listen and one by one we were all sucked into the awful whirlpool."

But it was not until Mr. Churchill drew away from his pessimism to say, "I do not believe that Soviet Russia wants another war," that the applause fell on him again.

The end was a faint, faraway note of hope . . . if men behave themselves, "the highroads of the future will be clear, not only for us, but for all for a century to come."

Mr. Churchill stood back from the stand. His shoulders slumped wearily. He was once again a lonely, tired old man.

When the wartime British leader sat down heavily, President Truman stepped forward to receive his degree. He was a small, humble figure. His voice rose with pleading: "We do live in perilous times. Never was leadership so necessary. The United Nations charter must be the law of the land, and the law of the world. We are either headed for complete destruction or a great stage in history. It is up to you to decide."

The deep tones of the organ filled the little hall. The black-robed figures moved down the aisle and into the warm, sun-filled afternoon.

The story was already on the wires. The calm, even voices of the British Broadcasting Corporation were spreading it across Europe. The United States had turned an abrupt postwar corner.

A few days later, a steady file of reporters trudged out of the drizzling morning and into the big lobby of the White House. The round table in the center was soon piled high with raincoats and hats. It was the largest Presidential press conference in many a week.

Since the last conference, Truman and Churchill had gone to Missouri. Across the street, the State Department had thrown on the desks in the press room blunt notes of warning to Moscow about Iran and Manchuria.

The President was standing cheerfully behind his desk this morning. John Snyder was at one side behind him, and Admiral Leahy on the other. A bright basket of roses was on a table.

A reporter, trying to phrase his question carefully, spoke slowly. "Mr. President, some people have suggested that your presence at Fulton gave added significance to Mr. Churchill's speech. Would you comment?"

Mr. Truman said coolly that he was Mr. Churchill's host. He had not read the speech beforehand. His guest had a perfect right to say what he pleased. This was a land of free speech.

Another correspondent tried to tackle the question from another angle. We had a combined chief of staff arrangement with the British. How long would this military union continue?

The President was not in a talkative mood. His answer was short and clipped – As long as the war emergency lasted.

A voice came in sharply, "What will you do after that?"

The President said that he would discuss it then, not before.

Several voices clamored for attention. Mr. Truman picked out the reporter who had spoken first and nodded for him to go ahead.

"Mr. President, did the Russians say anything at Potsdam about wanting to take over the Turkish provinces of Kars and Ardahan?" The answer was a flat no.

The questions kept hammering in. "Are there any plans if the Russians refuse to withdraw their troops from Iran?"

The President said he would discuss that when and if it came up. Then he added an earnest postscript. We must not let the United Nations collapse. Mr. Truman said he did not think the Russians really wanted to go down a one-way street.

A few hours later, the State Department conference room was filled with the same correspondents. They were waiting for Jimmy Byrnes. He swept into the room, sat down, arranged his papers, and looked up quizzically at the faces around him. A big crowd always meant troublesome questions.

The questions broke all over him. Did the subject of the Turkish provinces ever come up at Potsdam? Well, the Secretary said nervously, yes they had. It was not on the agenda. It came up casually, so it was very easy for the President not to recall it.

The reporters scribbled hurriedly on their folded sheets of paper. There was one story. Now, to clinch another. Was the Secretary of State informed about Mr. Churchill's speech in advance?

Byrnes looked like a worried father trying to explain to a neighbor about a broken window. Well, the Secretary said, Mr. Churchill had talked to him. The conversation was pretty general. The former Prime Minister had not asked for advice. The Secretary had not offered any.

The next question was, "To what extent does the United States associate itself with the Churchill speech?"

Byrnes spoke up with some irritation. The questioner could think what he pleased. Byrnes did not care to discuss it.

Chapter XXXII

(Henry Wallace was the most controversial figure in the first two years of the Truman Administration. To some, he was a dangerous fool with burning eyes, a Don Quixote with a broken lance riding a spavined horse. To thousands of others who were not so articulate, Henry Wallace was a great prophet. The final judgment rests with history.)

THE restless agreement on American foreign policy was kicked apart during a crazy two weeks in the late summer of 1946. Henry Wallace, the New Deal philosopher, emerged from a brooding silence to cry out a frightened warning.

On a bright Thursday morning as the mist was clearing over downtown Washington, a clerk dumped a big pile of mimeographed releases in the Department of Commerce press room. The title page said, "Released for use not earlier than 8 P.M., EST, September 12, 1946. An Address of Henry A. Wallace, Secretary of Commerce, 'The Way to Peace.'"

Yawning reporters began to look over the ten pages indifferently and then with almost feverish interest. This was the most exciting address to come out of Washington in nearly two years.

There was a provocative opening, "Tonight, I want to talk about peace – and how to get peace. Never have the common people of all lands so longed for peace. Yet, never in a time of comparative peace have they feared war so much. . . . We cannot rest in the assurance that we invented the atom bomb – and therefore this agent of destruction will work best for us. He who trusts in the atom bomb will sooner or later perish by the atom bomb – or something worse."

The words struck hard against an American alliance with "British balance-of-power manipulations," against our huge post-war military budget, against the get-tough-with-Russia policy, and against Communist political activity in western Europe, Latin America, and the United States.

One line stuck out like a sore thumb – "On our part, we should recognize that we have no more business in the *political* affairs of eastern Europe than Russia has in the *political* affairs of Latin America, western Europe and the United States."

The conclusion was a bleak prophecy: "I believe that peace is the basic issue, both in the Congressional campaign this fall and right on through the Presidential election in 1948. How we meet this issue will determine whether or not we live in 'one world' or 'two worlds' – or whether we live at all."

The writer of this speech was a lonely figure in the Washington of the Truman Administration. Only at the height of the New Deal did Henry Wallace seem a vital and real part of Washington. He translated a political doctrine into a religion, and for this he was hated as much as, if not more than, Franklin Roosevelt. While political doctrines wear out, religion is more enduring.

In his thirteen years in the Cabinet, Henry Wallace's indifferently combed brown hair had turned gray. Deep lines had carved into his forehead and the muscles of his face sagged. His gentle eyes had focused farther and farther away from the immediate political realities.

Talking with Henry Wallace has always been difficult. A curtain of thought excludes the visitor. Henry Wallace walks alone, brooding over the tragedy of mankind. He is indifferent to individuals and, from time to time, has surrounded himself with both brilliant and mediocre lieutenants, and always a string of eccentric camp followers.

Henry Wallace is filled with a misty love of humanity. Washington is essentially a cynical, irreligious city and has never understood Wallace. His enemies scornfully call him a "mystic with a Messiah complex." They convinced Mr. Roosevelt, with the help of influential New Dealers, that his Vice-President was fuzzy and unpredictable and a drag on the ticket.

All through his national career, Wallace has seemed to be searching for a great cause. He found it when a horribly bright flash exploded over an obscure Japanese city, Hiroshima. He developed a dreadful fascination in the atomic bomb. Wallace, the intense student, searched for all the knowledge available on atomic power. He spent hours talking with the atomic scientists and became infected with their sense of doom. There are few laymen in the world who know as much about atomic power as Henry Wallace.

Wallace walked alone with a sense of impending tragedy. He envisioned scenes of suffering and devastation. He could not take his thoughts away from them.

By midsummer of 1946, Henry Wallace could no longer endure his silence. He spoke out at a cabinet meeting. He said war in the atomic age was inconceivable, and yet the world was drifting in that direction. The United States was mixed up in British power politics and antagonizing Russia.

Jimmy Byrnes was scornful. Two other cabinet members mildly supported Wallace. Harry Truman was genuinely interested. He tartly reminded the Secretary of State that our policy was not tied to the British kite. The President asked Wallace to write out his thoughts in a memorandum.

The Secretary of Commerce tortuously searched his mind. He talked with atomic scientists, religious leaders, businessmen, and students of international affairs. The result was his famous letter of July 23.

Wallace began, "I have been increasingly disturbed by the trend of international affairs since the end of the war, and I am even more troubled by the apparently growing feeling among the American people that another war is coming and the only way that we can head it off is to arm ourselves to the teeth. . . . The months just ahead may well be the crucial period which will decide whether the civilized world will go down in destruction after the five or ten years needed for several nations to arm themselves with atomic bombs."

Half of the letter was devoted to the atomic bomb, with Wallace proposing, "We must be prepared to reach an agreement

Byrnes's independent attitude. White House friends were openly grumbling that Jimmy was a "poor appointment" and that the President regretted his "mistake."

Harry Truman liked Henry Wallace. The affection was as genuine as it was baffling. Both Wallace and Truman come from small towns in the Midwest, a bond that the President takes seriously. Wallace did not patronize Mr. Truman but addressed him with a flattering humility.

The President thought of Wallace as "a good sport." He showed no rancor at his defeat in Chicago, and did more campaigning for the Democratic ticket than any other national figure.

Henry Wallace was responsible for one of the great moments in Harry Truman's life. It happened in Madison Square Garden on election eve. Wallace was to introduce Mr. Truman. When the incumbent Vice-President stepped out in the center of the stage, the huge crowd deafened the auditorium with waves of cheers. Senator Truman stood in the background awed by the demonstration. Wallace pulled Mr. Truman forward, put his arm around him, and said, "I want you to support my friend."

The little fellow from Missouri felt for the first time that he belonged.

The letter of July 23 was followed by a series of Wallace-Truman "seminars" through the summer. Wallace talked simply and patiently with his "convert" for hours, preparing him for the final confession. He slowly and deliberately built President Truman into a belief in himself, a belief that he could step forward and be the great leader to prevent catastrophe.

Democratic Chairman Bob Hannegan encouraged the President to continue the talks. He was friendly to Wallace and considered him a political asset. The liberals were becoming discouraged with the Truman Administration, and Henry Wallace was the one man Hannegan believed could hold them.

Late in the summer, Hannegan gave a quiet dinner party. Both the President and the Secretary of Commerce were present. Harry Truman talked frankly and enthusiastically about foreign policy. He had been converted. Wallace enjoyed his triumph meekly.

which will commit us to disclosing information and destroying our bombs at a specific time or in terms of specific action by other countries, rather than on our unfettered discretion."

The latter part of the letter Wallace used to discuss American-Russian relations in some detail. He wrote, "I believe that for the United States and Russia to live together is the most important single problem facing the world today. We must recognize that the world has changed and that today there can be no 'one world' unless the United States and Russia can find some way of living together."

He analyzed the Russian suspicion of the Western world—the invasions of Russia by the Mongols, Turks, Swedes, Germans, and Poles over a thousand years, and attempts to interfere with the Bolshevik regime by Japan, Britain, and France; the Anglo-American military alliance, the monopoly of the atomic bomb, the expansion of American military bases.

Wallace recommended, "We should ascertain from a fresh point of view what Russia believes to be essential to her own security as a prerequisite to the writing of the peace and to co-operation in the construction of a world order. We should be prepared to judge her requirements against the background of what we ourselves and the British have insisted upon as essential to our respective security. We should be prepared, even at the expense of risking epithets of appeasement, to agree to reasonable Russian guarantees of security. . . . It is of the greatest importance that we should discuss with the Russians in a friendly way their long-range economic problems and the future of our co-operation in matters of trade."

Every point was a contradiction of the Truman-Byrnes-Leahy-Vandenberg policy.

The letter stirred vague apprehensions and resentment in Harry Truman. He felt uncomfortable and helpless about all the war talk he heard. The inference that Great Britain was pulling American diplomats around by their coattails disturbed him. Why hadn't Jimmy Byrnes told him these things?

President Truman did not have any great affection for Secretary Byrnes personally, and at that time he deeply resented

On Thursday afternoon after Wallace's New York speech had been turned over to the reporters, President Truman had a news conference. He had a moderately large crowd because of the maritime strike.

Toward the end of the session, a correspondent in the middle of the throng held up a copy of the Wallace speech and said, "Mr. President, I have a question about Secretary Wallace's address." Mr. Truman nodded his head agreeably.

The reporter read a paragraph from the mimeographed text, "I am neither anti-British, nor pro-British – neither anti-Russian nor pro-Russian. And just two days ago when President Truman read these words, he said they represented the policy of his Administration." The question was, "Do you subscribe to that statement, Mr. President?"

Mr. Truman said cheerfully that he had read the entire speech and approved all of it.

The storm broke that night! Communists shrilly screamed at Wallace's mild reproof of Russia and Communist activity. Editorials thundered virtuously that the Secretary of Commerce was butting into foreign affairs with the astonishing proposal to let the U.S.S.R. run wild in eastern Europe. Congressmen and politicians squealed like stuck pigs. Washington's liberal set was divided.

If Henry Wallace expected this reaction, certainly President Truman did not.

The next morning, Friday, the routine State Department press conference was on a standing-room-only basis. The Acting Secretary of State, Will Clayton, read through an announcement on lend-lease while the reporters waited impatiently with questions forming in their minds.

The first inquiry was, "Does the State Department still favor a policy of no spheres of influence?"

Clayton stared soberly at the correspondent and answered quietly that he believed that was right.

Was there anything to indicate that Wallace's speech had changed American policy in eastern Europe?

Again Clayton looked at the questioner and in that same subdued, faraway tone said he thought he had better not get into any detailed discussion of the subject.

"Can you say whether the Wallace speech was cleared with the Department?"

He replied it was not cleared with him.

"Was it cleared with Secretary Byrnes?"

Clayton did not know.

"Have you heard from Mr. Byrnes?"

No.

"Do you intend to talk with the President?"

No.

"Are you going to talk with the Secretary?"

No.

"Do you have any comment?"

No.

Clayton explained painfully that he thought he had better let the President say what he meant by approval of the speech. It was not clear to him, Clayton said.

By Saturday, the storm was raging against the White House. At one o'clock in the afternoon, a little note was pecked out on the news service wires. The President would read an announcement at two o'clock. No questions could be asked of him.

Saturday is a dead day in Washington with most of the news offices closed. The doors of government buildings are shut tight. So it was only a small crowd of reporters that gathered in the White House. Some had rushed from their homes and were dressed in sports clothes. In the lobby, a newspaper lay over a chair. Its headline bellowed, "Byrnes Boiling at Wallace Speech."

Linc White rushed over from the State Department. He had no more idea what was up than the rest of us.

When the correspondents walked into the President's office, Mr. Truman smiled and commented easily that not so many were there. He stood up and reading like a schoolboy reciting a lesson said, "There has been a natural misunderstanding regarding the answer I made to a question asked at the press conference on Thursday. The question was answered extemporaneously and my answer did not convey the thought that I intended it to convey. It was my intention to express the thought that I approved the right of the Secretary of Commerce to deliver the speech. I did not intend to indicate that I approved the speech as constituting a statement of the foreign policy of this country."

To be sure there was no mistake this time, the reporters were handed mimeographed copies of Mr. Truman's announcement.

The naïve White House statement did not satisfy anyone, particularly the enemies of Wallace. They were yelling for blood. Secretary Byrnes in Paris did not communicate directly with the President. He kept an injured silence, while stories poured out of Paris quoting "friends" or "persons close" to the Secretary as stating Byrnes felt that Wallace and Truman had torn up all his good work. Senator Tom Connally cabled the President asking what he thought he was doing.

The next Wednesday a red-haired secretary pinned the President's calling list on the White House press room bulletin board. Henry Wallace was down for an appointment at three-thirty. A milling crowd of photographers and reporters were waiting for him as he jumped out of his car and raced up the walk.

Four o'clock went by. The President and Wallace were still in conference. Every time a White House clerk walked across the lobby there was a scurry among the correspondents. Five o'clock. Still no word.

At a few minutes before six, Henry Wallace walked out of the President's office. He was smiling. The crowd bunched around him shouting questions. The throng was so large many reporters had to stand on the big center table to see and hear Wallace.

The Secretary of Commerce said cheerfully that he had agreed not to make any more foreign-policy statements until after the Paris Conference. The meeting with the President had been very cordial.

The agreement was made in the first fifteen minutes of the two and a half hour conference. The remainder of the time was spent discussing a proposed statement on foreign policy to be issued by the President. The theme of the announcement was to be that the United States stood for peace and was not aligned with any power against any other.

The President and Henry Wallace were still friends.

The following day, Thursday, Jimmy Byrnes called the President. His persuasion was skillful. Secretary Byrnes said his position in Paris had become untenable. The United States had lost its prestige at the international bargaining table. Tom Connally and Arthur Vandenberg were incensed and were going to walk out. There was no recommendation that Wallace be fired. But Jimmy made it plain that so long as Wallace remained in the Cabinet, America could not expect to be successful in its negotiations.

Friday morning was gray and sticky. At a few minutes before ten, the telephone rang in the Secretary of Commerce's office. The White House was calling.

Henry Wallace was happily talking to his assistants about the mail flooding his office from all over the nation. He picked up the phone, and waited for the President's voice. The conversation lasted two minutes. Mr. Truman said he was sorry, but he would have to ask for the Secretary's resignation.

The assistants noticed the surprised look on Wallace's face. He replied, "If that is your decision, Mr. President, I will be glad to abide by it. Peace is more important than any one person."

At the same moment, a steady file of reporters, columnists, commentators walked up the White House driveway. There were unfamiliar faces in this stream of newsmen, people who had not come to a White House press conference in weeks.

By ten-thirty, the White House lobby was filled. Reporters jammed up against the door leading to President Truman's office. Fifteen minutes later the door opened and the crowd scrambled into the President's office.

Bill Simmons, the tall Presidential usher, called out, "Move over to the left a little, gentlemen." This was greeted by a roar of laughter. President Truman smiled.

His mild, scratchy Midwestern voice was firm this morning. He said he would read a statement on foreign policy. All the little noises in the room ceased. Mr. Truman read, "The foreign policy of this country is the most important question confronting us today. Our responsibility for obtaining a just and lasting peace depends not only on the people of this country but on the nations of the world."

A few reporters had started to take notes, but they put down their pads and listened. The President continued, "The people of the United States may disagree freely and publicly on any question including that of foreign policy, but the government of the United States must stand as a unit in its relations with the rest of the world."

Mr. Truman paused, then said, "I have today asked Mr. Wallace to resign from the Cabinet."

A low whistle of surprise mixed in with the sound of Harry Truman's voice. "It had become clear that between his views on foreign policy and those of the Administration – the latter being shared, I am confident, by the great body of our citizens – there was a fundamental conflict."

His audience was only half listening. The men and women were trying to arrange the words of their stories. The President was reading steadily, "No change in our foreign policy is contemplated."

Mr. Truman concluded soberly, "That is all, gentlemen."

The cry ending every conference, "Thank you, Mr. President," rang out sharply. There was a wild rush for the door, as men raced out across the lobby and skidded into the press room to shout bulletins into their telephones.

Those who stayed behind saw Harry Truman, a little grimmer than usual, smiling and shaking hands. Admiral Leahy was sitting off at one side, a slightly bemused look on his face.

Many of the correspondents walked out of the White House and, half running, went down Fourteenth Street to the Commerce Department. A shaken publicity man was trying to answer a clamor of questions. Was Mr. Wallace surprised? The answer was – he was.

Upstairs in the fifth floor row, secretaries were trying to answer telephone calls. There were moments when every Department of Commerce line was tied up. Grave-faced associates of the Secretary stood dejectedly. A book with a red binding lay on a table. The title was, *Kicked In and Out of the President's Little Cabinet.*

The following Monday, Henry Wallace was saying good-by. A narrow hall on the fifth floor of the Commerce Department was filled with downcast men and women. They were lining up for the farewell. There was almost no conversation. Talk sometimes is a little cumbersome.

Only one person – a pretty young girl – was animated. She had been up and down the floors of the building all day getting signatures on a letter to the Secretary. Now she was waiting eagerly to present it to him.

The letter was simple: "It is with sincere regret that we bid you good-by. You have been an inspiration to the Department. We will carry over in our work the enthusiasm you have instilled in us."

As the people stood in the hall, first on one foot, then the other, an elderly Negro messenger pushed a cart toward the Secretary's office. It was filled with empty paper cartons. Every eye was fixed on this cart with a kind of horrible fascination.

Within an hour or two, the cartons would be filled with Henry Wallace's personal files, and the cart would be pushed down the hall again. Somehow, this cart was a symbol of Wallace's departure from the government after more than thirteen years.

There was a sigh of relief when the door closed behind the cart.

Inside this door, in the Secretary's outer office, the women and secretaries looked tired, too tired to feel anything.

Every desk, table, and filing cabinet was crowded with letters and telegrams, a part of the avalanche of mail that had fallen on Henry Wallace. They came from everywhere – Phoenix, Duluth, Brooklyn, and even Independence, Missouri. Most of the letters were scrawled handwriting. Very few were typed. A good many began, "This is the first letter I have ever written to a public official," or, "I'm not a very important person."

Editors and public officials and national leaders may not have liked the Wallace speech, but this was a tremendous outpouring of emotion from the country. The writers were veterans and mothers, machinists and dentists, lawyers and advertising men, ministers and doctors. The tone was reflected in two which started out, "Thank God for your talk tonight," and "You have my support in your courageous fight."

Harold Young, the heavy Texan who has been Wallace's closest associate for several years, came into the room. He looked as though he had not slept for two nights – circles under his eyes, his shirt wrinkled, shoes wet from the heavy afternoon rain.

In his own office, Henry Wallace stood before a huge bouquet of flowers on his desk, the most cheerful person in the room. He shook hands quietly, saying a few words to each visitor. In the dim light his hair seemed grayer than ever, the lines deeper in his forehead. He wore a gentle smile and his voice was husky from a bad cold.

Those with whom Wallace was shaking hands were solemn. They bobbed their heads and mumbled a few words. Then, they joined others in the room who stood around with long faces puffing cigarettes. One man who had been with Wallace ever since the old Department of Agriculture days shrugged his shoulders, sighed, and said, "Well, this is it."

There was not much else to say.

But for Henry Wallace this was not the end. It was just the beginning!

Chapter XXXIII

(Throughout the warm weeks of autumn, roses and cherry blossoms bloomed in the bright Washington sunlight. Bitterness and disillusion marched across a nation tired and sick of many fevers. The people had lost their faith.

A man from the Department of Agriculture returned from a tour of hungry Europe to hear at home the fevered cry of "Meat. Give us meat." The shock of seeing healthy and well-fed people complaining of food shortages made him violently ill.

Women stood wearily in long lines to buy food and clothing they could not afford. Discouraged veterans hunted for homes and good jobs, for automobiles and a sense of security. Businessmen listened uneasily to the prophets of depression. All heard the futile and little voices of quarreling statesmen.

Washington stood by helplessly as angry voices spoke impassioned or strange words in the political campaign. Alben Barkley rushed down to the Seventh District of Kentucky and cried, "Send Jack [Andrew] May back to Congress." Wayne Morse hustled around the Northwest campaigning for conservative Republicans. Henry Wallace blurted to reporters that an old-line Democrat was still better than a progressive Republican.

None of the profound issues – economic stability or world security – were seriously discussed. The issues of 1946, the second year of the atomic age, were "Communism" and shortages.

To be in Washington during this period was like reliving a bad dream. The weather and the situations were both reminiscent of spring. Controls were dumped overboard. Prices shot higher. Economists forecast a recession in the spring. John L.

Lewis called another coal strike. A New Dealer in the Justice Department was fired for slipping out confidential data on Americans who allegedly worked with the Nazis in the United States. As in the case of Henry Wallace's letter to the President, this report was first published by Drew Pearson.)

An old red brick Georgian mansion stares out indignantly over busy Connecticut Avenue.

Before the New Deal this aristocrat stood proud and alone. But with Roosevelt came the hustle of an expanding Capital. Now the mansion is wedged in between a row of fashionable women's dress shops and a café. It houses the offices of the Republican National Committee.

In the long, lean Roosevelt years, GOP headquarters had the forlorn and forsaken atmosphere of an old folks' home. Every two years the faithful gathered on a Tuesday night to share the misery. During the 1946 campaign, the offices had a subdued and tranquil air like those of the D.A.R. The reception hall was quiet and dimly lit, with pale green walls. From the doors opening on the hall came the soft clicking of noiseless typewriters. A gentle, white-haired lady sat at the reception desk.

The only political touch in the hall was a bold red, white, and blue poster which shouted, "Had Enough? Vote Republican, November 5." Campaign literature was neatly stacked on a polished, old-fashioned table.

There was a leisurely, timeless air in the offices. Workers leaned back in their chairs and seemed only too glad to break the monotony by talking with an occasional reporter. A placard leaned on top of a row of dog-eared books, arguing, 'End Controls, Confusion, Corruption, Communism, Vote Republican."

This was National Chairman Carroll Reece's favorite slogan.

The dominant figure in the headquarters was Clarence Brown, the large and hearty Congressman from Ohio. He has a great gift of making an intimate friend out of a complete stranger in five minutes. He is a lusty defender of the Old Guard and proud of it. For this Midwestern farmer there are two kinds of people – Republicans and Democrats. Farmer Brown is as earthy as a barnyard, as friendly as a big dog, and as noisy and shrewd as a crow.

At the Republican committee luncheons for groups of correspondents, Brown would put a big arm around the shoulder of the nearest reporter – he didn't care whether the boy was "fur or agin' " him – and bellow jokes and political wisecracks. His booming optimism was as infectious as the measles. Reporters went away from these affairs convinced the Democrats would have trouble carrying the South.

Carroll Reece, a pale carbon copy of Farmer Brown, was his enthusiastic yes-man. Another functionary in the headquarters was John Danaher, the round-faced former isolationist Senator from Connecticut. He still refers to himself as "Senator." The real strategy was turned out by Congressman Halleck. There was no disturbing voice of a GOP liberal in all the old mansion.

The Republican campaign was as simple and timeless as politics itself – to capitalize on every Administration blunder by blowing on each spark of resentment, and by methodically pulling apart the strange coalition Franklin Roosevelt gathered together under the New Deal.

The GOP was not bothered by any program. The only sign of one was slipped into a statement of House leader Joe Martin. It called for lower taxes, fewer people on the Federal payroll, home rule, removal of economic controls, and a halt to what was called "secret foreign dealings." This platform might have been copied from a speech by Senator Jim Watson fifteen years ago.

The consumer shortages were handmade for the Republican campaign. With every new gust of impatience from the country, Farmer Brown rubbed his hands gleefully and bawled, "Brother, the tide is sweepin' our way." After a swing through the Midwest Brown reported the Democrats were going to lose the President's own state of Missouri because of a local shortage of toilet paper. Republican nominees for Congress drove sound trucks before grocery lines and shouted, "Ladies, if you want meat, vote Republican."

GOP publicity jeered at Harry Truman. One pamphlet snickered, "Harry Truman for Governor." Another crowed, "Mr. Truman's Shoes Don't Fit."

The word "Communism" was whooped about like an Indian war cry. One campaign leaflet, entitled *Prophets of Planned Chaos*, showed an idiotic donkey staring into a crystal ball and wearing a turban with a Soviet hammer and sickle on it. Headquarters was piled high with recordings on "the Communist threat" to send out in the field. They were very popular.

Some campaigners suggested the confusion in the Truman Administration was not all accidental. Sh-sh, if you'll lean a little closer, you can get the inside dope. It was planned that way!

The word "radical" was whispered against Democrats. When Joe Martin's usual big plurality was threatened by the vigorous campaigning of his opponent, Mrs. Martha Sharp, a Unitarian social worker in Europe during the war, Ernie Adamson, the obliging counsel for the House un-American Activitics Committee, arrived in Catholic Massachusetts and leered that Mrs. Sharp was mixed up with radical views. When a Democratic nominee for Congress in Wisconsin was alleged to have had Communist connections, the Republican joy knew no bounds. The Soviet press made matters worse by lauding New Deal candidates.

The GOP campaign tugged away at the ties binding minority groups – Negroes, Catholics, Jews, Polish, and Italian-Americans. Placards, posters, literature, and speeches denouncing Senator Bilbo and Governor-elect Gene Talmadge of Georgia were thrown extravagantly into Negro wards. The failure of the Administration to force the issue of Palestine was pointed out in Jewish districts. Communism was the battle cry in Catholic areas.

John Lewis was given the job of stirring up labor in his own way. He announced abruptly late in October that unless the government managers of the coal mines reopened the agreement with the United Mine Workers there would be a strike November 1, four days before the election.

Several blocks down the street from the old mansion Democrats worked in a series of crowded hotel rooms. The atmosphere was one of frenzied confusion. Bathtubs were piled high with literature. Officials scampered in and out of conferences, bumping each other in the narrow corridor. Telephones rang all the time. Secretaries had to develop the knack of answering the phone with one hand and typing with the other. Visitors bounced impatiently on a lumpy divan.

Democratic headquarters was cursed almost from the beginning of the campaign. Striking hotel workers paced up and down in front of the Mayflower Hotel, and Democrats had to duck into a drugstore and from there into the lobby to miss the picket line.

Bob Hannegan's Irish face seemed to grow longer. It became the frowning and unsmiling countenance of a harassed man. He trotted in and out of the headquarters with quick, nervous steps. Pressure fell on him from all sides – get the Administration to throw off controls, throw out the New Dealers, bring them back in, get the President to make a statement on Communism. All the anguished cries and complaints of Democrats pushed on and over this man.

The busiest man in headquarters was Sam O'Neal, the Washington correspondent turned publicity agent. A constant stream of government officials, Congressmen, and reporters sat in his cluttered office. Their time was rationed by a worried secretary. Each evening she sighed as she looked at the long list of people whose telephone calls Sam had not had time to answer.

Sam's sharp face with its prominent nose and lines in his forehead was never free of some anxiety. His dark eyes usually wore the half-absorbed look of a man who has just remembered something important he should have done an hour ago.

On the wall of his corner office was a charcoal portrait of the old master of political propaganda, Charley Michelson, whose caustic jabs at Herbert Hoover helped put Franklin Roosevelt in the White House. A small eight-ball teetered on the edge of Sam's littered desk.

Sam O'Neal is a crusader cursed with intelligence and a streak of realism. His zeal drove him relentlessly until his staff ached with weariness. His intelligence made him curse the stupidity of the men he was trying to save. His realism made him admit he was fighting a losing battle.

Sam is a defiant liberal. He cheered the primary defeat of conservative Democrats in his column, "Dispelling the Fog," and argued in the conferences down the hall for a bold New Deal type campaign. When the politicians waved him aside, Sam stormed back into his office and hammered his typewriter. Out came speeches full of the poetry of the brave new world. They sounded incongruous coming from the lips of Bob Hannegan, Sam Rayburn, and Scott Lucas.

The Democratic campaign started off with all the dullness of a Sunday afternoon in a small town. Speakers dragged their 1944 speeches out of the files and virtuously shouted the praises of the glorious past. The name of Franklin D. Roosevelt was pulled in to wring applause from listless audiences.

On present issues the Democratic speakers were uneasily silent. They veered away from foreign policy.

Democrats tried to speak hopeful words on the shortages and to push the blame on Bob Taft.

But appeals to the past did not work and panic swept the Democratic campaign. It was every man for himself. Some tried to outdo the Republicans by saying they, too, were against Communism and shortages and war. Their only answer was a deep rumble of laughter from GOP headquarters and Clarence Brown's chuckling comment, "We've got 'em on the run."

Politicians begged the White House for help. Jimmy Roosevelt, the California Democratic chairman, pleaded for the President to say something decisive on foreign policy or his whole ticket would be beaten. The New York committee asked for a strong line on Palestine. Congressman McCormack yelled for an end to food price controls. Bob Hannegan plodded back and forth between the Mayflower Hotel and the White House with discouraging news.

For the first few weeks Harry Truman received the anguished cries calmly. He told one news conference he was not backing down on price controls. His jaw was set firmly and stubbornly. OPA publicity men happily told reporters the Administration was not going to give in.

By mid-October all the frightened squeals of Democratic candidates fell on the White House. On a sultry Monday night, Harry

Truman spoke to the nation. For ten minutes he was a grim and angry man. He turned his frustration vengefully on Bob Taft. Then his whole mood crumpled. Almost mechanically, the President announced his surrender. All meat controls were being lifted.

From the White House, Dr. Steelman ordered the wholesale dumping of other controls. But it was no use. The end of controls only brought another curse on the Administration – high prices.

The President dived headfirst into the campaign. He issued a statement on Yom Kippur eve demanding that 100,000 Jewish refugees be admitted into Palestine. But it was too late and followed too many indecisions.

Mr. Truman flew to the United Nations Assembly all dressed up in gray-striped trousers and black coat to read a message of hope to the world. But the time for believing was long since past and the noble words were wasted.

The White House dashed into the threatened coal strike. President Truman spoke with an air of boyish triumph when he told reporters there would be no strike. The White House had overruled "Cap" Krug, Secretary of the Interior, and advised John Lewis the government-miners contract could be reopened to discuss wages. The report of O. John Rogge, assistant to the Attorney General, accusing Lewis of taking part in a Nazi conspiracy to defeat President Roosevelt in the 1940 elections, was put in the confidential file and its author fired for talking out of turn.

Nothing the Administration could do seemed anything but clumsy and aimless. Even Jimmy Byrnes, who expected to be lionized and welcomed back from Paris, bustled into an antagonistic press conference late in October. It was the first since his return.

Byrnes's restless little eyes searched for a friendly face when he entered the long room. Every chair was taken and reporters stood up around the walls. The Secretary seemed to sense the mood for he wet his lips nervously.

A series of sharp questions jabbed at the heart of his policy – pressure on Russia and its bloc of dominated countries.

"Do you believe that the action requiring visiting Russian artists to register as agents of a foreign principle will lessen the tension?

. . . Is there a policy to deny economic aid to nations in the Soviet group and to give to such countries as Italy, Greece, and Turkey? . . . Isn't the State Department's action suspending the loan to Czechoslovakia drastic?"

Secretary Byrnes frowned. He pressed his lips tightly together. He tapped his fingers against the edge of the desk. His answers were brusque and his voice was edged with irritation.

With the correspondents still framing questions, Byrnes rose abruptly and said he had an appointment. He was halfway through the door as a voice said lamely, "Thank you, Mr. Secretary."

The left wing of the Democratic Party was dispirited. The day before election, "Beanie" Baldwin, the PAC's leading man, brushed off the 1946 campaign, saying, "Whatever the outcome, we independent progressives have got to start devoting all our energies now to make sure that in '48 the people have a chance to vote for a Presidential candidate who is *really* a progressive."

Baldwin, an old New Dealer from the Farm Security Administration, commented sadly, "The Democratic Party, the vehicle of progressivism in the past, seems to be coming to a dead halt." He spoke wistfully of the "exciting years" under Roosevelt and said, "Now all that is drifting away. It isn't just that Franklin Roosevelt is no longer there to direct the team. It isn't just that practically all his most loyal teammates have left, or been asked to leave. It's that the very spirit of what he stood for seems to have departed."

On election night, a happy crowd of Republican workers gathered around a long bulletin board in headquarters watching the early returns. Before nine o'clock a jubilant sign was posted. Connecticut was a clean GOP sweep. Within the next hour limousines swept up the avenue and stopped before the brick mansion. Chauffeurs opened the doors and well-dressed men and women rushed into the hall. There were women in expensive fur coats and orchids . . . a girl with a large Taft button . . . old Jim Watson, who had dominated the Senate almost a generation before.

That same night, a train rushed through the darkness on its way to Washington. There was only silence from the special car where Harry Truman and a few old friends listened to election returns. Reporters a few cars removed huddled over a battery radio. By the time the train stopped at North Vernon, Indiana, for a few clanging seconds, everyone knew how dark the night was for the little gray-haired man from Missouri.

Four days later the Cabinet met. The atmosphere, as one correspondent put it, was one of "desperate futility." The first Secretary out was ambitious W. Averell Harriman, the wealthy aristocrat who had taken over Henry Wallace's old job. His face looked thin and colorless this morning.

It was not until Armistice Day that Harry Truman spoke. Reporters trudged reluctantly up the White House driveway in the morning. The hour was early and this was a holiday. The sky was gray with overhanging clouds. Trees on the White House lawn rustled with the wind of an approaching storm.

The sleepy men sprawled out in the red leather chairs in the lobby watched George Allen waddle back toward the President's office. There was no smile on his broad clown's face. A few minutes later, Dave Niles trotted after him.

The large crowd of correspondents shuffled through a double lane of stern Secret Service men and into the familiar round office. Bill Simmons, the tall White House chief usher, was impatiently motioning correspondents to move over. But he was careful not to repeat his phrase of several weeks ago, "Gentlemen, please move over to the left."

The President stood up and began reading a prepared statement. He sounded like a schoolboy reciting his lesson. The mild, even voice said: "Only by the exercise of wisdom and restraint and the constant determination to place the interests of our country above all other interests can we meet and solve the problems ahead of us. . . . I shall devote all my energy to the discharge of my duty with a full realization of the responsibility which results from the present state of affairs. . . . I shall proceed in the belief that members of the Congress will discharge their duties with a full realization of their responsibility. . . ."

Halfway through the reading, the room grew restless. Reporters let their eyes wander—out the garden windows at the signs of storm, at the small bust of Franklin Roosevelt tucked away on top of the bookcase (what would he think?), at the solemn face of Presidential secretary Matt Connelly.

Mr. Truman read on doggedly, "Inevitably, issues will arise between the President and the Congress. When this occurs, we must examine our respective positions with stern and critical analysis to exclude any attempt to tamper with the public interest to achieve personal or partisan advantage."

When he had finished reading the statement, President Truman looked up for questions. To most of them he replied with a stiff, "No comment." The meeting had lasted exactly thirteen minutes.

The conference over, Harry Truman stood at his desk, a cheerful little gray-haired man in a blue suit. He wore a happy smile and he shook hands enthusiastically with visitors.

Later, friends of the President explained his good humor. After eighteen months of responsibility and criticism, Harry Truman was only too glad to move over for the Republicans.

On Capitol Hill the atmosphere was like that of a small college campus after defeat of a state university, on home-coming day. The voices of Republicans boomed in the quiet halls. GOP Senators and Congressmen clapped each other on the back and exchanged enthusiastic greetings. They pumped the hands of correspondents and called them by their first names.

The new leaders glibly rattled off their program – tax reduction, strict economy, an end to all economic controls, amendments to the Wagner Labor Act, investigations by the dozen, and no more foreign loans. There were a few lively quarrels. Wayne Morse and Kenneth Wherry swore they would stop Senator Taft if he tried to become floor leader. Clarence Brown and Charley Halleck fought lustily over the House leadership.

There were some regrets. One benevolent and portly Republican plaintively told a few reporters, "I was happy enough in the minority. We had lots of fun. Now, we've got the ball and I'm not sure we know what the hell to do with it." He shook his head. "Sixteen years is a long time."

On a bright Thursday afternoon, ten days after elections, the Republican Senate Steering Committee met. Reporters trooped down a long dark hall to find the little-visited minority caucus room.

John Danaher was there with a smile as wide as a slice of watermelon. He waved aside questions. The Senators drifted in—elegantly dressed Curly Brooks, gentle Wallace White, Styles Bridges, looking more than ever like a master of ceremonies at a night club; tall Harlan Bushfield and Bob Taft.

As a sign of the new eminence of the Republicans, two Capitol policemen stood conspicuously by the door.

Senator Taft's sharp eyes looked around with obvious amusement. He saw four Senators lined up self-consciously before a row of photographers, some thirty correspondents standing around with pencil and paper ready to take down each jeweled word, policemen to guard the sacred portals.

The Grand Old Party had come into its own after sixteen lean and hungry years!

As a sign of the times, a lively group of young New Dealers announced with mock seriousness that they were changing the name of their club to the "Rutherford B. Hayes Marching Association" and had adopted as the theme song, "Oh, Susanna, I want to be like Mark Hanna."

Chapter XXXIV

At the birth of the New Year Washington was shrouded with a mist of sleet and snow. Familiar objects blurred into the gray night. The White House behind its high steel fence faded into the mist.

The morning of December 31 had been cold and dreary. At the early hour (for Washington) of ten o'clock correspondents with their eyes half open bobbed along the White House driveway. President Truman had called a special news conference.

Reporters grumbled to each other in the lobby. The United Press men growled, "As long as he's going to do these things, why doesn't he have his press conferences at midnight?" The slim blond girl with the French news agency said brightly, "At least, I would be awake then."

President Truman was clearly awake and energetically cheerful. He wore a new Christmas tie. The handsome and well-groomed Clark Clifford sat on the President's left. Attorney General Tom Clark on the right was doing his best to look chipper.

Mr. Truman beamed at the small and sleepy crowd and said briskly that he would read a statement and proclamation terminating the legal period of hostilities. At the conclusion the President gaily wished his visitors a Happy New Year.

A press service reporter pleaded, "Can we ask a few questions?" The President did not think that was necessary. Another anxious voice said, "Some of us will have to start dictating before we have a chance to read your mimeographed statement."

Mr. Truman smiled sympathetically and the questions fell around him. The press conference had broken up into little casual groups. One was standing near the door waiting for the signal to run for the telephones. Another perplexed knot was murmuring over the meaning of the complicated announcement. Others pressed close to the President's desk.

A reporter asked, "Does this mean the final end of the war in the legal sense?"

Clark Clifford, who had been following the scene, like a producer in the wings hanging onto each word, slowly shook his head, "No," at this point. But Mr. Truman did not happen to be looking his way. He cheerfully replied in the affirmative.

Later, Clifford carefully explained to newsmen the meaning of the proclamation. This legal act would void taxes on luxury items. The move was considered a clever maneuver, stealing a march on the Republicans.

With the handsome Mr. Clifford at the forge, the White House was hammering out a reconstruction program to rebuild the prestige of Harry Truman. Changes were being fashioned in the Cabinet and Presidential circle. A conservative Administration program built around the cry, "Beat the Republicans to the punch," was introduced with sly smiles of triumph.

This was part of a stealthy stalking game between the Democratic White House and the Republican Hill, with each side trying to push the other out into the open. The players hid behind the bushes of generality and looked out cautiously toward 1948. The crux of this contest was labor legislation. The trick was to satisfy sentiment for restrictive bills without alienating the labor vote which might decide the next election.

President Truman was serenely confident of the ability of his helpers to pull a rabbit out of the hat. He told Senator Kilgore to pass the word around to liberals not to get excited and run off. The Administration would have a "moderate" program which could satisfy everyone.

But the National Association of Manufacturers sent glad tidings to its members in a newsletter just before Christmas. The NAM purred, "President Truman, his eye on the public's political temper, is shifting rapidly to the right. In the opinion of some Congressmen, he is already past center. The result will affect almost all legislation in the next Congress, labor and tax measures particularly. . . . [Some Republicans] are speculating whether the President may not be more conservative than some prospective Republican Presidential nominees. In any case this situation within the Administration is startlingly different than a year ago."

And John Rankin shouted proudly to the House of Representatives, "President Truman's popularity has increased tremendously within the last few weeks."

The most dramatic evidence of the reconstruction program was the change of expression on John L. Lewis's face within a week. One warm morning late in November after he had sent a defiant ultimatum to the government, Lewis walked from his office to the Carlton Hotel. His face was a mask of stern majesty. Reporters and photographers trotted respectfully by his side. A newsreel man said with elaborate politeness, "When you make your statement, Mr. Lewis, please don't forget us."

Lewis said not a word. Not a muscle in his face moved. His eyes were cold and regal. He carried a cane but it rarely touched the ground. He swung it jauntily.

A few days later John L. Lewis was in court facing a contempt penalty for violating a Federal judge's restraining order issued at the request of the Administration. He had failed to call off the strike. On this morning the muscles of his face sagged downward, giving his jowls a bloated look. His complexion was sallow. He rolled his tongue inside his mouth. He turned a quick, furtive glance at the crowd in the courtroom behind him. This was not his customary bold and scornful stare. Lewis avoided the curious gazes and like a sulky boy caught with his hand in the cookie jar shifted his eyes to the floor.

All Washington was feeling the new mood. Economic controls were pried loose. Dismissal notices were sent to thousands of government employees in the first sweep of the economy wave. The Cabinet discussed changes in the Wagner Labor Act. Housing expediter Wilson Wyatt lost a battle to keep his veterans' housing program, and resigned. The "trickle down" theory was adopted – wealthy home builders would move into new homes, thus vacating houses and apartments for veterans. According to this reasoning, there was no need for a low-cost priority housing for veterans.

The State Department tagged along with its new design for living and declined to support Fiorello LaGuardia's request to continue United Nations Relief with a $400,000,000 appropriation.

A big surprise was casually tossed out by the White House late one afternoon. Most of the correspondents had gone home to dinner. Government buildings were dark. Only four reporters were left when Charley Ross poked his head in the press room and said he would have a story.

The boys knew something bigger than a report on Indian affairs was coming up when Charley said, "I don't want any of you to leave the room until I finish talking."

The President had accepted the resignation of Jimmy Byrnes! He was appointing his hero, General George C. Marshall, to be Secretary of State!

For the next several weeks diplomats and correspondents scrambled around Washington trying to discover what kind of man was this four-star General and former chief of staff.

Actually, General Marshall is one of those members of American royalty – like the millionaire philanthropists whose pictures regularly bob into the rotogravure sections at opera openings – whose names and faces are popularly known but whose personalities are a mystery.

The General never encouraged familiarity, so that even those who worked closely with him knew little of George Marshall, the man. He is a gravely courteous Southern gentleman with a tempered and orderly mind, a clear sense of authority, and a great capacity for work. At all his press conferences and public appearances, General Marshall was always surrounded by his court – the attentive junior generals.

He is one of those rare individuals who can remain a figure of dignity in almost any predicament. Climbing out of a new tank being exhibited near Washington, the General caught the seat of his pants in the tread. While frantic generals, colonels, and enlisted mechanics worked feverishly to undo him, Marshall dangled with complete *sang-froid* for ten minutes.

The General has a broad knowledge of foreign affairs, and of Franklin Roosevelt's program for the world. He accompanied the

President to the Big Three meetings. FDR trusted him implicitly and was even willing to risk a personal break with Winston Churchill on his account. General Marshall coldly and dispassionately disagreed with Churchill's politico-military strategy to strike at the alleged "soft underbelly of Europe," and the PM never forgave him for it. Mr. Roosevelt wanted Marshall as the supreme commander of the European Theater of Operations over Churchill's violent objections. It was George Marshall, the diplomat, who personally asked FDR to withdraw his name.

Just three hours before the General's appointment as Secretary of State, his clear and forthright report on his unsuccessful mission to bring peace to China was put on the table in the press room. This report expressed the dilemma of modern times and showed General Marshall to be an objective reporter.

He wrote bluntly but not bitterly of "a dominant group of reactionaries" (within the Chinese Government) and "the innermost Chinese Communist circles" who had opposed all efforts to bring about peace through compromise. George Marshall looked, instead, to younger liberals in both the government and the Communist ranks as "the salvation of the situation."

The General rose above the fierce loyalty to his kind which most military men carry with them to the grave. His report said, "Though I speak as a soldier, I must here deplore the dominating influence of the military. Their dominance accentuates the weakness of civil government in China."

On New Year's Day, lights winked out from Capitol Hill. Through the mist government buildings down below spread out in line along Constitution Avenue like bowing subjects. The little world beneath the Capitol Dome was stirring with preparations for the Eightieth Congress.

Senator Bob Taft of Ohio was driving his Republican Steering Committee to complete its plans. With a furious gust of energy, Taft stamped out sparks of revolt and hammered and sawed on a new "moderate" front for the Grand Old Party. While Clifford and Company was trying to give the Democratic Party a respectable conservative look, Taft was looking for a little bolder color scheme so the Republicans would not look quite so stuffy. Not that he wanted a touch of red, but he was searching for some hue a little less reminiscent of Herbert Hoover and Alf Landon.

As he rushed briskly from meeting to meeting, Bob Taft wore the triumphant smile of the Cheshire cat. He looked like a schoolmaster who had organized his classes and put all the little boys in their places.

There were a few toots of protest. Senator Tobey crisply told reporters, "We fought this war against centralization of power. I object to centralization of power in the Republican Party, to which I have belonged for some time."

One of the boys slyly suggested that perhaps Bob Taft was this "centralization of power." Tobey's frosty blue eyes twinkled and his pink face broke into a smile. He commented, "Bob Taft is the brainiest man in Washington, but don't you tell him I said so."

As Tobey was talking, the Steering Committee was meeting. When the doors opened, the first man out was Wallace White of Maine, the Republican floor leader. Reporters and cameramen crushed around him in the dark hall. He said sheepishly, "Taft is the man you want to see."

Senator Taft stood at the head of the table in the committee room. Seated at his right was Eugene Millikin, whom Taft had pulled into the inner circle as one of his lieutenants. The Colorado Senator began reading through the agenda in the deliberate manner of a judge. Taft would impatiently interrupt and expand a point just as a teacher stops a pupil and explains parts of the text he is reciting.

Someone asked about the Tobey objections. Bob Taft replied scornfully, "I haven't heard that point raised, and I don't think anything of it."

That same afternoon, all fifty-one Republican Senators met to approve the Taft program. Millikin judicially pounded down the protests. The slate went through . . . Taft, chairman of the Policy Committee and Senate Labor Committee; Vandenberg, president pro tem and chairman of the Foreign Relations Committee; Millikin, chairman of the Republican Conference and Senate Finance Committee. Wallace White, who plaintively told a friend, "I don't see why they want me for floor leader. I'm not mean enough," was elected to the job. (A few weeks later, sympathetic reporters in the press gallery were talking of taking up a collection to buy White a rear-vision mirror. They were afraid he might get a stiff neck from turning around so often to get his signals from Taft.)

All the assignments were parceled out so that Bob Taft would have a finger in every stew and his thumb on any potential troublemaker. He took the troublesome labor issue under his own wing and divided membership on the Labor Committee so that neither liberals nor conservatives could jerk control away from him.

This busy man still had time to elaborate to correspondents his program for the Republican Party. He smoothly praised Harry Truman's "change of heart." His labor policy carefully skirted the edges and asked for a mediation board, sixty-day cooling-off period, authority to sue unions for breach of contract, and prohibitions against jurisdictional strikes, secondary boycotts, and unions of supervisory employees. He wanted spending reduced, especially "foreign" loans and grants. He favored a 20 per cent cut in income taxes.

At every session of the Republican Steering Committee, a Negro lobbyist waited patiently outside. He would wait until the doors opened and then plead with Taft to bar Theodore Bilbo from the Senate. This ballooned into the big issue as Congress opened.

At ten o'clock on the morning the new Congress was to convene, Tom Connally, dressed in a long black coat and wide-brimmed hat, poked along a back corridor of the Senate Office Building. He was looking for a rump session of Southern Democrats to defend "The Man" Bilbo. Others, thirteen in all, straggled along to the meeting called by Senator Ellender of Louisiana. John McClellan of Arkansas drawled to a few reporters in the hall, "Chalk up one more Southern rebel." But some Southerners were conspicuously absent – McKellar, Hill, Byrd, Sparkman, Pepper, Fulbright.

At eleven the meeting broke up and Ellender, a small, black-haired man with a dark complexion, outlined the strategy to the correspondents. He began his explanation calmly, "An effort will be made to have Mr. Bilbo sworn in without prejudice. We propose to argue the constitutional questions involved." He added carefully, "There has been no talk of a filibuster but we propose, if necessary, to spend a few days developing the law."

The mere act of talking and thinking about the Bilbo issue heated Ellender's temper. His voice rose angrily. "If the Republicans want to continue this and not see the light, we'll talk some more. We won't let them trample over Bilbo. This is nothing but rotten, putrid politics."

There were several questions. Ellender glared and his voice became husky. "I can't believe the Senate of the United States would stoop so low. . . . Selfish groups are trying to destroy our government. . . . It's nothing but the Republicans trying to get the nigger vote." He hit the word "nigger" spitefully and added brusquely, "I mean nigger."

Half an hour later the Senate galleries were jammed. Crowds moved about restlessly in the lobby trying to push past the ushers. On the floor Senators milled around in little groups. When Bilbo pushed through a cloakroom door with Ellender by his side whispers spread through the gallery like a series of sparks. "That's him. That's Bilbo."

When the two hands on the gold clock at the rear of the chamber met at twelve, the gavel pounded down. The Senate was in session. Clerk John Crockett started to call out in his auctioneer's voice the names of Senators to be sworn in. As Bilbo's was read, two voices from different sides of the chamber were clamoring, "Mr. President, Mr. President." On the right or Democratic side was Glen Taylor. His handsome long face was drawn tensely. On the left side, Homer Ferguson leaned forward anxiously. Les Biffle in the chair recognized Taylor.

In a ringing voice, Taylor offered a resolution – to deny Bilbo his seat until all charges were thoroughly investigated. While Bilbo glowered at him and muttered "that Idaho cowboy," Taylor argued that the Mississippi primary had been conducted "in an atmosphere redolent of the odors of hate, of burning flesh, of tar, of feathers, of gunpowder." (Bilbo had yelled in the primary, "I call upon every red-blooded white man to use any means to keep the nigger away from the polls.")

Many Senators had left for lunch, but this pale and dramatic speaker was calling out into the corners of the gallery, "We've known for years there was a mess in our own back yard. It remained for Bilbo to rub our noses in it."

The scene shifted into a series of debates and legal arguments. The audience upstairs in the wooden benches responded with laughter, flurries of applause, and dark mutterings.

Across the Capitol in the larger House of Representatives chamber, there was an aura of great good humor . . . roars of laughter and waves of applause as Sam Rayburn turned over the Speaker's gavel to Joe Martin with elaborate ceremony.

Harold Knutson introduced House Bill Number 1, the Republican tax program. It would slice most income taxes 20 per cent at a cost of three and a half billion dollars to the Treasury. (A *Washington Post* cartoon the next morning showed Knutson leaning out of a window tossing a big bag marked with a dollar sign to a man in a top hat down below. At the same time, Knutson flipped a single coin to a ragged character labeled "Lower Bracket Incomes." The heading on the cartoon was, "Something for Everybody.")

Back in the Senate, Bob Taft suddenly called a test of his strength. It was a motion to swear in new Senators and gain Republican votes before Bilbo was seated. John Crockett called the ayes and nays. The first surprise was the low, even, "Aye" from Bill Fulbright. The young Southerner was voting his convictions as did nine other Democrats.

The friends of Bilbo were licked but stubbornly they began the filibuster. The shadows over Capitol Hill darkened into night. Taft let them talk on until six o'clock. Then he arose with a warning, "I favor a recess until tomorrow. But if, by that time, those who block the organization of the Senate continue their efforts, I say the Senate should meet continuously until this is disposed of." There was no grim or threatening note in his voice. He was simply stating a fact. Taft added, "The only thing is to see this through."

An agitated Alben Barkley rose heavily from his chair and said, "I disapprove of the filibuster. I deplore anything that might lower the estimate of the people in the United States Senate. I do not believe the people are in any mood to approve of frivolity."

There was the silence of attention over the chamber as Barkley added, "I hope the Senate can preserve itself from the contempt and condemnation of the people, if we have to stay here for a week. This is a solemn moment in the history of the Senate."

The next afternoon while Ellender slammed his desk and shouted to an almost empty Senate, Barkley slipped across the aisle and whispered to Taft. He was building a compromise. In the early evening the filibuster broke. Bilbo's name was withdrawn temporarily and the Senate was organized.

Two days later, on Monday, brilliant floodlights slanted down from the gallery rail on the dais of the Speaker of the House. The light stared into the blinking eyes of Joe Martin and Senator Vandenberg on the top level of the stand, looked impersonally at Secretary of State Byrnes with his arms folded rigidly across his chest, and gleamed on the bald head of Sam Rayburn. The Congress was in joint session to hear the President's state of the Union message.

At two minutes after one, Martin tapped the gavel and said, "The President of the United States." The galleryites peered into the brightly lit chamber as welcoming applause beat on Harry Truman. He trotted down the middle aisle, a trim little figure in a black suit. Harry Vaughan, loops of gold braid over his shoulder, lumbered behind.

The President began his message with a gay, *ad lib* remark, "It seems to me a lot of you moved over to the left [Republican] side since I was here last."

For the first few minutes the Congressman and Senators on the floor listened with respectful indifference. Bob Taft, sitting in the front row, fiddled with his hands. There was an epidemic of coughing.

But when the President said, "Private enterprise must be given the greatest possible freedom to continue the expansion of our economy," there was a wild and enthusiastic burst of applause which began from the Republican side.

When Mr. Truman announced, ". . . the balancing of the

budget in the next fiscal year, and the achieving of a substantial surplus to be applied to the reduction of the public debt," the GOP members started the hearty hand clapping. This happened again on the sections on labor and governmental economy. Democrats began the applause while most Republicans sat silently as the President said, "We will vigorously enforce the antitrust laws."

Through most of the reading Bob Taft followed the mimeographed text in his lap. He underlined sections with a long yellow pencil, and wrote notes on the margin. At the last paragraph Taft uncrossed his legs and put the pencil back in his pocket. Then he stood with the rest of the Congressmen and applauded politely.

He walked back to the Senate with a reporter trotting on each side during the journey through the long gray hall. He was asked if he thought the message showed "a spirit of co-operation."

The Midwestern twang of the Senator rasped with scorn. "Oh, it's all right, except for some points he was committed to make. That Wagner-Dingell health bill. Just socialized medicine. I'll never go along with that. . . . I don't see what he wants with all that money. . . . No, Congress will never go along with compulsory military training."

One of the reporters, being extra respectful, momentarily forgot his words and said, "Thank you, Mr. President."

Bob Taft either did not hear, or pretended not to. The tall figure strode onward with long and purposeful strides.

The author wishes to express his thanks to the Columbia Broadcasting System, *Coronet*, the *Nation* and the *New Republic* for permitting the use of material originally prepared for broadcasts or articles.